TOP TRAILS™

Yellowstone & Grand Teton
National Parks

Written by
Andrew Dean Nystrom

WILDERNESS PRESS · BERKELEY, CALIFORNIA

Top Trails Yellowstone & Grand Teton National Parks

1st EDITION June 2005

Copyright © 2005 by Andrew Dean Nystrom

All photos copyright by Andrew Dean Nystrom, except where noted
Maps: Fineline Maps
Cover design: Wilderness Press
Book design: Frances Baca
Book production: Pease Press
Book editor: Rebecca Freed

ISBN: 0-89997-368-X
UPC: 7-19609-97368-3

Manufactured in the United States of America

Published by: **Wilderness Press**
                1200 5th Street
                Berkeley, CA 94710
                (800) 443-7227; FAX (510) 558-1696
                info@wildernesspress.com
                www.wildernesspress.com

Visit our website for a complete listing of our books and for ordering information.

Cover photos: Teton Range; bighorn sheep (inset)

SAFETY NOTICE: Although Wilderness Press and the author have made every
attempt to ensure that the information in this book is accurate at press time, they are not
responsible for any loss, damage, injury, or inconvenience that may occur to anyone while
using this book. You are responsible for your own safety and health while in the wilderness. The fact that a trail is described in this book does not mean that it will be safe for
you. Be aware that trail conditions can change from day to day. Always check local conditions and know your own limitations.

The Top Trails™ Series

Wilderness Press

When Wilderness Press published *Sierra North* in 1967, no other trail guide like it existed for the Sierra backcountry. The first run of 2800 copies sold out in less than two months and its success heralded the beginning of Wilderness Press. In the past 35 years, we have expanded our territories to cover California, Alaska, Hawaii, the U.S. Southwest, the Pacific Northwest, New England, Canada, and Baja California.

Wilderness Press continues to publish comprehensive, accurate, and readable outdoor books. Hikers, backpackers, kayakers, skiers, snowshoers, climbers, cyclists, and trail runners rely on Wilderness Press for accurate outdoor adventure information.

Top Trails

In its Top Trails guides, Wilderness Press has paid special attention to organization so that you can find the perfect hike each and every time. Whether you're looking for a steep trail to test yourself on or a walk in the park, a romantic waterfall or a city view, Top Trails will lead you there.

Each Top Trails guide contains trails for everyone. The trails selected provide a sampling of the best that the region has to offer. These are the "must-do" hikes, walks, runs and bike rides, with every feature of the area represented.

Every book in the Top Trails series offers:

- The Wilderness Press commitment to accuracy and reliability
- Ratings and rankings for each trail
- Distances and approximate times
- Easy-to-follow trail notes
- Maps & permit information

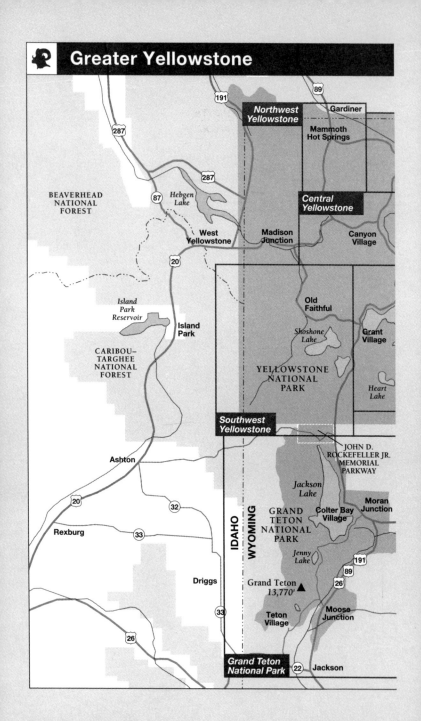

Greater Yellowstone

191

89

Gardiner

Northwest Yellowstone

Mammoth Hot Springs

287

287

87

Hebgen Lake

BEAVERHEAD NATIONAL FOREST

Central Yellowstone

West Yellowstone

Madison Junction

Canyon Village

20

Island Park Reservoir

Island Park

Old Faithful

Shoshone Lake

Grant Village

CARIBOU– TARGHEE NATIONAL FOREST

YELLOWSTONE NATIONAL PARK

Heart Lake

Southwest Yellowstone

Ashton

20

JOHN D. ROCKEFELLER JR. MEMORIAL PARKWAY

Jackson Lake

32

IDAHO

WYOMING

Colter Bay Village

Moran Junction

Rexburg

33

GRAND TETON NATIONAL PARK

Jenny Lake

191

89

26

Driggs

Grand Teton 13,770'

Moose Junction

33

Teton Village

26

Grand Teton National Park

22

Jackson

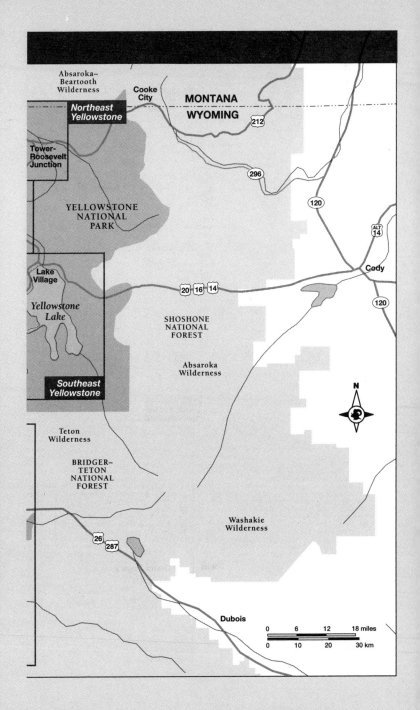

Absaroka–
Beartooth
Wilderness

Cooke
City

MONTANA
WYOMING

Northeast Yellowstone

(212)

(296)

(120)

Tower-
Roosevelt
Junction

YELLOWSTONE
NATIONAL
PARK

ALT (14)

Cody

Lake
Village

(20) (16) (14)

(120)

Yellowstone Lake

SHOSHONE
NATIONAL
FOREST

Absaroka
Wilderness

N

Southeast Yellowstone

Teton
Wilderness

BRIDGER–
TETON
NATIONAL
FOREST

Washakie
Wilderness

(26) (287)

Dubois

| 0 | 6 | 12 | 18 miles |
| 0 | 10 | 20 | 30 km |

Yellowstone & Grand Teton Trails

TRAIL NUMBER AND NAME	Page	Difficulty -12345+	Length in Miles	Type	Hiking	Bicycling	Horses	Backpacking	Handicap Access	Child	Permit
1. Northwest Yellowstone—Mammoth/Gallatin Country											
1 Beaver Ponds Loop	37	3	5.5	↻	🚶					👫	
2 Boiling River	43	1	1.0	↗	🚶				♿	👫	
3 Bunsen Peak	47	4/5	4.2	↗	🚶						
4 Howard Eaton Trail	53	3/4	4.0	↘	🚶						
5 Mammoth Hot Springs	57	1	1.0	↻	🚶				♿	👫	
6 Osprey Falls	63	5	10.2	↗	🚶	🚴					
2. Northeast Yellowstone—Tower/Roosevelt Country											
7 Black Canyon of the Yellowstone	77	5	18.5	↘	🚶		🐎	🎒			✔
8 Lower Blacktail Deer Creek	87	4	8.0	↗	🚶		🐎				
9 Fossil Forest	91	4	3.0	↗	🚶						
10 Tower Fall	97	1	1.5	↗	🚶				♿	👫	
11 Yellowstone River Picnic Area Overlook	101	2	4.0	↗	🚶					👫	
3. Central Yellowstone—Norris/Canyon Country											
12 Artists Paint Pots	115	1	1.2	↻	🚶					👫	
13 Grand Canyon of the Yellowstone: North Rim	119	2	3.8	↘	🚶				♿	👫	
14 Grand Canyon of the Yellowstone: South Rim	125	2	3.2	↘	🚶				♿	👫	
15 Hayden Valley: Mary Mtn. East	129	4	10.0	↗	🚶						
16 Monument Geyser Basin	135	3	3.0	↗	🚶						
17 Mt. Washburn	139	4	6.0	↗	🚶	🚴					
18 Norris Geyser Basin: Porcelain & Back Basins	145	2	2.0	↻	🚶				♿	👫	

USES & ACCESS
- 🚶 Hiking
- 🚴 Bicycling
- 🐎 Horses
- 🎒 Backpacking
- 👫 Child Friendly
- ♿ Handicap Access
- Backcountry Permit Required
- ⚠ Camping

TERRAIN
- Canyon
- Mountain
- Summit
- Stream
- Waterfall
- Lake
- Geothermal

FLORA & FAUNA
- Autumn Colors
- Wildflowers
- Birds
- Wildlife

OTHER
- Cool & Shady
- Great Views
- Photo Opportunity
- Swimming
- Secluded
- Historic
- Geologic Interest
- Moonlight Hiking
- Steep

DIFFICULTY
- 1 2 3 4 5 +
less   more

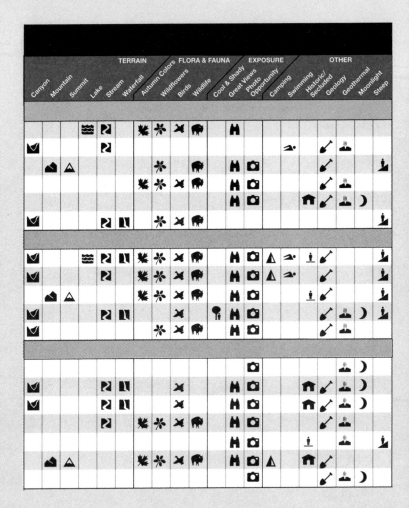

TRAIL NUMBER AND NAME	Page	Difficulty 1-2-3-4-5+	Length in Miles	Type	Hiking	Bicycling	Horses	Backpacking	Handicap Access	Child	Permit
4. Southeast Yellowstone—Lake Country											
19 Avalanche Peak	161	4	4.0	↗	✓						
20 Elephant Back Mountain	165	3	3.5	↻	✓					✓	
21 Heart Lake & Mt. Sheridan	169	5	15.0	↗	✓			✓			✓
22 Pelican Valley	173	4	15.3	↻	✓		✓				
23 West Thumb Geyser Basin	179	1	0.6	↻	✓				✓	✓	
5. Southwest Yellowstone—Cascade and Geyser Country											
24 Bechler Meadows	197	3	7.8	↻	✓		✓	✓			
25 Bechler River	203	5	29.7	↘	✓		✓	✓			✓
26 Cave Falls & Bechler Falls	213	3	7.3	↻	✓		✓			✓	
27 Dunanda & Silver Scarf Falls	217	5	16.4	↗	✓		✓	✓			
28 Fairy Falls & Imperial Geyser	223	3	6.8	↗	✓	✓		✓		✓	
29 Lone Star Geyser	229	2	5.0	↗	✓	✓		✓	✓	✓	
30 Mystic Falls	235	3	4.0	↻	✓					✓	
31 Old Faithful & Observation Point	239	2	2.4	↻	✓				✓	✓	
32 Shoshone Lake & Shoshone Geyser Basin	245	5	17.0	↗	✓			✓			✓
33 Terraced Falls	251	2	3.6	↗	✓					✓	
34 Union Falls & Mountain Ash Creek	257	5	15.8	↗	✓		✓	✓			✓
6. Grand Teton National Park											
35 Bradley & Taggart Lakes	275	3	5.8	↻	✓		✓			✓	
36 Cascade Canyon	279	4	9.1	↗	✓		✓	✓		✓	
37 Hermitage Point	285	4	9.4	↻	✓		✓	✓		✓	
38 Huckleberry Hot Springs	291	1	1.0	↗	✓					✓	
39 Jenny Lake	295	3	7.0	↻	✓		✓		✓	✓	
40 Leigh, Bearpaw, & Trapper Lakes	301	2/3	2.2/8.4	↗	✓		✓	✓		✓	
41 Phelps Lake	305	2/3	4.0	↗	✓		✓			✓	
42 Rendezvous Mtn. to Granite Canyon	309	4/5	12.4	↻	✓		✓	✓			
43 String Lake	317	2	3.4	↻	✓		✓		✓	✓	
44 Surprise & Amphitheater Lakes	321	5	9.6	↗	✓			✓			
45 Two Ocean Lake	327	3/4	6.4	↻	✓		✓				

Trails table (icons indicate features present for each trail):

Canyon	Mountain	Summit	Lake	Stream	Waterfall	Autumn Colors	Wildflowers	Birds	Wildlife	Cool & Shady	Great Views	Photo Opportunity	Camping	Swimming	Historic/Secluded	Geology	Geothermal	Moonlight	Steep
	✓	✓					✓				✓	✓			✓				✓
	✓	✓				✓	✓		✓		✓	✓							✓
	✓	✓	✓	✓				✓	✓		✓	✓	✓				✓		
				✓		✓	✓	✓	✓		✓	✓		✓			✓		
			✓						✓		✓	✓					✓	✓	
				✓	✓			✓	✓				✓	✓	✓				
✓	✓			✓	✓	✓	✓	✓	✓	✓	✓	✓	✓	✓	✓		✓		
				✓	✓	✓		✓	✓			✓		✓					
				✓	✓	✓		✓	✓			✓	✓	✓	✓		✓		
					✓							✓	✓	✓			✓		
				✓					✓	✓		✓	✓				✓	✓	
✓				✓	✓		✓				✓	✓					✓		✓
											✓	✓					✓	✓	✓
			✓	✓		✓	✓	✓	✓		✓	✓	✓				✓		
✓				✓	✓	✓				✓	✓	✓			✓	✓			
✓				✓	✓	✓						✓	✓	✓	✓	✓			
			✓			✓	✓	✓	✓		✓					✓			
✓			✓	✓	✓	✓	✓	✓	✓	✓	✓	✓	✓			✓			✓
			✓			✓		✓	✓	✓	✓	✓	✓						
				✓				✓	✓					✓		✓			
✓			✓				✓		✓	✓	✓	✓				✓			
			✓			✓	✓	✓	✓	✓	✓	✓	✓	✓		✓			
			✓	✓		✓	✓	✓	✓	✓	✓	✓	✓	✓		✓			
✓	✓	✓		✓		✓	✓	✓	✓		✓	✓	✓			✓			✓
			✓	✓		✓	✓	✓	✓	✓	✓	✓		✓		✓			
✓	✓		✓			✓	✓	✓	✓		✓	✓	✓			✓			✓
		✓	✓			✓	✓	✓	✓		✓	✓			✓	✓			

Contents

CHAPTER 5

Southwest Yellowstone– Cascade & Geyser Country 185

CHAPTER 6

Grand Teton National Park 263

Using Top Trails™

Organization of Top Trails

Top Trails is designed to make identifying the perfect trail easy and enjoyable, and to make every outing a success and a pleasure. With this book you'll find it's a snap to find the right trail, whether you're planning a major hike or just a sociable stroll with friends.

The Region

Top Trails begins with the **Greater Yellowstone Map** (pages iv-v), displaying the entire region covered by the guide and providing a geographic overview. The map is clearly marked to show which area is covered by which chapter.

After the Regional Map comes the **Yellowstone & Grand Teton Trails Table** (pages vi-ix), which lists every trail covered in the guide along with

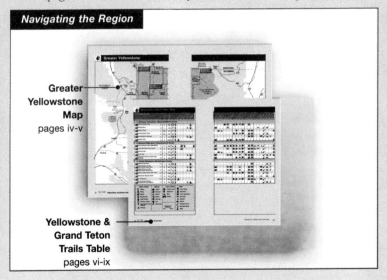

Navigating the Region

Greater Yellowstone Map
pages iv-v

Yellowstone & Grand Teton Trails Table
pages vi-ix

attributes for each one. A quick reading of the Regional Map and the Trail Table will give a good overview of the entire region covered by this book.

The Areas

The region covered by this book is divided into Areas, with each chapter corresponding to one area in the region.

Each Area chapter starts with information to help you choose and enjoy a trail each time out. Use the Table of Contents or the Regional Map to identify an area of interest, then turn to the Area Chapter to find the following:

- An Overview of the Area, including maps and permits
- An Area Map with all trails clearly marked
- A Trail Feature Table providing trail-by-trail details
- Trail Summaries, written in a lively, accessible style

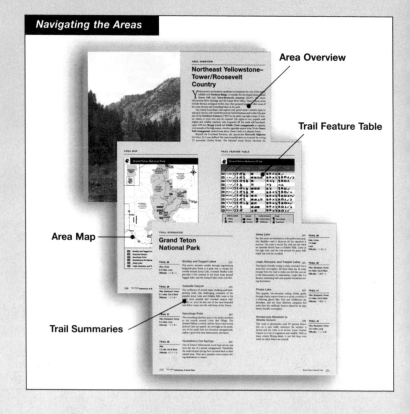

Navigating the Areas

Area Overview

Trail Feature Table

Area Map

Trail Summaries

The Trails

The basic building block of the Top Trails guide is the Trail Entry. Each one is arranged to make finding and following the trail as simple as possible, with all pertinent information presented in an easy-to-follow format:

- A Trail Map
- Trail Descriptors covering difficulty, length, and other essential data
- Narrative Trail Text
- Trail Milestones, providing easy-to-follow, turn-by-turn trail directions

Some Trail Descriptions offer additional information:

- An Elevation Profile
- Trail Options
- Trail Highlights
- Trail Teasers

In the margins of the Trail Entries, look for icons that point out notable features at specific points along the trail.

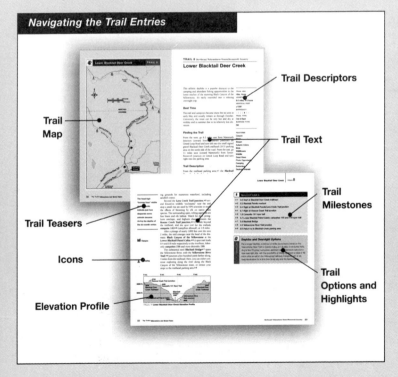

Choosing a Trail

Top Trails provides several different ways of choosing a trail, presented in easy-to-read tables, charts, and maps.

Location

If you know in general where you want to go, Top Trails makes it easy to find the right trail in the right place. Each chapter begins with a large-scale map showing the starting point of every trail in that area.

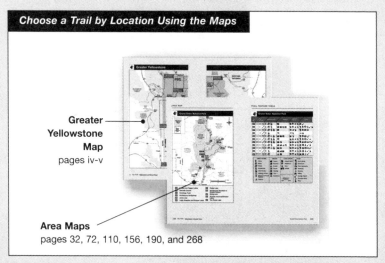

Choose a Trail by Location Using the Maps

Greater
Yellowstone
Map
pages iv-v

Area Maps
pages 32, 72, 110, 156, 190, and 268

Features

This guide describes the Top Trails of Yellowstone and Grand Teton National Parks, and each trail is chosen because it offers one or more features that make it appealing. Using the trail descriptors, summaries, and tables, you can quickly examine all the trails for the features they offer, or seek a particular feature among the list of trails.

Season and Condition

Time of year and current conditions can be important factors in selecting the best trail. For example, an exposed low-elevation trail may be a riot of color in early spring, but an oven-baked taste of hell in midsummer. Wherever relevant, Top Trails identifies the best and worst conditions for the trails you plan to hike.

Difficulty

Each trail has an overall difficulty rating on a scale of 1 to 5, which takes into consideration length, elevation change, exposure, trail quality, etc., to create one (admittedly subjective) rating.

The ratings assume you are an able-bodied adult in reasonably good shape, using the trail for hiking. The ratings also assume normal weather conditions—clear and dry.

Readers should make an honest assessment of their own abilities and adjust time estimates accordingly. Also, rain, snow, heat, wind, and poor visibility can all affect the pace on even the easiest of trails.

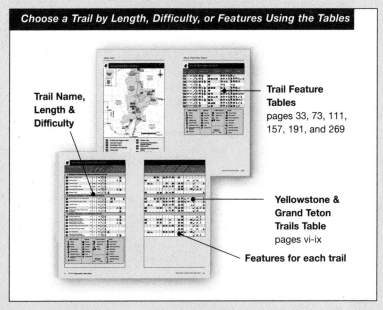

Choose a Trail by Length, Difficulty, or Features Using the Tables

Trail Name, Length & Difficulty

Trail Feature Tables
pages 33, 73, 111, 157, 191, and 269

Yellowstone & Grand Teton Trails Table
pages vi–ix

Features for each trail

Vertical Feet

Every trail description contains the approximate trail length and the overall elevation gain and loss over the course of the trail. It's important to use both figures when considering a hike; on average, plan one hour for every 2 miles, and add an hour for every 1000 feet you climb.

This important measurement is often underestimated by hikers when gauging the difficulty of a trail. The Top Trails measurement accounts for all elevation change, not simply the difference between the highest and lowest points, so that rolling terrain with lots of up and down will be identifiable.

The calculation of Vertical Feet in the Top Trails series is accomplished by a combination of trail measurement and computer-aided estimation. For routes that begin and end at the same spot—i.e. Loop or Out & Back—the vertical gain exactly matches the vertical descent. With a point-to-point route the vertical gain and loss will most likely differ, and both figures will be provided in the text.

Finally, all Trail Entries with more than 1000 feet of elevation gain include an **Elevation Profile**, an easy means for visualizing the topography of the route. These profiles graphically depict the elevation throughout the length of the trail.

Surface Type

Each Trail Entry describes the surface of the trail. This information is useful in determining what type of footwear is appropriate. Surface Type should also be considered when checking the weather—on a rainy day early or late in the hiking season a dirt surface can be a muddy slog; a boardwalk jaunt or gravel surface might be a better choice.

 Top Trails Difficulty Ratings

1 A short trail, generally level, that can be completed in one hour or less.

2 A route of 1 to 3 miles, with some up and down, that can be completed in one to two hours.

3 A longer route, up to 5 miles, with significant uphill and/or downhill sections.

4 A long or steep route, perhaps more than 5 miles or climbs of more than 1000 vertical feet.

5 The most severe, both long and steep, more than 5 miles long with climbs of more than 1000 vertical feet.

Map Legend

Trail	-------		River	——
Other Trail	- - - -		Stream	——
			Seasonal Stream	—·—·—
Freeway	▬▬▬		Body of Water	
Major Road	▬▬▬			
Minor Road	——		Marsh/Swamp	
Tunnel	- - - -		Dam	
Ski Lift/Tramway	┼┼┼┼┼			
Railroad	┼┼┼┼┼		Peak	▲
Bridge	)(		Park/Forest	
Building	■ ▮		Boundary	—·—·—

Trailhead Parking	🅿
Picnic	🛆
Camping	▲
Gate	●—●
Birds	🕊
Wildlife	🦬
Great Views	M
Photo Opportunity	📷

Start/Finish — start & finish

North Arrow

Morgan Konn

Yellowstone's Lower Falls (*Trail 14*)

Introduction to Yellowstone & Grand Teton National Parks

Yellowstone and Grand Teton National Parks form the wild core of the Greater Yellowstone Ecosystem (GYE), one of the world's largest intact temperate-zone ecosystems. The Greater Yellowstone concept originated in the early 1970s, based on a pioneering study of grizzly bear population dynamics directed by brothers John and Frank Craighead. After 12 years of field research, the year-round range of the bears was calculated to exceed 5 million acres.

Jazz lovers may beg to differ, but many have called the National Park system "the best idea America ever had." Yellowstone was set aside as the world's first National Park in 1872, named a United Nations World Biosphere Reserve in 1976, and added to the World Heritage Sites in Danger list in 1995. The establishment of National Elk Refuge near Jackson in 1912 opened up public access to the region's southern flank. Much of the area eventually set aside as Grand Teton in 1929 was part of a proposed enlargement to Yellowstone in 1918.

These two landmark national parks are surrounded by a buffer zone composed of seven national forests, six wilderness areas, three national wildlife refuges, 125,000 acres of Bureau of Land Management rangeland, and more than 1 million acres of tribal lands and private property.

Estimates of the total area of this vast wildlands complex range from 19,000 to 28,000 square miles (12 to 18 million acres), about the size of West Virginia. Yellowstone protects 2.22 million acres (3468 square miles), roughly the same size as Puerto Rico, or Delaware and Rhode Island combined. In contrast, Grand Teton packs its concentrated wilderness punch into a mere 310,000 acres.

To give you a better idea of just how big the region is, Yellowstone's Thorofare patrol cabin in the park's far southeast corner is 32 miles by trail from the nearest road—a long day's horseback ride—making it one of the most remote wilderness outposts in the Lower 48 US states.

Long-range planning for holistic management of the buffer zone, home to a rapidly growing human population of more than 200,000 people, is increasingly considered by experts to be the key to preserving this unique region (often described as "an island of mountains in the high, dry plains").

Geography and Topography

The topography of Greater Yellowstone is the result of an underlying magmatic hot spot, and millions of years of volcanic influence. The massif of high moist plateaus, peaks, and valleys is surrounded by arid plains.

The region contains the headwaters of several of the continent's grandest waterways: two of the three forks of the **Missouri**; the headwaters of the **Snake River**, which flows into the Columbia and eventually into the Pacific Ocean; and the **Yellowstone River**, the longest free-flowing river in the USA, which runs north and drains approximately 70,000 square miles.

The **Continental Divide**, the crest of the North American continent, zigzags across the southwest corner of Yellowstone. The region's landforms channel westerly storm systems onto Yellowstone's **Central Plateau**, where most of the region's snow drops. The Tetons' topographic extremes create their own unique, semiarid microclimate, with most storms approaching from the southwest. Here, snowfall averages 191 inches, but annual rainfall hovers around just 10 inches.

The majority of Yellowstone consists of broad volcanic plateaus scored by deep river canyons, with an average elevation of 8000 feet. There are 370 miles of paved roads, and more than 1100 miles of maintained hiking trails. Five percent of Yellowstone is covered by water, 15 percent by grassland, and 80 percent by forest. The highest point is the seldom-scaled Eagle Peak (11,358'), near the park's southeast corner. The lowest point is near the North Entrance at Reese Creek (5282'), just north of the prominent Electric Peak (10,992').

Grand Teton's centerpiece is the 40-mile long **Teton Range**, an active fault-block mountain front. Twelve peaks exceeding 12,000 feet tower over the **Snake River Plain**, and the valley known as **Jackson Hole**, which averages 6800 feet in elevation, and tilts subtly southward towards the gateway town of **Jackson**. In addition to the string of morainal piedmont lakes at the

Larry Van Dyke

Teton Range *and Jackson Hole*

base of the range, the park is home to more than 100 alpine and back-country tarns (steep-banked glacial lakes). In Yellowstone, over 600 lakes and ponds cover approximately 107,000 surface acres: 94 percent of which can be attributed to Yellowstone, Lewis, Shoshone, and Heart lakes. Some 1000 rivers and streams account for over 2000 miles of running water.

Geology and Hydrothermal Activity

Glaciers and **supervolcanoes** are the primary influences in Greater Yellowstone's dramatic, ever-evolving landscape. Three cataclysmic eruptions have rocked the region in the past 2.1 million years. The most recent massive volcanic explosion, which occurred around 640,000 years ago, created the gigantic **Yellowstone Caldera**, a vast, collapsed crater that defines the park's Central Plateau.

Since 2001, the **Yellowstone Volcano Observatory** has tracked the uplift of the dome beneath Yellowstone Lake resulting from the pressure exerted by superplumes of near-surface magma in what it calls the "largest volcanic system in North America." Multiple earthquakes are recorded daily, but a swarm of 400 temblors centered in the park's northwest sector in 2004 sparked renewed speculation about the possibility of another gigantic volcanic event, and the possible resulting global climate disruption. Volcanologists downplay the possibility of such an event in our lifetime. However, some say its likelihood is 5 to 10 times greater than that of a globally destructive asteroid impact.

Also related to the hot spot are Yellowstone's unique, superheated **hydrothermal features**. An ongoing inventory, sponsored by the Yellowstone Center for Resources, estimates that the park is home to more than 18,000 distinct geothermal features. The most common surface expressions of the park's extensive but little-studied subterranean plumbing network are **hot springs**, where colorful **thermophiles** (heat-loving microorganisms, also known as extremophiles) and **cyanobacteria** (single-celled photosythetic bacteria) thrive in pools of geothermally heated water. These springs are often linked to **geysers** (from the Icelandic *geysir*, literally "to

Morgan Konn

Boardwalks *provide close access to many frontcountry hot springs.*

gush or rage"), where highly pressurized water rockets towards the surface and often flashes to steam. **Fumaroles** are dry, hissing vents that issue hydrogen sulfide (the source of that "rotten egg" odor), hydrochloric acid, and other gases. A **solfatara** is a sulfur-emitting fumarole. **Mudpots** (also known as paint pots when tinted by minerals) form in thermal areas where precipitation mixes with fine volcanic soils to create a bubbling, viscous— and often very acidic—slurry, sometimes forming **mud volcanoes**.

For hikers, all this ancient ice sculpting and geothermal hyperactivity translates into many unusual geologic features to explore, including multi-layered fossil forests, lava flows, dramatic U-shaped canyons, glacial boulder fields, and black mountains of obsidian. These wild and varied landscapes form numerous ecological niches that support an amazing diversity of plants and wildlife.

Flora

Some 1100 native species of flowering plants are found in Yellowstone alone, but there are only two endemic species: Yellowstone sand verbena and Ross' bentgrass. There are more than 200 nonnative species, some of which are starting to invade the backcountry. An additional 600 species of fungi, lichens, mosses, and liverworts have been cataloged. It's legal to collect small quantities of edible plants and berries for personal consumption, but keep it to a minimum to maintain your good bear karma.

Elevation has the most influence over which plant species flourish where. Though the vegetation varies significantly throughout the ecosystem, it's mostly typical of the Rocky Mountains. The observant hiker may notice elements of seven distinct biomes from the surrounding deserts, plains, montane forests, and arctic tundra.

Thanks to their shallow root systems, vast tracts of drought-tolerant **lodgepole pines** dominate the nutrient-poor, volcanic soils within the Yellowstone Caldera. In sharp contrast, the clayey glacial lakebeds beyond the caldera encourage a much more diverse flora.

Botanists group Rocky Mountain vegetation in five zones: foothills, riparian, montane, subalpine, and alpine. These zones overlap considerably and are not strictly defined. The altitude and width of each zone increases progressively as you move from north to south. **Fall colors** peak around the autumnal equinox in the Tetons, a bit later on Yellowstone's relatively low-lying Northern Range.

Most of Yellowstone's lower-elevation hikes begin in sagebrush-blanketed **foothills** (5500'-6500'). A prime example of this type of habitat is the arid Northern Range, where the annual precipitation hovers around 20 inches. Unique species found here include cacti and Rocky Mountain

Larry Van Dyke

Bison *graze in Fountain Flats, in the Southwest Yellowstone area.*

juniper. In the absence of foothills in the Tetons, most trails begin near Jackson Hole and the Snake River Plain, where porous soils support sagebrush, grasses, and numerous wildflowers.

Riparian or **wetland** communities prosper around year-round streams. Typical moisture-loving plants in this zone include rushes, sedges, colorful deciduous trees like cottonwoods, and shrubs such as willow, quaking aspen, dogwood, mountain ash, and Rocky Mountain maple. These lush but narrow areas are often home to rare, water-loving wildflowers and provide a transition between aquatic and upland steppe environments. North-facing slopes, which receive less sunlight and thus retain more moisture, are favored by most plants. Several rare aquatic plants thrive in Yellowstone's hydrothermal areas, such as the Shoshone Geyser Basin.

Semiarid **steppe** vegetation is primarily scrubby and is dotted by lots of fragrant Big Mountain sagebrush, open woodlands, and more than a hundred species of sparse grasses. Prime, wildlife-rich examples of this habitat occur in Yellowstone's Hayden Valley, Pelican Valley, and Swan Lake Flats. Conspicuous blooms of **wildflowers** like the pungent yellow arrowleaf balsamroot; snow-white, mat-forming phlox; flaming scarlet-orange Indian paintbrush; and pastel lupines and penstemons festoon hillsides in late June and early July.

Sagebrush-interspersed meadows mark the transition between rolling prairies and the forested **montane zone** (6000'-9500'). Snow persists at higher elevations until July or August around the highest passes. The resulting short, cool growing season limits the number of plant species. Snowmelt on warmer south-facing slopes waters hearty conifer (cone-bearing) species, such as Douglas-fir, Englemann spruce, which dominate older forests, and the higher-ranging subalpine fir. The damp understory is dominated by shrubs and berries. If there is a prolonged absence of fire, spruce-fir forests should begin to succeed the currently dominant lodgepole stands.

Morgan Konn

Aspen grove *near Taggart Lake (Trail 35)*

Beyond the upper montane zone, the wild **subalpine zone** (7500'-10,000') continues up to timberline. Isolated spruce-fir stands dominate where snow lingers longest. Short-lived wildflower displays can be fantastic after the spring snowmelt. At higher elevations, such as around Mt. Washburn, the nuts of whitebark pine (which is sometimes confused with limber pine) are a favored but erratic source of prehibernation nutrition for ravenous grizzly bears.

Above timberline, the **alpine zone** (above 9000 to 10,000 feet) is the preserve of the most robust species of both plants and humans. The exposed meadows and rocky outcrops host bountiful but short-lived wildflower shows in late July and August. Wind-stunted krummholz trees abide in sheltered areas of southern exposure. More than 200 plant species have been cataloged just beyond Yellowstone's northeast entrance on the untamed Beartooth Plateau, one of largest swaths of alpine tundra in the Lower 48 US states.

Fauna

Let's face it: Geyser gazing and rambling around alpine peaks aside, a trip to Yellowstone and the Tetons isn't complete without spotting—and photographing—a root-grubbing bear with her cute yearling cub, a bugling eight-point elk, a drooling moose or, at the very least, a wallowing bison.

Besides the iconic thermal features that earned Yellowstone its early nickname Wonderland, the park's photogenic wildlife are the main draw for most visitors. Thanks to the successful wolf reintroduction effort (see below), Greater Yellowstone now supports all of the 61 native mammal species that it historically has hosted. With such an incredible concentration of charismatic megafauna, these parks are easily one the world's foremost wildlife watching hot spots.

The comparison that's frequently drawn between Yellowstone's Lamar Valley and the Serengeti Plains in northern Tanzania isn't frivolous. Both parks are grappling with similar issues: managing large migrating wildlife herds, reducing the spread of disease, curbing invasive species, and coping with ranching and human development in their shrinking buffer zones.

Subalpine habitat *below Rendezvous Mountain in the Teton Range (Trail 42)*

If Greater Yellowstone has a totem species, it's the great **grizzly bear** (also known as the brown bear). Yellowstone constitutes the heart of their range, which is estimated to have expanded by as much as 40 percent since 1975, when the 200 remaining animals in the region were listed as endangered. Current estimates of the region's population range from 300 to as high as 650, by those who would like to see the grizzly removed from the list of animals protected by the Endangered Species Act, so that hunting can be reinstated in surrounding national forests. The region in northern Montana around Glacier National Park harbors the only other grizzly population in the Lower 48 states. A final ruling on a proposal to delist grizzlies is expected in late 2005.

Besides poaching near park boundaries, current threats to grizzlies include a decline in cutthroat trout caused by the so-called whirling disease and illegally introduced lake trout; as well as a fungus that's been decimating the supply of whitebark pine nuts, a prime source of late-season sustenance. Researchers have found that wolf reintroduction has actually increased the bears' food supply: Since 2000, all wolf-killed ungulate carcasses in the Pelican Valley have ultimately been taken over by grizzlies.

In 2004, the most bear sightings were reported in the vicinity of Tower-Roosevelt Junction. Other areas with frequent sightings included Bridge Bay, and from Fishing Bridge to Yellowstone's East Entrance. Less frequent sightings occurred around dawn and dusk in Mammoth, on the north slopes of Mt. Washburn, and in the Hayden and Lamar valleys. In recent years, grizzly sightings have become more common than black bear sightings.

Yearling black bear cubs *never stray far from their mothers.*

Yellowstone's abundant, omnivorous **black bear**, at an estimated population of 500 to 650, exists primarily in niches not filled by territorial grizzlies. Sightings (and resulting roadside "bear jams") are common around Tower and Mammoth. Despite their name, their coloration actually ranges from black to cinnamon. Both black bears and grizzlies start denning around mid-November, emerging from hibernation five months later, starting in April.

In both Yellowstone and Grand Teton, black bears have become quite pesky in seeking food from garbage cans, dumpsters, and campgrounds. However, the majority of bears you might see in the backcountry remain timid and are wary of human encounters. See the Bear Safety Guidelines (page 16) for advice about how to best avoid or manage potentially hazardous encounters with bears and other wildlife.

Thirty-three Canadian **gray wolves** were reintroduced to Yellowstone in 1995, marking the beginning of an unprecedented effort to restore them to their historic range in the Northern Rockies. Wolves are now found throughout Yellowstone and increasingly around the fringes of Grand Teton. As of the winter of 2004-'05, 171 individuals were roaming the park in 14 distinct packs; a grand total of 301 of the primo predators were tallied in 31 packs in Greater Yellowstone.

Outside of sunny winter days, the best times to spot wolves are at dawn and dusk. The most reliable method of finding them? Scan roadside turnouts for an array of high-powered binoculars and spotting scopes, telephoto lenses mounted on camouflage tripods, and CB radio antennas on the roofs of expedition-equipped four-wheel-drive vehicles. Then stop and ask if you can take a look; devoted wolf watchers are usually quite happy to share their knowledge and passion with passersby.

The highly adaptable, omnivorous **coyote** is often seen loping across meadows, fields, and other open grasslands. The coyote population has decreased by as much as 50 percent in Yellowstone since wolf reintroduction, which has been shown conclusively to have relegated coyotes to a scavenger role. The nighttime chorus of yelps (sometimes mistaken for wolf howls), however, still reverberates through backcountry campsites.

Estimates of the numbers of the seven species of native **ungulates** (hooved mammals) vary as widely as the large animals' migratory range. Counts of Yellowstone's bugling **Rocky Mountain elk** (also known as wapiti, or red deer in Europe) vary seasonally from 10,000 to 20,000, with seven distinct herds. In summer, you can hardly toss a bison chip without hitting a member of the largest elk herd in North America: Look around Gibbon Meadows or the Lamar Valley. During the autumn rut (mating season), elk take over the lawns around Mammoth Hot Springs and flock to meadows around Norris Geyser Basin. In Jackson Hole, Timbered Island becomes a no-go zone during the rut. In winter, they migrate south to the National Elk Refuge, or north and east to Gardiner and West Yellowstone, where hunters await just beyond the park boundaries.

Yellowstone's population of persistent **bison** (often used interchangeably with buffalo), the largest land animal in North America, was estimated at 4000 during the spring of 2004. Watch year-round for the United States' largest free-roaming herd in the Hayden and Lamar valleys, in summer in open meadows and grasslands, and in winter in thermal areas and along the Madison River. In Grand Teton, smaller herds roam the sagelands around Mormon Row.

Common, floppy-eared **mule deer** prefer open forests and grassy meadows, where they munch on leaves, shrubs, and sedges. Watch for them browsing around dusk near forest edges. The furtive, less common **white-tailed deer** is only occasionally spotted near waterways in Yellowstone's Northern Range.

A declining population of moody, drooling **moose** lurk in willow thickets in riparian zones, mainly in marshy meadows, near lake shores, and along rivers. In Yellowstone, they are most frequently seen browsing in the Bechler region, and in the Soda Butte Creek, Pelican Creek, Lewis River, and Gallatin River drainages. They are more common in Grand Teton, wherever willows colonize marshes and ponds. Appearances are deceptive: They are superb swimmers and can—and will—charge at up to 35 miles per hour, so give them wide berth.

A drastically diminished population of around 250 fleet-footed **pronghorn** are more closely related to goats than antelope. They are found in

*Stay clear of bull **bison** like this fellow in Pelican Valley (Trail 22).*

summer in sage flats and grasslands in the Lamar Valley, Jackson Hole, and near Yellowstone's North Entrance. Their numbers have declined by approximately 50 percent in Yellowstone since 1991, and their long-distance winter migration routes around Grand Teton are jeopardized by large-scale energy developments outside of the park.

A few hundred hardy **Rocky Mountain bighorn sheep** are often spotted scampering along cliffs and roaming Yellowstone's alpine meadows. In summer, the are most easily found on the slopes of Mt. Washburn, and year-round in Gardner Canyon between Mammoth and the North Entrance. Also watch for their silhouettes on cliff tops along the Yellowstone River, and above Soda Butte in the Lamar Valley.

Invasive, nonnative **mountain goats** are increasingly common and thought to be colonizing rocky slopes in Yellowstone's northern reaches.

The expanding **American cougar** (also known as the mountain lion) population is estimated at 20 to 35, with 15 to 17 resident adults, making it Yellowstone's most common cat species. They are primarily nocturnal and stealthily patrol a vast range.

The solitary, nocturnal, and reclusive **bobcat** is poorly studied but thought to be widespread. You're more likely to hear its blood-curdling scream at night while snuggled inside your sleeping bag than to see it from the trail. Most reports are from the northern half of Yellowstone in sagebrush and conifer forests.

Other common small mammals include the wily, weasel-like **marten** in coniferous forests; the playful **river otter** found in rivers, lakes and ponds; and two species of **weasel** (also known as **ermine**) both widespread in willows and spruce/fir forests. **Beavers** dam watercourses and cobble together lodges adjacent to trails in both parks.

Animals rarely seen by hikers include sagebrush-loving **badgers**, and the **red fox**, found in the Lamar Valley and around Canyon Village at the edges of forest and sagelands. A recent three-year study confirmed the presence and reproduction of the wide-ranging **Canadian lynx**, which hide out in remote subalpine forests and feed primarily on **snowshoe hare**, on the east side of Yellowstone.

Rare mammals include the relatively scarce **raccoon**; carnivorous, forest-dwelling **fisher**; weasel-like **mink**, occasionally seen in riparian forests;

striped skunk, seen flitting between the forest and riparian zones; and the fierce, seldom-seen **wolverine**, the largest land member of the weasel family.

Three territorial species of **chipmunk** are common in conifer forests. Four **squirrel** species, which are similar to but larger than chipmunks, are common in around rocky outcroppings in forests. The **yellow-bellied marmot** is commonly seen, or at least its high-pitched whistle is heard, where trails traverse rocky slopes. The bleating **pika** is also common in this kind of landscape. Other rodents often spotted scurrying about the forest understory include **gophers**, **mice**, several species of **voles**, and **shrews, muskrats**, **bushy-tailed wood rats**, and **porcupines**.

At last count, 319 bird species were winging around the skies above Greater Yellowstone, with 148 of those observed nesting. Early morning in spring (from mid-May through early July) is the best time for birding. While hiking around lakes and waterways, keep your eyes peeled for big raptors like the threatened but recovering **bald eagle** and trout-loving **osprey** swooping around hunting for prey. Majestic but imperiled **trumpeter swans** range between Montana's Paradise Valley and the Madison River. The reintroduced **peregrine falcon**, which preys on songbirds and waterfowl, nests in Yellowstone and well is on its way to recovery but is rarely seen.

Other common species that exhibit entertaining antics include the boisterous **Clark's nutcracker**, the diminutive **mountain chickadee**, the **mountain bluebird**, and the **Steller's jay**, a bold scavenger. Monitored species of special concern include **American white pelicans**, **common loons**, **harlequin ducks**, and **great gray owls**.

Yellowstone contains one of the most significant aquatic ecosystems in the United States. It's home to 16 fish species: 11 native and 5 nonnative. Since 2001, regulations have required the release of all native sport fishes hooked in park waters. The fishing season runs from Memorial Day weekend through the first Sunday of November.

The three subspecies of native **cutthroat trout** are an essential source of grizzly sustenance. They are being eaten out of house and home by the proliferation of illegally introduced, nonnative **lake trout**, also known as Mackinaws. Other native sport fish are the rare, protected **Arctic grayling** and the slender, silver **mountain whitefish**. Introduced sport fish include **brook trout**, **brown trout**, **rainbow trout**, and **lake chub**.

Coyote *populations have halved since wolves were reintroduced.*

Six species of **reptiles** (prairie rattlesnake, bull snake, valley garter snake, wandering garter snake, rubber boa, and sagebrush lizard) and four species of **amphibians** (boreal toad, chorus frog, spotted frog, and tiger salamander) are found in Yellowstone. It's possible, but encountering a poisonous **prairie rattlesnake** in Yellowstone's low-lying Northern Range is unlikely.

More than 12,000 **insects**, including 128 species of butterflies, provide fodder for many quick-tongued predators. Of greatest concern to hikers are **mosquitoes** (see Trail Safety, page 17).

When to Go

As two of the North America's most popular summer destinations, both parks have the unfortunate reputation of being overcrowded. This certainly can be true on major holiday weekends and on heavily trafficked roads and at must-see attractions, but solitude is not hard to come by—if you know where to look.

Both parks are four-season recreation destinations. Less than 5 percent of Yellowstone's visitors arrive between November and April. Likewise, in Grand Teton 80 percent of visitors come between June and September. Annual Yellowstone visitor numbers have hovered around 3 million for the past 15 years, while Grand Teton averages around 2.5 million.

Thankfully, even in summer, escaping the crowds is reasonably easy—especially in Yellowstone. If you head for the backcountry, you can find solitude. Surveys by the Park Service found that only 1.5 percent of visitors apply for a backcountry permit in Yellowstone, and only half of 1 percent do in Grand Teton.

To avoid the crowds, all the usual rules of thumb apply about visiting midweek instead of on weekends, and during spring and fall shoulder periods. Luckily, some of the finest hiking conditions coincide with the peak of fall foliage colors and the crowds diminishing after Labor Day weekend.

Weather and Seasons

Throughout the region, conversations (and tall tales told by the fireplace over a post-hike pint) are peppered with anecdotes about the famously mercurial weather. Snowfall has been recorded every single day of the year in Greater Yellowstone, so the best advice is to always come prepared for the possibility of extreme conditions. Locals claim there are nine months of winter and three months of relatives. This isn't that far from the truth. Perhaps the most reliable climate-related axiom is, "If you don't like the weather, just wait five minutes."

Always be ready for afternoon thundershowers (locally called "rollers"), and to beat a hasty retreat from the higher elevations when lightning threatens. Since conditions on the trails change as quickly as the weather, it's best to check in with a ranger station before hitting the trail, even if you're only going for a dayhike.

Given the right disposition, conditions, and over-snow travel gear, **winter** can be the ideal time to explore the parks in relative tranquility. Yellowstone's Winter Daily Report (www.nps.gov/yell/dailyreports) is essential reading at this time of year.

During winter, the mercury hovers around 0°F during the short daylight hours, with occasional highs in the 20s. Subzero overnight lows are the norm. Infrequent warm "chinook" winds push daytime highs into the 40s. Annual snowfall averages 150 inches in most of Yellowstone, with 200 to 400 inches routinely recorded at higher elevations.

Based on a new winter use plan, all snowmobilers in Yellowstone are required to be accompanied by an authorized commercial guide. This temporary ruling—in effect through the winter of 2006-'07—permits a maximum of 720 snowmobiles per day in Yellowstone, plus an additional

140 unguided snowmobiles in Grand Teton. In addition, 16 operators offer increasingly popular guided tours by snowcoach (vehicles such as vans or buses that have been adapted to travel over snow). Skiers and snowshoers don't need a guide, and they have many groomed and ungroomed trails to choose from in several areas of the parks.

Though February sees some frosty but crystal-clear days of sunshine, snow blankets most of both parks well after the **vernal equinox** (March 21). The appearance of migrating mountain bluebirds, and the emergence of Uinta ground squirrels, are reliable indicators of the arrival of spring, usually in the second half of March. Depending on snow conditions, nonmotorized exploration (including hiking, bicycling, jogging, in-line skates, and roller skis) is permitted in

Bald eagle nest: *Eagles are often seen fishing for trout around Heart Lake (Trail 21).*

Yellowstone between the West Entrance and Mammoth Hot Springs from mid-March through the third week in April. Contact the NPS to verify opening dates and road conditions.

The **spring hiking season** begins as snow starts to melt from the lowest-lying trails—as early as May on Yellowstone's Northern Range, a bit later around Jackson Hole—and after trail maintenance crews clear winter deadfall. Early-season hiking coincides with the appearance of ravenous bears (and their newborn cubs) from their dens. Many of Yellowstone trails that pass through Bear Management Areas are off-limits during this period. Hiking can be superb before crowds begin to arrive for Memorial Day, when both parks are a hive of calving, nesting, spawning, and blooming activity. River fords are most dangerous in May and June, when snowmelt-fed waterfalls are also the most spectacular. Daytime temperatures average in the 40s and 50s in May. By June they reach the 60s and 70s, but nighttime lows still occasionally dip below freezing. The most precipitation (an average of around 2 inches per month) falls during May and the "June monsoon."

The prime **summer hiking and backpacking season** starts as the snow line retreats progressively up mountainsides until the highest elevations are clear, typically by late July in Yellowstone, and early August around the highest Teton passes. Elk and bison continue to drop calves until the **summer solstice** (June 21), the longest day of the year. The opening of Yellowstone's **fishing season** (the first Saturday of Memorial Day weekend) coincides with the start of the stonefly hatch—when mosquitoes and biting flies really hit their stride! **Wildflower watching** heats up soon after snowmelt, and peaks around mid-July in Yellowstone, a bit later at higher elevations and in the Tetons. Midsummer, daytime temperatures are typically in the 70s (and 80s at lower elevations). Nights remain cool, in the 40s and 30s, with the odd frosty spell.

The courting and **mating season** ("the rut") begins as early as late July. During this period, it's especially important to give elk and bison a wide berth on trails. Mosquitoes and other biting pests finally die down in August; that's also when berries are ripe for the picking in riparian zones. July and August are the driest months, but afternoon showers are still fairly common. Blooming goldenrod and gentians are reliable indicators of the coming of autumn.

Mature **bighorn rams** *with horns in full curl are often seeen around Bunsen Peak (Trail 3).*

Fall colors start to appear in the riparian zone by mid-August, and peak around the **autumnal equinox** (September 21), with slight variations according to elevation. Vibrant yellows, reds, and oranges persist on Yellowstone's Northern Range until early October, when the first significant snowfall usually occurs. Temperatures can remain surprisingly pleasant through October, but nighttime lows often plunge into the teens. Squirrels, chipmunks, and other rodents frantically preparing winter seed caches are a sure sign of another impending lo-o-o-ong winter.

Trail Selection

Three criteria were used during the selection of trails for this guide. Only the premier dayhikes and overnight backpacking trips are included, based upon **beautiful scenery**, **ease of access**, and **diversity of experience**. Many of the selected trails are very popular, while several others see infrequent use. If you are fortunate enough to be able to complete all the trips in this book, you will gain a comprehensive appreciation for the complex beauty of one of the world's most scenic and intact temperate-zone ecosystems.

Nearly half of the trails included in this guide are out-and-back trips, requiring you to retrace your steps back to the trailhead. Forty percent of the routes are full or partial loop trips, with the remaining six routes being point-to-point trips that are worthy of the required vehicle shuttle.

Key Features

Top Trails books contain information about "features" for each trail. Yellowstone and the Tetons are blessed with a wide diversity of terrain—no matter what your interests, you're sure to find a trail to match them.

Water lovers and anglers will find plenty of pristine lakes, rivers, and streams, while peak-baggers will be spoiled by the choice of world-class alpine panoramas. The abundance of open meadows are graced with riotous wildflower displays, and aspen groves provide plenty of fall color. All these features combine to make Greater Yellowstone a photographer's paradise. With a bit of planning, the opportunities for camping, fishing, boating, swimming, and wildlife watching are endless.

Multiple Uses

All the trails described in this guide are suitable for **hiking**. Although all the trails are equally legal for jogging, the vast majority of them are not suited for such a purpose, since running can incite predatory behavior in some wildlife. The only exceptions are the few gravel and paved roads in more

Bear Safety Guidelines

Restrictions in Yellowstone's 16 **Bear Management Areas** include seasonal closures, recommendations on minimum party size, and off-trail travel and camping prohibitions. Several trails in this book pass through these areas. No matter where you hike, it's always wise to take the following precautions:

• Ask at a ranger station or visitor center about recent bear activity before heading out.
• Do not travel alone or at night, when most bear feeding occurs. Parties of three or more are ideal.
• Stay alert for bear signs. Make noise and stay on marked trails; half of all attacks occur off-trail.
• Avoid carcasses and do not carry smelly food.
• Never leave your pack unattended on the trail.
• Follow NPS guidelines for proper camping and food storage techiques, as outlined in free hiking and backcountry camping brochures available at ranger stations and backcountry offices.
• Report any incidents to park rangers.

Even if you follow all of these guidelines, it's still quite possible that you will encounter a bear, especially if visiting the backcountry. If you see a bear before it sees you, keep out of sight and backtrack the way you came, or detour downwind as far as possible. There are various schools of thought about what to do in case of an encounter. Here's an executive summary what the NPS recommends:

• Stay calm. Do not run or make sudden movements— you cannot outrun a bear!
• Back away slowly. Do not drop your pack.
• Talk quietly to the bear, do not shout. Avoid looking directly at the bear.
• Only climb a tree if it's nearby and you can climb at least 15 to 20 feet.

If you are charged, the NPS recommends standing still (easier said than done!) since most charges are bluff charges. If the bear makes physical contact, drop to the ground, face down with your hands behind your neck. In the case of a nighttime attack on a tent (these are extremely rare), you should fight back aggressively and use pepper spray.

developed areas that also allow **bicycling**. Where applicable, trail descriptions note where routes receive heavy **stock use** by horse packers and llama outfitters. As in most national parks, **pets** and **mountain biking** are not allowed on any of the trails. Winter use is limited but growing in both parks, with **cross-country skiing**, **snowshoeing**, and **snowcoach tours** becoming more popular as snowmobiling is increasingly restricted.

Trail Safety

Dramatic elevation changes pose a possible danger to visitors arriving from near sea level. Signs of **altitude sickness** to watch for include headache, fatigue, loss of appetite, shortness of breath, nausea, vomiting, drowsiness, dizziness, memory loss, and diminished mental acuity. A rapid descent generally alleviates any symptoms if they develop. The best advice is to eat lots of carbohydrates prior to the trip, acclimatize slowly, avoid alcohol and heavy foods, and drink plenty of fluids.

    Burns from thermal features are a common cause of death and serious injury in Yellowstone. Follow posted regulations about off-trail travel, don't traverse thermal areas after dark, and don't bathe in thermal waters that aren't NPS-approved (see "Bathers Beware" in this section).

YOU Can Help Save Our Bears!

This bear found unattended coolers and backpacks in the Jenny, String, and Leigh Lake areas. It was killed 7/24/04 because it became aggressive trying to get more human food.

PLEASE

Help us save other bears in this area by **NEVER** letting your food out of your sight!

Bear Responsibility *To avoid tempting food-conditioned black bears, please follow all park regulations.*

    Ticks are a nuisance from mid-March through mid-July in the lowest-lying areas. Wear repellent, tuck your shirt and pant legs in, and check your body often. Depending on elevation and the rate at which the previous winter's snowpack melts, the peak of the **mosquito season** hits the backcountry in June and July, and abates in mid- to late August. Repellents, netting, and protective clothing are your best forms of protection.

    Most of Yellowstone's backcountry **river crossings** intentionally lack bridges, and many fords are dangerous (over thigh-deep) until at least July. Check current conditions during trip planning, and when in doubt, pick another route or turn back.

Dehydration is a concern on longer trails where water is lacking. The presence of *Giardia* means that all water should be boiled, filtered, or otherwise treated before drinking. Keep your hands clean to avoid transmitting nasty microbes to your hiking companions.

Sunburn is a concern, especially at higher altitudes. Sun protection, sunglasses, and a good wide-brimmed hat are essential. Due to the possibility of rapid weather changes, **hypothermia** is a concern year-round. Most hypothermia cases happen when air temperatures are between 30° and 50°F. Always check the weather forecast before heading out, and carry extra warm and waterproof gear. It's not uncommon to experience four seasons during a midsummer hike!

 Bathers Beware

Soaking directly in thermal waters is not allowed, in order to protect bathers' skin and the park's unique thermophilic microbiological resources. Swimming *is* allowed in a few places where thermal runoff mixes with cold water sources, such as the Boiling River (Trail 2, page 43), and the Firehole River Canyon near Madison Junction.

Cell phone coverage is sketchy at best throughout both parks, though emergency calls have aided recent rescues in Grand Teton. That said, you should not count on your phone as a reliable means of communication in an emergency.

Fees, Camping, and Permits

The combined **entrance fee** ($20 per car, $15 per motorcycle, $10 per hiker or bicyclist) is valid for seven days' admission to Yellowstone and Grand Teton national parks. The annual **National Parks Pass** ($50) grants entrance to most parks for one year from the date of purchase, and is often available at a slight discount from NPS partners. Year-long **park-specific passes** ($40) allow entrance to a single park. The **Golden Age Passport** ($10 one-time fee) allows US citizens 62 years old and older lifetime entrance to all National Park System areas. Similarly, the **Golden Access Passport** grants lifetime entrance to all NPS areas to US citizens with proof of permanent disability.

Myriad camping opportunities exist throughout the Greater Yellowstone region. The challenge can be securing a spot, as the most popular campgrounds fill to capacity early in the day during the summer, especially on weekends. Where available, reservations are strongly advised between the Memorial Day and Labor Day weekends.

In Yellowstone, the NPS runs seven first-come, first-served campgrounds ($12-$14 per night). Call (307) 344-2114 for details. Concessionaire **Xanterra** manages four reservable campgrounds ($18 per night) and the Fishing Bridge RV Park ($31). Call (307) 344-7311 or see www.travelyellowstone.com for more information. With the exception of Slough Creek, all campgrounds have a few hiker/biker sites ($4). The NPS sites are much smaller and less developed, most with basic vault toilets and prohibitions against generators. The more developed sites allow generators and have flush toilets, dump stations, and showers and laundry nearby. There's a 14-day limit on camping between June 15 and September 15 everywhere except Fishing Bridge, with a 30-day limit the rest of the year.

In Yellowstone, advance reservations for the more than 300 **backcountry campsites** are accepted (for a $20 fee) only by mail or in person, starting April 1. Fortunately, a portion of backcountry sites in each area of the park are left open for in-person reservations, which can be made not more than 48 hours in advance of the first date of the trip. Contact Yellowstone's **Backcountry Office** to request a free Backcountry Trip Planner (or download it from the park's Web site) for a full rundown of the extensive regulations. Call (307) 344-7381 or see www.nps.gov/yell/publications/-pdfs/backcountry.

Backcountry Use Permits are available at most ranger stations and dedicated backcountry offices: separate information desks in Grant Village, Lake Village, and Mammoth, staffed by specialized rangers. The permits are also occasionally available at the Northeast and East Entrance Stations, depending on seasonal staffing levels. Contact the main backcountry office (see above) and consult the Backcountry Trip Planner for current updates.

In Yellowstone, trailheads are sometimes referred to on maps (and in this book, where applicable) according to an alphanumeric naming system, such as "Lone Star (OK1)"; a complete list of these trailhead names appears in the park's Backcountry Trip Planner brochure.

In Grand Teton, there are five first-come, first-served **frontcountry campgrounds** ($15 per night), with hiker/biker sites ($5 per night) at Jenny Lake and Colter Bay. There are also concessionaire-operated **"trailer villages"** (reservable RV parks with showers, laundry, and full hook-ups) at Colter Bay and between Grand Teton and Yellowstone at Flagg Ranch. **Backcountry camping reservations** ($15 fee) are accepted from January 1 through May 15. Download the Backcountry Camping brochure from the park's Web site (www.nps.gov/grte/trip/activities/back.htm) for details on current reservation procedures.

Beyond the parks, there are plenty of private campgrounds and ample opportunity for primitive and dispersed camping in the nearby national forests and wilderness areas. The NPS maintains a handy chart of campgrounds outside of Yellowstone and Grand Teton. See www.nps.gov/yell/planvisit/services/campoutofpark.htm.

Free permits, available at ranger stations and visitor centers, are required for all overnight trips into the backcountry in both parks. Fees are charged for mandatory boating and fishing permits.

On the Trail

Every outing should begin with proper preparation, which usually takes only a few minutes. Even the easiest trail can turn up unexpected surprises. People seldom think about getting lost or injured, but unexpected things can and do happen. Simple precautions can make the difference between a good story and a miserable outcome.

Use the Top Trails ratings and descriptions to determine if a particular trail is a good match with your fitness and energy level, given current conditions and time of year.

Have a Plan

Choose Wisely The first step to enjoying any trail, no matter the activity or the degree of difficulty, is to match the trail to your abilities. It's no use overestimating your fitness or experience—know your abilities and limitations, and use the Top Trails Difficulty Rating that accompanies each trail.

Leave Word About Your Plans The most basic of precautions is leaving word of your intentions with friends or family. Many people will hike the backcountry their entire lives without ever relying on this safety net, but establishing this simple habit is free insurance.

It's best to leave specific information—location, trail name, intended time of travel—with a responsible person. However, if this is not possible or if plans change at the last minute, you should still leave word. If there is a registration process available, make use of it. If there is a ranger station, trail register, or visitor center, check in.

Prepare and Plan

- **Know your abilities and limitations**
- **Leave word about your plans**
- **Know your route and the area**

Review the Route Before embarking on any hike, read the entire description and study the map. It isn't necessary to memorize every detail, but it is worthwhile to have a clear mental picture of the trail and general area.

If the trail or terrain are complex, augment the trail guide with a topographic map. Maps and current weather and trail condition information are available from local ranger stations and backcountry offices, and these resources should be utilized (see Appendix, page 333).

Carry the Essentials

Proper preparation for any type of trail use includes gathering the essential items to carry. The checklist will vary tremendously by trail and conditions.

Clothing When the weather is good, light comfortable clothes are the obvious choice. It's easy to believe that little in the way of spare clothing if needed, but a prepared hiker has something tucked away for the unexpected, ranging from a surprise shower to an emergency overnight in more remote areas.

Clothing includes proper footwear, essential for hiking and backpacking. As a trail becomes more demanding, you will need footwear that performs. Running shoes are fine for shorter trails. If you will be carrying substantial weight or encountering sustained rugged terrain, step up to hiking boots.

In hot, sunny weather, proper clothing includes a hat, sunglasses, long-sleeved shirt, and sunscreen. In cooler weather, particularly when it's wet, carry waterproof outer garments and quick drying undergarments (avoid cotton). As general rule, whatever the conditions, bring layers that can be combined or removed to provide comfort and protection from the elements in a wide and highly changeable variety of conditions.

 Trail Essentials

- **Dress to keep cool, but be ready for cold**
- **Carry plenty of water**
- **Have adequate food (plus a little extra)**

Water Never set out on a trail without water. At all times, but particularly in warm weather, adequate water is of key importance. Experts recommend at least two quarts of water per day, and when hiking in heat a gallon or more may be more appropriate. At the extreme, dehydration can be life-threatening. More commonly, inadequate water brings fatigue and muscle aches.

For most outings, unless the day is very hot or the trail very long, you should plan to carry sufficient water for the entire trail. Unfortunately in North America, natural water sources are questionable: often contaminated with bacteria, viruses, and fertilizers.

Water Treatment If you have to use trailside water, you should filter or treat it. There are three methods for treating water: boiling, chemical treatment, and filtering. Boiling is best, but it's often impractical: It requires a heat source, a pot, and time. Chemical treatments, readily available in outdoor stores, handle some problems—including the troublesome *Giardia* parasite—but they will not combat many of the chemical pollutants. The preferred method is filtration. A good filter system removes Giardia and other contaminants and doesn't leave any unpleasant aftertaste.

If this hasn't convinced you to carry all the water you need, one final admonishment: Be prepared for surprises; water sources described in the text and shown on maps can change course or dry up completely. Never run your water bottle dry in expectation of the next source; fill up when water is available and always keep a little in reserve.

Food While not as critical as water, food is energy and should not be underestimated. Avoid foods that are hard to digest, such as sugary candy bars and fatty potato chips. Carry high energy, fast-digesting foods: nutrition bars, dehydrated fruit, jerky, trail mix. Bring a little extra food—it's good protection against an outing that turns unexpectedly long, perhaps due to foul weather or losing your way.

Useful But Less than Essential

Map and Compass (and the know-how to use them) Many trails don't require much navigation, so a map and compass aren't always as essential as water or food—but it's a close call. If the trail is remote or infrequently visited, a map and compass should be considered necessities.

A handheld GPS (Global Positioning System) receiver can also be a useful trail companion, but it's really no substitute for a map and compass; knowing your longitude and latitude is not much help without a map.

Cell Phone Most parts of the country, even remote destinations, have some level of cellular coverage, but service is sketchy at best in much of Yellowstone and the Tetons. In extreme circumstances, a cell phone can be a lifesaver. But don't depend it; where available, coverage is unpredictable and batteries fail. And be sure that the occasion warrants the phone call—a blister doesn't justify a call to search and rescue.

Gear Depending on the remoteness and rigor of the trail, there are many additional useful items to consider: pocket knife, flashlight, fire source (waterproof matches, lighter, or flint), and first-aid kit.

Every member of your party should carry the appropriate items described above; groups often split up or get separated along the trail. Solo hikers should be even more disciplined about preparation, and carry more gear. Traveling solo is inherently more risky. This isn't meant to discourage solo travel, simply to emphasize the need for extra preparation. Solo hikers should make a habit of carrying a little more gear than is absolutely necessary.

Trail Etiquette

The overriding rule on the trail is **"Leave No Trace."** Interest in visiting natural areas continues to increase in North America, even as the quantity of unspoiled wilderness continues to shrink. These pressures make it ever more critical that we leave no trace of our visits.

Never Litter If you carried it in, it's just as easy to carry it out. Leave the trail in the same, if not better condition than you found it. Try picking up any litter you encounter and packing it out—it's a great feeling! Just one piece of garbage and you've made a difference.

Stay on the Trail Paths have been created, sometimes over many years, for many purposes: to protect the surrounding natural areas, to avoid dangers, and to provide the best route. Leaving the trail can cause damage that takes years to undo. Never cut switchbacks. Shortcutting rarely saves time or energy, and it takes a terrible toll on the land, trampling plant life and hastening erosion. Moreover, safety and consideration intersect on the trail. Its hard to get truly lost if you stay on the trail.

Share the Trail The best trails attract many visitors, and you should be prepared to share the trail with others. Do your part to minimize impact. Commonly accepted trail etiquette dictates that **bike riders yield to both hikers and equestrians, hikers yield to horseback riders, downhill hikers yield to uphill hikers**, and **everyone stays to the right.** Not everyone knows these rules of the road, so let common sense and good humor be your ultimate guide.

Leave It There Removal or destruction of plants or animals; or historical, pre-historic, or geological items is certainly unethical and almost always illegal.

 Trail Etiquette

- Leave no trace—Never litter
- Stay on the trail—Never cut switchbacks
- Share the trail—Use courtesy and common sense
- Leave it there—Don't disturb plants or wildlife

Getting Lost If you become lost on the trail, stay on the trail. Stop and take stock of the situation. In many cases, a few minutes of calm reflection will yield a solution. Consider all the clues available; use the sun to determine direction if you don't have a compass. If you determine that you are indeed lost, stay on the main trail and stay put. You are more likely to encounter other people by staying in one place.

A Note from the Author

During the summer of 2002, I had the privilege of living inside the park while working for the Yellowstone Center for Resources in Mammoth. While collecting baseline scientific and Geographic Positioning System (GPS) data for an ongoing Geographic Information Systems (GIS) database project focused on mapping the park's microbial diversity, I surveyed several well-known frontcountry and seldom-seen backcountry thermal areas. When I wasn't in the field doing research, I was out exploring trails.

Between May 2002 and October 2004, I hiked every trail included in this book at least once. In many cases, I rehiked my favorite trails in both parks in several different months. With that in mind, please note that the only consistency in the seasons and trail conditions in Greater Yellowstone is inconsistency. Thus, despite my best efforts, this book's trail descriptions represent a snapshot, not a comprehensive picture, of this supremely dynamic region.

CHAPTER 1

Northwest Yellowstone–Mammoth/Gallatin Country

Northwest Yellowstone–Mammoth/Gallatin Country

The northwestern quadrant of Yellowstone National Park includes the developed area around the park's headquarters at **Mammoth Hot Springs** and, to the east, the soaring peaks of the **Gallatin Range**. It is also the park's lowest and driest region.

The **North Entrance**, near the sociable gateway town of Gardiner, Montana, is the only park entrance that remains open year-round; the Grand Loop Road remains open year-round between Gardiner and Cooke City. Halfway between the North Entrance and Mammoth Hot Springs, the first-come, first-served **Mammoth Campground** is the park's only year-round campground. Eight miles south of Mammoth, the smaller, NPS-run **Indian Creek Campground** is in the thick of moose country and is often closed in the spring season by bear activity.

The region's diverse terrain includes some of the park's topographic extremes, ranging from desertlike corridors between 5300 and 6000 feet near the park's northern boundary to several peaks that top out over 10,000 feet. Yellowstone's low-lying **Northern Range**, which straddles the Montana-Wyoming state line, is a vital overwintering area for migrating wildlife such as pronghorn, elk, bighorn sheep, mule deer, bison, and coyotes between November and May. Just like the animals, early- and late-season hikers migrate here to seek refuge from the rest of the park's extreme weather. These relatively mild conditions also make Mammoth a popular base camp for winter sports such as snowshoeing and cross-country skiing.

In Mammoth, the main Visitor Center and Backcountry Office (where permits are issued) are housed adjacent to the park headquarters in the **Fort Yellowstone-Mammoth Hot Springs Historic District**, in buildings constructed by the US Army during its tenure (1886–1918) as park custodians. Nearby, portions of the updated **Mammoth Hot Springs Hotel** date back to 1911. Room rates run from $69 to $306; call (307) 344-7311 for information and reservations.

Just outside the North Entrance, which was the park's first major gateway, the large stone **Roosevelt Arch** was designed by Old Faithful architect Robert Reamer in 1903 to commemorate the completion of the Northern Pacific railway spur line from Livingston to Gardiner, Montana, and the subsequent visit of President Theodore Roosevelt. The top of the arch is inscribed FOR THE BENEFIT AND ENJOYMENT OF THE PEOPLE, a quote from the Organic Act of 1872, the enabling legislation for what was then the world's first national park. Inside the arch is a sealed time capsule that includes period postcards and a photo of Roosevelt.

The railroad's plans to lay spur lines through the fragile geyser basins and monopolize public access to the park were countered by the lobbying efforts of avid outdoorsman President Roosevelt's Boone & Crockett Club, a politically influential pro-hunting group. By 1905 the US Army Corps of Engineers had established the beginnings of today's Grand Loop Road, and in 1915 the first private automobiles were admitted to the park. In 1916 the newly constituted National Park Service banned horse-drawn wagons from all park roads.

Today, you can still travel the original gravel stagecoach road (one-way only, except for bicycles and hikers) from Mammoth to Gardiner. It starts behind the Mammoth Hot Springs Hotel and winds down for 5 miles to the North Entrance gate.

Overleaf: *Author on Bunsen Peak (Trail 3)*

Permits and Maps

The year-round **Albright Visitor Center and Museum** sells a good selection of maps and field guides. Rangers also hand out free dayhiking brochures and are a great source of trail updates and general advice. Call (307)-344-2263; open daily 8 AM to 7 PM in summer, 9 AM to 5 PM in winter. The museum, housed in former bachelor officers' quarters, focuses on history and has a good exhibit on predators and prey upstairs. The art gallery has reproductions of watercolor sketches by Thomas Moran and original William Henry Jackson photographs from the 1871 Hayden Survey. The visitor center's theater shows a couple of short videos about the history and evolution of Yellowstone.

Under the same roof and next door to the visitor center, the summer-only **Backcountry Office** issues boating, fishing, and backcountry camping permits, and is a wealth of hiking and backpacking information. Call (307) 344-2160; the office is open from 8 AM to 4:30 PM. In spring, fall and winter, call the park's operator at (307) 344-7381 for advice about where to obtain permits.

National Geographic's Trails Illustrated *Mammoth Hot Springs* (no. 303, scale 1:63,360) map depicts all of the trails, trailheads, and campsites mentioned in this chapter. The similar Trails Illustrated *Yellowstone National Park* (no. 202, scale 1:126,720) map, with trails and mileage waypoints, has sufficient detail for trip planning and frontcountry hiking, but does not depict trailheads or backcountry campsites.

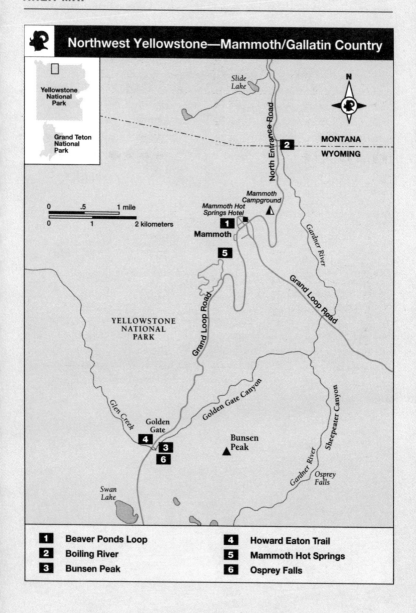

Northwest Yellowstone—Mammoth/Gallatin Country

Yellowstone National Park

Grand Teton National Park

Slide Lake

North Entrance Road

N

MONTANA

WYOMING

0   .5   1 mile

0   1   2 kilometers

Mammoth Campground

Mammoth Hot Springs Hotel

1

Mammoth

5

Gardner River

Grand Loop Road

YELLOWSTONE NATIONAL PARK

Grand Loop Road

Glen Creek

Golden Gate

4

3

6

Golden Gate Canyon

Bunsen Peak ▲

Gardner River

Sheepeater Canyon

Osprey Falls

Swan Lake

1	Beaver Ponds Loop	**4**	Howard Eaton Trail
2	Boiling River	**5**	Mammoth Hot Springs
3	Bunsen Peak	**6**	Osprey Falls

Northwest Yellowstone—Mammoth/Gallatin Country

TRAIL	Difficulty	Length	Type	USES & ACCESS	TERRAIN	FLORA & FAUNA	OTHER
1	3	5.5	↻	Hiking, Child Friendly	Lake, Stream	Wildflowers, Autumn Colors, Birds, Wildlife	Great Views, Swimming
2	1	1.0	↗	Hiking, Handicap Access, Child Friendly	Canyon, Stream	Wildflowers, Wildlife	Swimming, Geologic Interest
3	4/5	4.2	↗	Hiking	Mountain, Summit	Wildflowers, Wildlife	Great Views, Photo Opportunity, Geologic Interest, Secluded
4	3/4	4.0	↘	Hiking		Wildflowers, Autumn Colors, Birds, Wildlife	Great Views, Photo Opportunity, Historic, Geologic Interest
5	1	1.0	↻	Hiking, Handicap Access, Child Friendly			Great Views, Photo Opportunity, Swimming, Historic, Moonlight Hiking
6	5	10.2	↗	Hiking, Bicycling	Canyon, Stream, Waterfall	Wildflowers, Birds, Wildlife	Secluded

USES & ACCESS
- Hiking
- Bicycling
- Horses
- Backpacking
- Child Friendly
- Handicap Access
- Backcountry Permit Required
- Camping

TERRAIN
- Canyon
- Mountain
- Summit
- Stream
- Waterfall
- Lake
- Geothermal

FLORA & FAUNA
- Autumn Colors
- Wildflowers
- Birds
- Wildlife

DIFFICULTY
- 1 2 3 4 5 +
less   more

OTHER
- Cool & Shady
- Great Views
- Photo Opportunity
- Swimming
- Secluded
- Historic
- Geologic Interest
- Moonlight Hiking
- Steep

Northwest Yellowstone– Mammoth/Gallatin Country

Howard Eaton Trail 53
This short downhill section of Yellowstone's longest trail traverses good wildlife habitat and a wide variety of picturesque terrain, including geothermal areas, boulder fields, and the scenic shoulder of Terrace Mtn. It's most enjoyable if you can arrange a shuttle.

TRAIL 4

Hike
4 miles, Point-to-Point
or 6.6 miles, Loop
Difficulty: 1 2 **3 4** 5

Mammoth Hot Springs 57
A network of wooden boardwalks offers a close-up look at the most accessible thermal area in the northern half of the park. While Yellowstone's most famous geysers wow audiences with their predictable, instantly gratifying performances, Mammoth's mercurial hot-spring terraces are impressive for both their human history and drawn-out natural development.

TRAIL 5

Hike
1 mile, Loop
Difficulty: **1** 2 3 4 5

Osprey Falls 63
A strenuous add-on to the Bunsen Peak Loop, this infrequently visited waterfall awaits at the head of the impressive Sheepeater Canyon. After a long, flat stretch along an abandoned service road through a regenerating burn area, you plunge 800 feet into the deep, narrow canyon.

TRAIL 6

Hike, Bike
9.8 miles, Out & Back,
or 10.2 miles, Loop
Difficulty: 1 2 3 4 **5**

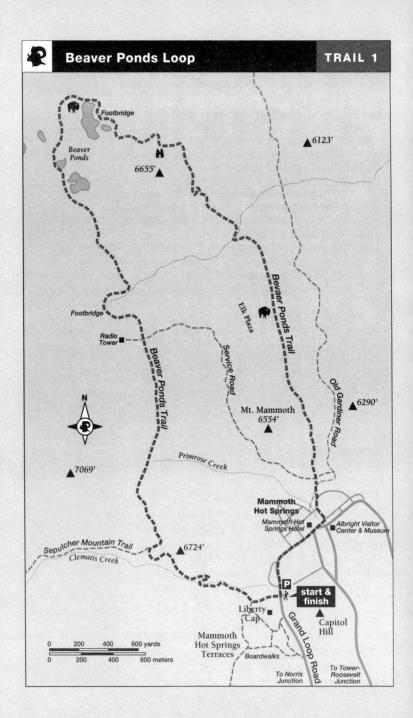

Beaver Ponds Loop

TRAIL 1

Footbridge

Beaver Ponds

▲6123'

6655' ▲

Footbridge

Radio Tower ■

Beaver Ponds Trail

Elk Plaza

Beaver Ponds Trail

Old Gardiner Road

▲6290'

N

Service Road

Mt. Mammoth 6554' ▲

▲7069'

Primrose Creek

Mammoth Hot Springs

Mammoth Hot Springs Hotel ■

Albright Visitor Center & Museum ■

Sepulcher Mountain Trail

Clematis Creek

▲6724'

| 0 | 200 | 400 | 600 yards |
| 0 | 200 | 400 | 600 meters |

P

start & finish

Liberty Cap ■

Capitol Hill ▲

Grand Loop Road

Mammoth Hot Springs Terraces

Boardwalks

To Norris Junction

To Tower-Roosevelt Junction

Beaver Ponds Loop

The most popular moderate-difficulty loop near Mammoth traverses a range of habitats and provides the opportunity to see a wide variety of wildlife, including the occasional black bear.

Best Time

The trail is hikable from May to October: During the summer the exposed portions of the route are hot and dry. Wildflowers bloom early here and aspen groves color the hillside starting in September. Wildlife is most abundant in spring, fall and winter. The beavers are at their busiest in the late afternoon.

Finding the Trail

From the Grand Loop Road junction in front of the Albright Visitor Center, the Sepulcher Mountain/ Beaver Ponds trailhead (1K1) parking area is 0.25 mile south toward Norris Junction. The signed trailhead is at the foot of Clematis Gulch, between an old stone park-employee residence and the dormant hot-spring cone known as Liberty Cap. There are parking lots on both sides of the road, but private vehicles are not allowed to park in the tour bus parking area next to the new restroom facilities.

Logistics

This dayhike is one of the only short loop hikes in the northern half of the park and is frequently recommended by rangers at the Mammoth Visitor Center. It's also a favorite with park employees early

TRAIL USE
Hike

LENGTH
5.5 miles, 2.5-3 hours

VERTICAL FEET
±400

DIFFICULTY
– 1 2 **3** 4 5 +

TRAIL TYPE
Loop

SURFACE TYPE
Dirt

FEATURES
Child Friendly
Stream
Lake
Autumn Colors
Wildflowers
Birds
Wildlife
Great Views

FACILITIES
Visitor Center
Restrooms
Picnic Tables
Phone
Water

If you're staying at the Mammoth Campground, the closest hot showers ($3) are up the hill at the Mammoth Hot Springs Hotel. Sign up and grab a towel at the hotel's reception desk.

Birds

and late in the season. Given all this, it can get busy at times.

Trail Description

From the trailhead parking areas►1 near the northern base of the **Mammoth Hot Springs terraces**, look for a trailhead sign on the main road pointing the way up Clematis Gulch, between the dormant **Liberty Cap** hot spring cone (to your left) and the old stone house next to the restroom facility and tour bus parking area (to your right).

Beyond the **Sepulcher Mountain trailhead,►2** the path crosses **Clematis Creek** a couple of times on wooden footbridges as it climbs into shady mixed spruce-fir forest. Ignore the unofficial trail that cuts uphill just before the second bridge and continue to your right across the creek.

Beyond this bridge, the trail swings away from the north bank of the creek and switches back sharply around a juniper- and sagebrush-studded ridge to the **Howard Eaton/Golden Gate Trail junction►3** after 0.3 mile. Keep to your right to finish the calf-stretching 350-foot climb up to the **Beaver Ponds Loop Trail junction,►4** 0.7 mile from the parking areas.

Beyond this junction, views of Mammoth Hot Springs, Bunsen Peak, and the Lava Creek Bridge on the Mammoth-Tower road open up to the east, with Mt. Everts (7842') tilting to your left in the north. Watch and listen here for strutting sage grouse alongside the trail, especially in early spring.

The slope eases up as it rolls through sageland and bird-rich meadows accented by stands of aspen that exhibit the tell-tale blackened, head-high browsing marks on their trunks, left by sustenance-starved ungulates each winter. As the trail flattens out, it parallels, then passes under, some power

Male grouse *court mates in spring with low-frequency drumming noises they create by rapidly vibrating their wings.*

lines. Ignore the numerous game trails that branch off the main trail here. Where the trail swings east and the views really open up, watch for elk, mule deer, and pronghorn antelope grazing in the sage-lands below to your right.

 Wildlife

After passing several mature stands of heavily browsed aspen and crossing an NPS service road (which leads up the hill to a radio tower), the trail descends gently through meadows and spruce-fir forest. You cross a seasonal stream via a bridge before reaching the first of several shallow, cattail-fringed **beaver ponds**▶5 after 2.5 miles. Look for evidence of the amphibious, hydrological engineers in the form of gnawed-down logs around the shore. The paddle-tailed rodents lie low during the day and are busiest beavering away in the late afternoon. Moose are also occasionally spotted browsing nearby in the willow thickets.

The trail undulates and meanders past a couple

of small, marshy ponds and crosses four seasonal streams on footbridges over 0.5 mile before arriving at the last and **largest of the unnamed ponds.**▶6 Listen for birds as you approach through the trees. The edges of the mixed forest are also a favored haunt of black bears: Make plenty of noise to avoid unpleasant surprises. The trail loops around along the shore, passing a variety of idyllic spots to stop for a picnic lunch. At the outlet, you can admire some of the beavers' handiwork before carefully crossing over the stream on a logjam.

Wildlife

The trail climbs away from the ponds through open grassland and shady forest, back under more power lines, and past the ruins of an old log cabin, before entering a wide-open plateau known as **Elk Plaza** and more rolling sagelands. Here, you get an eye-level view of the ridgelike Mt. Everts's geologic layers, across the Gardner River Valley to the north (left).

Beyond the Mammoth Area Trails notice board, a trailhead sign▶7 announces your return to civilization. Continue straight ahead at the old service road intersection▶8 and drop down a hundred yards on a narrow, rocky trail to the beginning of the gravel, one-way **Old Gardiner Road,**▶9 an early stagecoach route that drops 1000 feet in 5 miles to the park's North Entrance station.

To return to the trailhead parking areas,▶10 walk behind the **Mammoth Hot Springs Hotel** and left out to the main road, then turn right and head for **Liberty Cap**.

MILESTONES

▶1 0.0 Start at Sepulcher Mountain/Beaver Ponds parking areas

▶2 0.1 Sepulcher Mountain/Beaver Ponds trailhead

▶3 0.3 Right at Howard Eaton/Golden Gate Trail junction

▶4 0.8 Right at Beaver Ponds Trail junction

▶5 2.5 First of several beaver ponds

▶6 3.0 Last and largest beaver pond

▶7 5.0 Beaver Ponds/Clematis Creek trailhead

▶8 5.1 Straight through old service road intersection

▶9 5.25 Start of Old Gardiner Road

▶10 5.5 Return to trailhead parking areas

OPTIONS

Starting from Mammoth Hot Springs Hotel

If you'd rather not start out with the steepest part of the hike first, you can do the loop in reverse with no difference in elevation gain.

Map Room, Music, and Espresso at Mammoth Hot Springs Hotel

If you have a few minutes to spare, check out the **Map Room** off the Mammoth Hot Springs Hotel lobby. Constructed in 1937, it features a unique map of the United States fashioned from 16 types of wood from nine different countries. The map was designed by architect Robert Reamer, who also envisioned the Old Faithful Inn. If you're staying in the area, check out the schedule of **evening talks**, **slide shows**, and live **piano music**. In the morning, there's an **espresso** cart in the lobby to get you going.

Old Gardiner Road

If you're headed north out of the park after the hike, consider taking the scenic, 5-mile gravel stagecoach route down to the North Entrance station in Gardiner.

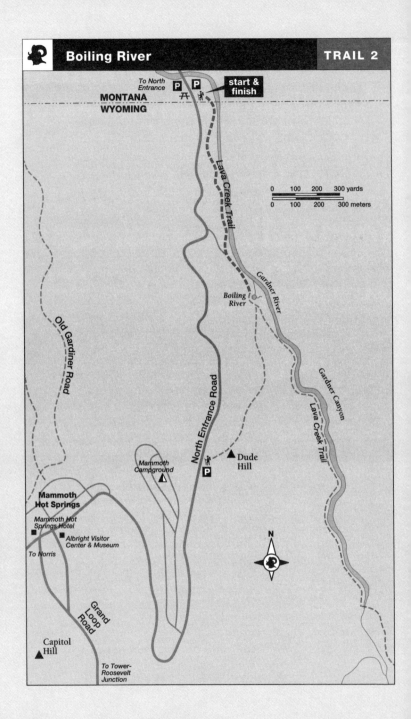

Boiling River

TRAIL 2

To North
Entrance

start &
finish

MONTANA
WYOMING

Lava Creek Trail

0   100   200   300 yards
0   100   200   300 meters

Gardner River

Boiling
River

Old Gardiner Road

North Entrance Road

Lava Creek Trail

Gardner Canyon

Mammoth
Campground

Dude
Hill

Mammoth
Hot Springs

Mammoth Hot
Springs Hotel

Albright Visitor
Center & Museum

To Norris

N

Grand
Loop
Road

Capitol
Hill

To Tower-
Roosevelt
Junction

Boiling River

Yellowstone's premier frontcountry soak is a dynamic series of five-star hot pots formed by the confluence of an icy river and an impressive thermal stream. It's fun for the entire family and, as one of few remaining places to legally soak in the US National Parks, it's definitely not to be missed.

Best Time

Soaking in the mix of cool and near-boiling water is most enjoyable in early morning or late afternoon, and best avoided in the midday summer sun. Visiting in the winter is a special treat. The area is normally open for soaking from around mid-June through April, but access is restricted by the NPS during periods of high spring runoff.

Finding the Trail

The springs do not appear on official NPS park maps and are not named on most other maps, but they are still easy to find. The unsigned turnoff for the parking areas is off the North Entrance Road, almost exactly halfway between the North Entrance gate and the Mammoth Hot Springs Junction, 2.3 miles from either point. Officially, these are the parking areas for the Lava Creek Trail, which leads to the bathing area. The only signs near the parking areas—the main one on the east side and an over-flow lot with shady picnic tables on the west side of the road—announce the Wyoming/Montana state line (if headed south from Gardiner) and 45TH PAR-ALLEL OF LATITUDE: HALFWAY BETWEEN EQUATOR AND

TRAIL USE
Hike
LENGTH
1.0 mile, 1-2 hours
including soaking
VERTICAL FEET
Negligible; ±300'
DIFFICULTY
– **1** 2 3 4 5 +
TRAIL TYPE
Out & Back
SURFACE TYPE
Dirt

FEATURES
Child Friendly
Handicap Access
Canyon
Stream
Swimming
Geothermal
Geologic Interest

FACILITIES
Restrooms
Picnic Tables

NORTH POLE (if headed north from Mammoth). The signed Lava Creek trailhead (1N3) is on the northeast side of the road, behind the restrooms on the far east side of the gravel parking lot.

Logistics

The Boiling River is generally open for soaking from dawn to dusk, or as late as 5 AM to 9 PM in the high season. Check with the Visitor Center in Mammoth for the current status. Even though there are few signs, the area is one of the park's worst kept secrets and receives up to 200 visitors per day.

Bring drinking water, hiking sandals (flip-flops will fall off in the river), and a towel, plus a flashlight if visiting around sunset. The only changing area is inside the toilet at the trailhead.

Trail Description

From the far east side of the main parking area▶1 on the east side of the North Entrance Road, a wide, flat gravel path heads upstream alongside the **Gardner River** (yes, the river and the town of Gardiner are spelled differently, for no good reason, except that Montana is quirky) for about half a mile.

The steep, unnamed path from the **Mammoth Campground▶2** joins the Lava Creek Trail just

Mammoth Campground Trail

OPTIONS

From the Mammoth Campground, a steep path, which is roughly as long as the trail from the parking lot, descends several hundred feet in elevation from the far northeastern corner of the camping area. The unsigned trailhead is across the North Entrance Road, to the left of the prominent Dude Hill. It's not uncommon to confuse this route with the Lava Creek Trail that forks off to the right. The campground office can point you in the right direction.

before the main trail winds around the thermal source that emanates from an off-limits cave, thought to be resurfacing runoff from distant Mammoth Hot Springs. The official Boiling River **soaking area,▶3** indicated by split-rail log fencing, is at the far end of the trail, 0.5 mile from the trailhead.

Signs warn of the possible presence of the path-ogenic bacteria *Naegleria fowleri*, but no cases of the rare meningitis caused by the microscopic amoeba have ever been reported after bathing here. Just to be safe, do not submerge your head or nose below the water—the amoeba enters the brain via the nasal passages. Symptoms include a runny nose, sore throat, severe headache, and in the worst cases, possible death within a few days.

Bathing in the near-scalding main thermal channel would be fatal and is prohibited. (See **Bathers Beware** on page 18). The actual composi-tion of the dynamic bathing area changes daily and with the seasons. Seek out spots where other soak-ers are congregating and beware of direct contact with undiluted thermal water. If you have trouble finding a calm spot where the current does not wash you downstream, try placing a big river stone in your lap.

Do not overdo the soaking, especially if you have to make the steep hike back up to Mammoth Campground afterwards. When finished, retrace your steps to the campground or parking areas.**▶4**

To keep the Boiling River a family-friendly place, a couple of rules are strictly enforced: Bathing suits are required and alcohol is forbidden.

● Swimming

🚶	MILESTONES
▶1	0.0 Start at Boiling River/Lava Creek trailhead
▶2	0.4 Junction with trail from Mammoth Campground
▶3	0.5 Boiling River soaking area
▶4	1.0 Return to parking lots

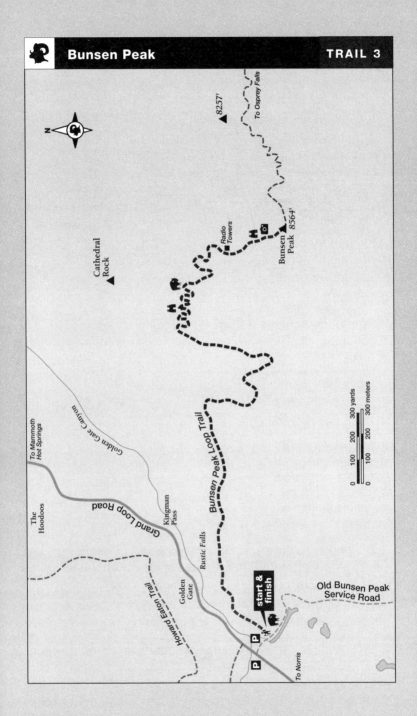

8257'

To Osprey Falls

Radio Towers

Bunsen Peak 8564'

Cathedral Rock

To Mammoth Hot Springs

Golden Gate Canyon

The Hoodoos

Grand Loop Road

Kingman Pass

Rustic Falls

Bunsen Peak LOOP Trail

Howard Eaton Trail

Golden Gate

start & finish

Old Bunsen Peak Service Road

To Norris

| 0 | 100 | 200 | 300 yards |
| 0 | 100 | 200 | 300 meters |

Bunsen Peak

This scenic cardio ascent is a popular early-season altitude acclimatization route. Many folks hike in jeans and tennis shoes, but boots and trekking poles come in handy for the scree slopes, especially if you opt for the full loop or the steep side-trip to Osprey Falls.

Best Time

The trail is hikable from May through October: Snow lingers on the trail near the summit as late as June, but the south-facing slope is free of heavy snow earlier than most peaks in the park. Other than snowmelt, there is no water along the entire route. There is precious little shade along the way, so it is best to hike early in the morning or late in the afternoon. Early afternoon thunder showers (locally known as "rollers")—and lightning—are common. No matter what the weather is like at the trailhead, pack a jacket for the typically brisk weather up top.

Finding the Trail

From the north, go 4.5 miles south on Grand Loop Road from Mammoth Junction (just past the Golden Gate) and turn left into the gravel Bunsen Peak trailhead (1K4) parking area on the east side of the road. From the south, go 16.5 miles north from Norris Junction on Grand Loop Road and turn right into the parking area. If the parking area is full, try the smaller Glen Creek trailhead (1K3) turnout across the road.

TRAIL USE
Hike
LENGTH
4.2 miles, 3 hours or
7.0 miles, 5.5 hours
VERTICAL FEET
±1300'
DIFFICULTY
– 1 2 3 **4 5** +
TRAIL TYPE
Out & Back or Loop
SURFACE TYPE
Dirt

FEATURES
Mountain
Summit
Wildflowers
Wildlife
Great Views
Photo Opportunity
Geologic Interest
Steep

FACILITIES
None

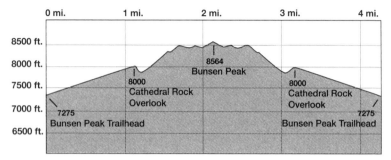

0 mi.	1 mi.	2 mi.	3 mi.	4 mi.

8500 ft.

8000 ft.

7500 ft.

7000 ft.

6500 ft.

8564
Bunsen Peak

8000
Cathedral Rock
Overlook

8000
Cathedral Rock
Overlook

7275
Bunsen Peak Trailhead

7275
Bunsen Peak Trailhead

TRAIL 3 Bunsen Peak Elevation Profile

Trail Description

The patchwork "burn mosaic" pattern left by the 1988 fires, most evident from Grand Loop Road, demonstrates how supposedly catastrophic fires can actually open up new ecological niches.

 Great Views

From beyond the service road barrier at the **Bunsen Peak trailhead▶1** parking area, the single-track earthen trail divides off from Old Bunsen Peak Road at a signed junction▶2 opposite a few waterfowl-rich ponds. Just up the hill through some sagebrush, a notice board▶3 has a map of trails in the Mammoth region.

The double-wide gravel trail winds gently up through lodgepole pines in a regenerating burn mosaic created by the 1988 North Fork Fire. Thanks to the burn, in spring and summer this section is often festooned with wildflowers. The trail climbs scenically above Rustic Falls and the Golden Gate, with the Howard Eaton Trail sometimes visible off to the left above the rocky white jumble known as The Hoodoos.

From here, you can also spot your destination atop Bunsen Peak, just to the right of the telecommunications equipment. Behind you are expansive views back over Gardner's Hole, Swan Lake Flats, and beyond to the Gallatin Range. The trail flattens out through an area dotted with snags as it swings away from the Grand Loop Road and heads for the summit.

As you climb through remnants of a mature spruce-fir forest on the southwest facing slope, heading toward the first switchbacks, watch for the

Looking southwest from Bunsen Peak *over Gardner's Hole and Swan Lake Flats*

stoic bighorn sheep (some with radio collars) that inhabit the scree slopes below the summit. In the fall, you can sometimes even hear rutting elk bugling as far away as Mammoth. A little bit more than halfway up, after a couple of gentle switchbacks, there is a good overlook of the Mammoth Hot Springs area; this is near the **Cathedral Rock▶4** outcropping after 1.2 miles.

Beyond the overlook, the trail traverses several scree slopes. Avoid the temptation to shortcut switchbacks here as they get shorter, steeper and more frequent. The trail tread remains good, but it is slow going—all the better to look for ripe raspberries. As the trail wraps around the northwest slope of the summit, it passes under a power line that feeds the antennae on the first of **three small summits,▶5** at 2 miles from the trailhead.

Expansive panoramic views of the Absaroka Range and Beartooth Wilderness open up to the

Osprey Falls and Loop Trails

To make this trail into a loop, continue past Bunsen Peak and return to the parking area via the Old Bunsen Peak Road, a wide, relatively flat paved service road that is now unused. This abandoned service road is also a popular cross-country ski route; the northern end is an alternative trailhead that is used by park employees but is largely inaccessible to park visitors. Plan on about five hours for the full loop, plus 2.8 miles and an extra couple of hours if you opt to take the steep detour to Osprey Falls.

Geologists theorize that Bunsen Peak, which dates back some 50 million years, is the eroded remains of a volcano. Evidence of the lava and volcanic rocks that once enclosed the peak is visible far below in the Gardner River Canyon.

north and northeast as you pass several precariously anchored antennae. The true summit, **Bunsen Peak** (8564'),▶6 is a few hundred yards farther along, down through a small rocky saddle. At last check, the summit register consisted of a rusty metal box filled with dog-eared scraps of paper, tucked under some rocks in the middle of the remains of a lookout foundation.

Whoa! The unobstructed, 360° views here are superb: Electric Peak and the Gallatin Range to the northwest and west; Mt. Holmes to the southeast and the Central Plateau to the south; Mt. Washburn and the southern Absarokas to the southeast; and Sheep Mtn. and the vast Gallatin National Forest to the north. Far below to the northeast is the Yellowstone River drainage, with Swan Lake Flat and the upper Gardner River drainage to the south.

After absorbing the views, it is time to make your first and only real decision of the hike. Your options are: Retrace your steps back to the trailhead parking area,►7 or descend the rocky, marginally steeper northeast slope on an unsigned but well-blazed and well-maintained route through heavily burned elk habitat to complete a longer loop. The later option includes the possibly of a detour to seldom-seen **Osprey Falls** (described at the end of Trail 6, page 63).

 Summit

| 🚶 | **MILESTONES** |

- ►1   0.0 Start at Bunsen Peak trailhead parking area
- ►2   0.1 Left at Bunsen Peak/Osprey Falls trail junction
- ►3   0.2 Straight past Mammoth Area Trails notice board
- ►4   1.2 Cathedral Rock overlook
- ►5   2.0 Telecommunications equipment; first of three summits
- ►6   2.1 Bunsen Peak
- ►7   4.2 Return to parking area

Bunsen, Geysers, and Burners

HISTORY

The peak was named after the German chemist and physicist, Robert Wilhelm Bunsen—just like his invention, the "burner" (remember high school science lab?). Bunsen also did pioneering theoretical research about the inner workings of Iceland's geysers, which his burner resembles.

Absaroka Range

The Absaroka (pronounced *ab-SOR-ka*) Range is named after one the region's numerous Native American tribes, known today in English as the Crow.

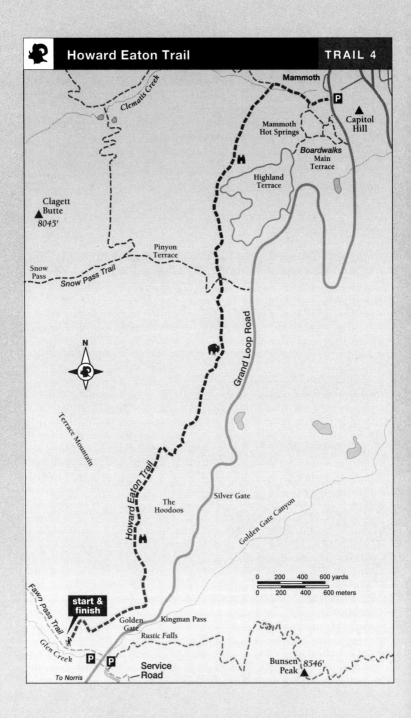

Howard Eaton Trail

Named after a pioneering Yellowstone outfitter and guide, this short downhill section of Yellowstone's longest trail (much of which is no longer maintained since it parallels the Grand Loop Road) traverses a wide variety of scenic terrain from the Golden Gate to Mammoth Hot Springs.

Best Time

The trail is hikable from May through October: Some exposed stretches make early morning and late afternoon the most pleasant times to hike here.

Finding the Trail

From the north, go 4.6 miles south on Grand Loop Road from Mammoth Junction and turn right into the Glen Creek trailhead (1K3) parking turnout (just past the Golden Gate) on the west side of the road. From the south, go 16.4 miles north from Norris Junction on Grand Loop Road and turn left into the parking turnout. If the small turnout is full, try the larger Bunsen Peak trailhead parking area on the opposite side of the road.

Logistics

Arranging a car shuttle is the first order of business to make this an easy hike; leave a car in one of the parking turnouts near the bottom of the Mammoth Hot Springs Terraces. Otherwise, you can try to arrange a ride from Mammoth uphill to the Glen Creek trailhead before you start hiking.

TRAIL USE
Hike
LENGTH
4 miles, 2 hours or
6.6 miles, 4 hours
VERTICAL FEET
+250'/-850'
DIFFICULTY
– 1 2 **3 4** 5 +
TRAIL TYPE
Point-to-point or Loop
SURFACE TYPE
Dirt

FEATURES
Autumn Colors
Wildflowers
Birds
Wildlife
Great Views
Photo Opportunity
Geologic Interest
Geothermal Features

FACILITIES
None

Trail Description

The Hoodoos were named for their ghostly appearance, but bear little resemblance to the park's other natural rock pinnacles, which are more classical examples of the form.

 Geologic Interest

 Wildlife

From the **Glen Creek trailhead,**▶1 head west through the sagelands of Swan Lake Flat toward Quadrant Mt. (10,216') and the Gallatin Range.

After a few hundred yards you reach a notice board and the **Howard Eaton/Fawn Pass Trail junction.**▶2 Turn right and climb sharply several hundred feet into the forest. Bunsen Peak juts up to your right, with the lichen-encrusted Golden Gate and Rustic Falls gorge far below.

Stop to admire the expansive views of the Gallatins to the west where the trail reaches its high point (7500') along the shoulder of Terrace Mtn. (8006'). After 1.3 miles, the trail drops down into the eerie rockscape known as **The Hoodoos,**▶3 a massive jumble of ancient limestone hot-spring deposits that sheered off of Terrace Mtn. during landslides. The travertine boulder field provides prime habitat for yellow-bellied marmots (also known as rockchucks) and is a favorite playground of rock climbers.

Beyond The Hoodoos, the trail jogs left, away from the Grand Loop Road, and starts to descend gradually through a burn area and aspen groves to another notice board and the **Snow Pass Trail junction,**▶4 2.8 miles from the trailhead. Watch for moose and, in late summer, black bears (and less frequently grizzlies) prowling this scenic stretch for buffalo berries. To be safe, make plenty of noise where sightlines are restricted.

Snow Pass and Terrace Mountain Loop

OPTIONS

If you are unable to arrange a car shuttle, you can loop around between Clagett Butte and Terrace Mtn. on the Snow Pass Trail, instead of finishing the hike in Mammoth. This option adds 2.6 miles and up to two hours due to the added elevation gain of over 1000 feet, nearly doubling the difficulty of the hike.

If you are not completing the loop option, keep going straight downhill for 0.5 mile past the junction, through pine and juniper forest, to reach a short spur trail for the **Mammoth Hot Springs Terraces.▶5** You can take a detour here along the Upper Terrace Drive, but the most interesting thermal features are more accessible at the end of the hike, near Liberty Cap. As the trail wraps around the upper terraces, you will enjoy views to the north of the historic Fort Yellowstone area.

Drop down for another 0.5 mile past the travertine Narrow Gauge Terrace through sagebrush and shady Douglas-fir forest to the **Beaver Ponds Trail junction.▶6** Turn right and continue 0.2 mile down Clematis Gulch to end up at the **Sepulcher Mountain trailhead.▶7**

Sixty-five thousand years ago, Terrace Mtn. was an active thermal area. Notice how the bright grayish-white travertine of The Hoodoos is similar to the dormant areas around the Mammoth Hot Springs terraces.

| 🚶 | MILESTONES |

▶1 0.0 Start at Glen Creek trailhead parking turnout
▶2 0.3 Right at Howard Eaton/Fawn Pass Trail junction
▶3 1.3 The Hoodoos
▶4 2.8 Straight at Snow Pass Trail junction
▶5 3.3 Straight past Mammoth Hot Springs Terraces
▶6 3.8 Right at Beaver Ponds Trail junction
▶7 4.0 Arrive at Sepulcher Mountain trailhead

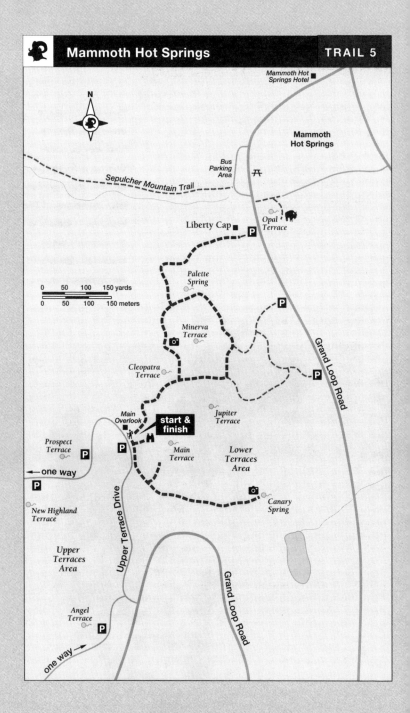

Mammoth Hot Springs

TRAIL 5

Mammoth Hot
Springs Hotel

Mammoth
Hot Springs

Bus
Parking
Area

Sepulcher Mountain Trail

Opal
Terrace

Liberty Cap

Palette
Spring

0   50   100   150 yards
0   50   100   150 meters

Minerva Terrace

Cleopatra
Terrace

Main
Overlook

start &
finish

Jupiter
Terrace

Prospect
Terrace

Main
Terrace

Lower
Terraces
Area

one way

New Highland
Terrace

Canary
Spring

Upper Terrace Drive

Upper
Terraces
Area

Grand Loop Road

Angel
Terrace

one way

Grand Loop Road

Mammoth Hot Springs

While many of Yellowstone's most famous hydrothermal areas wow audiences with their dramatic antics and predictable, instantly gratifying performances, Mammoth's mercurial hot-spring terraces are impressive more for their important place in the history of the park and their long-term natural development. A network of boardwalks provides numerous options for exploring the most accessible thermal area in the northern half of the park.

Best Time

At least some portion of the terraces can be explored year-round. When boardwalks are iced over in winter, the fringes of the thermal area are fascinating to explore via skis or snowshoes. There is no shade on the boardwalks, so bring plenty of water and sun protection.

Finding the Trail

From Mammoth Junction, either walk 0.25 mile south to the Lower Terraces boardwalk or drive 2 miles south on the Grand Loop Road toward Norris. Go past a paved overlook turnout, and turn right at the well-signed entrance gate to reach the main Upper Terrace Drive parking lot, where the route begins.

Logistics

All visitor facilities are located near the parking lots at the Upper and Lower Terraces. Rangers lead free, 90-minute walks (no reservations necessary) that

TRAIL USE
Hike
LENGTH
1.0 mile, 1-1.5 hours
VERTICAL FEET
±300'
DIFFICULTY
– **1** 2 3 4 5 +
TRAIL TYPE
Loop
SURFACE TYPE
Boardwalk

FEATURES
Child Friendly
Handicap Accessible
Great Views
Photo Opportunity
Historic
Geologic Interest
Geothermal Features
Moonlight Hiking

FACILITIES
Visitor Center
Restrooms
Picnic Tables
Phone
Water

depart from the Upper Terraces parking lot at 5 PM daily between Memorial Day and Labor Day.

Before heading out, pick up a helpful *Mammoth Hot Springs Trail Guide* (50¢ donation requested) from the Visitor Center or the metal box below the map on the east side of the main parking area.

Trail Description

After surveying the views of Fort Yellowstone and the **Main Terrace** from the **overlook** (6590') near the main parking area,►1 follow the boardwalk to the right, past the short boardwalk leading to the inactive **Cupid Spring**, down to the first of three platforms overlooking the travertine terraces below the source of **Canary Spring**.►2 Note: a less steep, wheelchair-accessible boardwalk begins closer to the entrance gate.

Named for its bright yellow color, Canary Spring owes its brilliance to filamentous bacteria living around its vent. The rest of the impressive geothermally heated runoff channel exhibits more oranges, browns and greens, indicating the presence of thermophiles that prefer cooler temperatures. The lower overlook platform provides the best up-close look at how calcium carbonate, which dissolves from the sedimentary limestone layers, crystallizes on the plant matter that falls onto the terraces.

It's estimated that as many as 65 species of algae and bacteria live in Mammoth's hot springs, and that up to two tons of travertine are deposited here daily.

Retrace your steps along the boardwalk back up to the parking area and main overlook,►3 where a different boardwalk►4 leads straight ahead to another overlook of the mostly dormant New Blue Spring. Follow the stairs down to the Lower Terraces and another junction►5 where there is yet another trail map signboard. To your left is the multilayered **Cleopatra Terrace**; to your right is **Minerva Terrace**, definitely a highlight of the tour.

Geologic Interest

Geothermal

Canary Spring: *Family standing in the steam from a runoff channel at the lower Canary Spring Overlook*

Named for the Roman goddess of artists and sculptors, many of Minerva's ornately layered terraces took shape in the early 1990s. At last look the spring was inactive, but a photo on the interpretive sign shows what the area looked like during a period of activity in 1977. Believe it or not, during one particularly active cycle, minerals deposited by Minerva buried the boardwalk you are now standing on. In the dry areas, look for elk tracks in the gravel and evidence of how fragile the crust is where bison hoofs have caused cave-ins.

From the junction, follow the paved path down to your right for about 100 yards to **Palette Spring**, ▶6 a good example of how thermophiles (heat-tolerant bacteria) lend different colors to runoff channels.

Back at the trail map sign, detour to your right down the steep gravel path for a close-up look at the dormant, 37-foot-tall hot spring cone that was named **Liberty Cap**▶7 in 1871, for its resemblance to the peaked caps worn during the French Revolution. There are picnic tables across the road

Mineral deposits *in thermal runoff channel near Canary Spring*

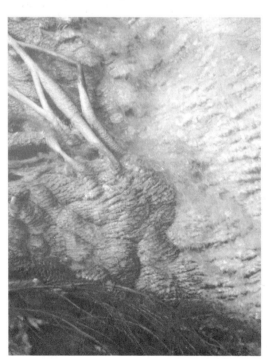

near the dormant **Opal Terrace** (a favorite spring-time hangout of elk), and restrooms to the left past the bus parking area.

Retrace your steps back past Palette Spring and turn left on the boardwalk at the junction►8 to loop around the lower side of Minerva Terrace. Even where all appears dry and dormant, watch closely for steam puffing out of small cracks in the hillside, hinting at future hydrothermal activity. At **Jupiter Terrace,**►9 interpretive signs display historic photos and explain the terrace's varied cycles of activity.

Head right (uphill) on the boardwalk and climb the stairs starting at the foot on the Main Terrace to return to the Upper Terrace overlook and parking area.►10

⚐ MILESTONES

►1 0.0 Start at Upper Terrace Drive parking area

►2 0.1 Right on boardwalk to Canary Spring

►3 0.2 Back at parking area and overlook

►4 0.25 Straight on boardwalk to New Blue Spring overlook

►5 0.4 Left on paved path at Cleopatra/Minerva Terrace junction

►6 0.5 Right down gravel path at Palette Spring junction

►7 0.6 North (right) on gravel path to Liberty Cap; return by retracing your steps

►8 0.7 Left on boardwalk at Palette Spring junction

►9 0.85 Right on boardwalk at Mound/Jupiter terraces junction

►10 1.0 Return to Upper Terrace Drive parking area

OPTIONS

Lower Terraces from Mammoth

You can walk five minutes from the Visitor Center in Mammoth and join this hike halfway, at Liberty Cap. If you want to explore more, you can bicycle or drive around the 1.5-mile, one-way Upper Terrace Drive past several more active hot springs terraces.

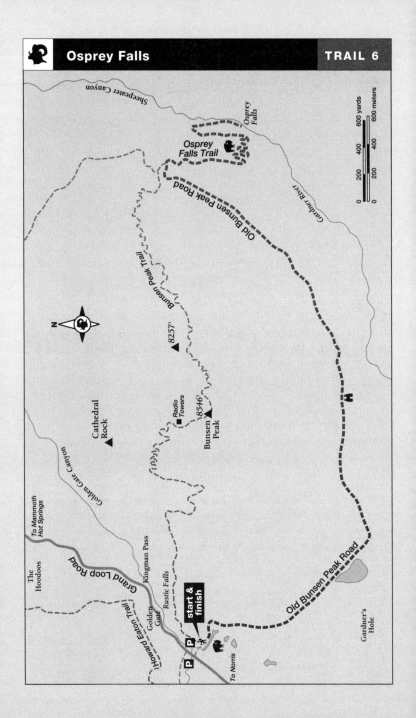

Sheepeater Canyon

Osprey Falls

Osprey Falls Trail

Old Bunsen Peak Road

Gardner River

600 yards

600 meters

0   200   400   600

0   200   400   600

Bunsen Peak Trail

N

8257'

Radio Towers

8546'

Bunsen Peak

Cathedral Rock

Golden Gate Canyon

To Mammoth Hot Springs

The Hoodoos

Grand Loop Road

Golden Gate

Howard Eaton Trail

Kingman Pass

Rustic Falls

start & finish

P   P

To Norris

Old Bunsen Peak Road

Gardner's Hole

Osprey Falls

An easy (though fairly long) hike on an old service road ends with a steep out-and-back drop to secluded base of the scenic falls at the head of an impressive canyon. The route can be extended to a slightly longer and more strenuous loop by combining it with Trail 3 to see both sides of Bunsen Peak, which makes for an all-day trek.

Best Time

Old Bunsen Peak Road is open for travel whenever the park is open to visitors. The hiking and biking season runs roughly May to October. On hot days and for spotting wildlife, it's best to hike in the early morning or late afternoon.

Finding the Trail

From the north, go 4.5 miles south on Grand Loop Road from Mammoth Junction and turn left into the Bunsen Peak trailhead parking area on the east side of the road (just past the Golden Gate). From the south, go 16.5 miles north from Norris Junction on Grand Loop Road and turn right into the parking area. If the parking area is full, try the smaller Glen Creek trailhead turnout on the opposite side of the road.

Logistics

There's no water at the trailhead and the only water along the trail is at the falls. If doing this hike as part of the full Bunsen Peak Loop (starting as described in Trail 3), watch carefully for orange blazes (metallic

TRAIL USE
Hike, Bike

LENGTH
10.0 or 10.2 miles,
5-7 hours

VERTICAL FEET
±850'

DIFFICULTY
– 1 2 3 4 **5** +

TRAIL TYPE
Out & Back or Loop

SURFACE TYPE
Dirt

FEATURES
Canyon
Stream
Waterfall
Wildflowers
Birds
Wildlife
Steep

FACILITIES
None

flags tacked to tree trunks) marking the way to the cutoff for Osprey Falls as you finish the descent off the backside of Bunsen Peak. Bicyclists are allowed on the gravel service road, but must park their bikes before descending to Osprey Falls. The northeast end of Old Bunsen Peak Road is an alternative trailhead, used primarily by park employees.

Trail Description

Beyond the service road barrier at the **Bunsen Peak trailhead parking area,▶1** continue straight ahead on Old Bunsen Peak Road at the signed Bunsen Peak **Trail junction▶2** across from some waterfowl-rich ponds.

 Great Views

The relatively level gravel service road heads east out across the rolling sagebrush meadows of **Gardner's Hole** and passes through prime bison and elk habitat. Watch for scats and tracks along the road. This stretch of abandoned road is also a popular mountain bike and cross-country ski track.

After skirting a couple of ponds, the road swings around the foothills and southern base of **Bunsen Peak** (8564'). The regenerating forest is more than head high here, obscuring the views in places. Eventually the road approaches an overlook that affords a glimpse of the **Gardner River** at the bottom of **Sheepeater Canyon**.

Canyon

The canyon is named after the park's only original year-round residents, a subgroup of the Shoshone Nation who referred to themselves as the

Bunsen Peak Loop

OPTIONS

Ambitious hikers looking for a full-day ramble can tack a detour to Osprey Falls onto the full Bunsen Peak Loop (a combination of this route and Trail 3, page 47). Plan on at least an extra two hours for the steep 1300-foot climb to Bunsen Peak.

Tukuarika, but were called the Sheepeater by Western settlers. In 1871, the year before Yellowstone was declared a park, they were forcibly relocated to the Wind River Reservation.

Although osprey rarely nest near their namesake falls, if you're lucky you might spot them circling over the river looking for prey, as well as bald eagles.

At the signed **Osprey Falls/Bunsen Peak Trail junction,▶3** 3.4 miles from the trailhead, turn right where the old road continues straight ahead and drops down into an NPS maintenance area. The road dead-ends at an alternative trailhead, used by NPS employees but which visitors are discouraged from using. The rim of **Sheepeater Canyon▶4** is several hundred yards beyond the bike parking rail. Bikes are not allowed beyond this point due to the extreme steepness of the trail to Osprey Falls.

Do not let the posted signs warning about treacherous conditions on the Osprey Falls Trail scare you. Yes, the steep trail's tread is in poorer condition than most of the superbly maintained trails in the park, but with a reasonable dose of caution it is safely manageable under normal circumstances. It plunges nearly 800 feet in a little over 0.5 mile, to the base of the impressive 150-foot **Osprey Falls,▶5** a total of 5 miles from the trailhead.

The misty area near the base of the falls makes a fine spot for a picnic as you ponder the stiff climb back out to the trailhead parking area.**▶6**

> Besides bighorn sheep, the Tukuarika hunted bison, elk, and deer with bows fashioned from ram's horns, ornamented with porcupine quills, and tipped by arrows pointed with obsidian. Evidence of chutes used to herd bighorn off cliffs has been uncovered near Rustic Falls.

 Waterfall

🚶	**MILESTONES**
▶1	0.0 Start at Bunsen Peak trailhead parking area
▶2	0.1 Straight on road at Bunsen Peak/Osprey Falls trail junction
▶3	3.4 Right at Osprey Falls/Bunsen Peak trail junction
▶4	3.8 Sheepeater Canyon rim
▶5	5.0 Osprey Falls
▶6	10.0 Return to trailhead parking area

CHAPTER 2

Northeast Yellowstone–Tower/Roosevelt Country

Northeast Yellowstone– Tower/Roosevelt Country

Yellowstone's northeastern quadrant encompasses the core of the park's wildlife-rich **Northern Range**. It includes the developed areas around **Tower Fall** and **Tower-Roosevelt Junction** (6270'), the lower **Yellowstone River** drainage and the Lamar River Valley. These unique areas include distinct ecological niches, but when grouped together offer some of the most diverse and rewarding hikes in the park.

The Grand Loop Road—the region's only paved route—remains open to wheeled vehicles year-round between the North Entrance and Cooke City, just east of the **Northeast Entrance** (7365') in the park's top-right corner. In winter, chains or snow tires may be required. The region is very popular with anglers and wildlife watchers, who frequently fill the small and less-developed, NPS-run **Slough Creek** and **Pebble Creek campgrounds** to capacity, even outside of the high season. Another agreeable option is the 32-site **Tower Fall Campground**, tucked away above Tower Creek in a pleasant forest.

Beyond the Northeast Entrance, the spectacular **Beartooth Highway** (US Hwy. 212) was dubbed "the most beautiful drive in America" by roving TV journalist Charles Kuralt. The National Scenic Byway traverses the **Beartooth Pass** (10,947'; typically open from Memorial Day weekend through mid-October; call 888-285-4636 for recorded travel condition and construction updates) and a total of 65 stunning miles en route to the appealing outdoor base camp of Red Lodge, Montana. The route also provides easy access to many US Forest Service campgrounds, trailheads, and scenic alpine hikes in the Absaroka-Beartooth Wilderness.

Wildlife flocks to Yellowstone's northeast corner for its lush riparian zones, wide-open expanses of grazing meadows and attractive denning habitat. The **Lamar Valley**, often referred to as "the Serengeti of America," is one of the most popular places in Greater Yellowstone for spotting wolves, elk, bison and coyotes. Both black and grizzly bears frequently cause roadside "bear jams" around Tower-Roosevelt Junction.

The hiking terrain here runs the gamut, from low-lying overnight routes that trace the depths of the **Black Canyon of the Yellowstone** to high-altitude ascents that top out above timberline for never-ending views of the surrounding wildlands.

The rustic cabins at the summer-only **Roosevelt Lodge** (circa 1916; rates $59-$95), near President Theodore Roosevelt's favorite campsite, are a popular base camp for families and anglers. The Yellowstone Association Institute bases many of its field study seminars nearby at the historic **Lamar Valley Buffalo Ranch** complex, where the United States' last known mountain bison once survived in captivity. After the Yellowstone herd was counted at 23 in 1902, Great Plains bison were reintroduced and ultimately the two species were allowed to interbreed in 1915.

The last of Yellowstone's once-extensive gray wolf population was exterminated in the Lamar Valley in the 1920s. In 1995, an unprecedented **wolf reintroduction** effort began with the release of 14 wild-captured Canadian gray wolves near Soda Butte and Druid Peak. The Montana state legislature unceremoniously responded to the federally sponsored reintroduction efforts by proposing that wolves be reintroduced smack dab in the middle of pro-wolf territory: Central Park in New York City, the Presidio in San Francisco, and on the National Mall in Washington, D.C.

The last two of Yellowstone's 31 reintroduced wolves died in early 2004, but the 2003 year-end radio tracking count tallied 306 wolves (including 21 breeding pairs) roaming in 30 distinct packs in Greater Yellowstone. For seasonal wildlife watching tips, pick up a free copy of the newspaper Yellowstone Tracker at any ranger station or visitor center.

Heading south toward Canyon Village, the **Grand Loop Road** and **Dunraven Pass** (8859') are scheduled to be closed year-round from the Chittenden Road parking area (which provides access to the north slope of Mt. Washburn) to Canyon Junction through the summer of 2005, due to ongoing major construction. The Mt. Washburn trailhead, however, will remain open. Call (307) 344-2117 for Yellowstone road construction updates.

Overleaf: *Looking down-river, deep inside the lower Black Canyon of the Yellowstone*

Permits and Maps

The only permits required here are for fishing and backcountry campsites along the Blacktail Deer Creek and Yellowstone River trails.

There's no visitor center in the region, but the **Tower Ranger Station** (open 8 AM to 4:30 PM daily in summer), housed in a reconstruction of a historic soldier station near Roosevelt Lodge, issues backcountry and fishing permits and can advise about current hiking conditions. The rustic, log-cabin-style **Northeast Entrance Ranger Station**, a National Historic Landmark and fine example of NPS parkitecture built between 1934 and 1935, may issue permits as well, depending on seasonal staffing levels.

The Trails Illustrated *Tower/Canyon* (no. 304, scale 1:63,360) map covers all of the hikes, trailheads, and campgrounds described in this chapter, with the exceptions of the Blacktail Deer Creek Trail and the western half of the Yellowstone River Trail, which appear on the *Mammoth Hot Springs* (no. 303, scale 1:63,360) and *Yellowstone National Park* (no. 202, scale 1:126,720) sheets in the same series.

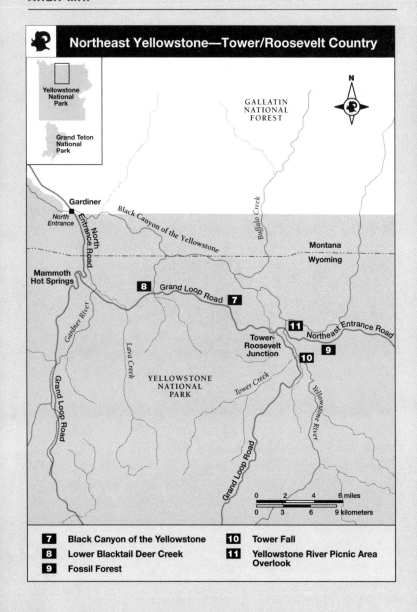

Northeast Yellowstone—Tower/Roosevelt Country

Yellowstone National Park

Grand Teton National Park

N

GALLATIN
NATIONAL
FOREST

Gardiner

North Entrance

Black Canyon of the Yellowstone

Buffalo Creek

Montana

Wyoming

Mammoth Hot Springs

North Entrance Road

8 Grand Loop Road **7**

Gardiner River

Lava Creek

11 Northeast Entrance Road

Tower-Roosevelt Junction

9

10

YELLOWSTONE
NATIONAL
PARK

Tower Creek

Yellowstone River

Grand Loop Road

Grand Loop Road

0   2   4   6 miles
0   3   6   9 kilometers

7	Black Canyon of the Yellowstone	**10**	Tower Fall
8	Lower Blacktail Deer Creek	**11**	Yellowstone River Picnic Area Overlook
9	Fossil Forest		

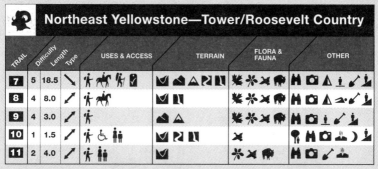

Northeast Yellowstone—Tower/Roosevelt Country

TRAIL	Difficulty	Length	Type	USES & ACCESS	TERRAIN	FLORA & FAUNA	OTHER
7	5	18.5	↘	🚶🚴🐎🎒☑	☑🏔△🏞💧	🍁❀🦅🦬	🔭📷△⬆✦⬇
8	4	8.0	↗	🚶🐎🎒	☑💧	🍁❀🦅🦬	🔭📷△⬇✦⬇
9	4	3.0	↗	🚶	🏔△	🍁❀🦅🦬	🔭📷⬆✦⬇
10	1	1.5	↗	🚶♿👪	☑🏞💧	🦅	🌳🔭📷☕🌙⬇
11	2	4.0	↗	🚶👪	☑	❀🦅🦬	🔭📷⚒♨

USES & ACCESS	TERRAIN	FLORA & FAUNA	OTHER
🚶 Hiking	☑ Canyon	🍁 Autumn Colors	🌳 Cool & Shady
🚴 Bicycling	🏔 Mountain	❀ Wildflowers	🔭 Great Views
🐎 Horses	△ Summit	🦅 Birds	📷 Photo Opportunity
🎒 Backpacking	🏞 Stream	🦬 Wildlife	⬆ Swimming
👪 Child Friendly	💧 Waterfall		⬇ Secluded
♿ Handicap Access	≋ Lake		🏠 Historic
☑ Backcountry Permit Required	♨ Geothermal		✦ Geologic Interest
△ Camping		DIFFICULTY - 1 2 3 4 5 + less more	🌙 Moonlight Hiking
			⬇ Steep

Northeast Yellowstone–Tower/Roosevelt Country

TRAIL 7

Hike, Backpack, Horse

18.5 miles, Point-to-Point

Difficulty: 1 2 3 4 5

Black Canyon of the Yellowstone 77

Though a shuttle is required, this classic downhill hike through the park's most impressive river canyon is an early- and late-season favorite of park employees. It's a popular fishing and wildlife-watching route and is just far enough away from the road to give the illusion of being in the wilderness.

TRAIL 8

Hike, Horse

8.0 miles, Out & Back

Difficulty: 1 2 3 4 5

Lower Blacktail Deer Creek 87

This hearty dayhike is a popular shortcut to the fishing and camping opportunities that abound in the depths of the stunning Black Canyon of the Yellowstone. It's an enjoyable descent through wildflower meadows along Blacktail Creek and is easily extended into a relaxing overnighter.

TRAIL 9

Hike

3.0 miles, Out & Back

Difficulty: 1 2 3 4 5

Fossil Forest 91

This short but steep and lightly traveled heart-thumping ascent is the most direct of several unmarked but well-beaten paths that access Yellowstone's most extensive petrified forest, high up a ridge with endless views.

Tower Fall 97
This easygoing hike to an impressive waterfall is a perfect multigenerational affair. Views from the wheelchair-accessible overlook are good up top, but it's worth a wander down to the river to really appreciate the fall's grandeur.

**Yellowstone River
Picnic Area Overlook** 101
Bring your binoculars: This family-friendly jaunt provides quick access to unobstructed views of the Grand Canyon of the Yellowstone and the Absaroka Range. There's also intriguing geology, plus a good chance of spotting coyote and several different ungulates outside of the summer months.

Arrowleaf: *When in full bloom, it's easy to confuse the pungent yellow Arrowleaf Balsamroot with sunflowers.*

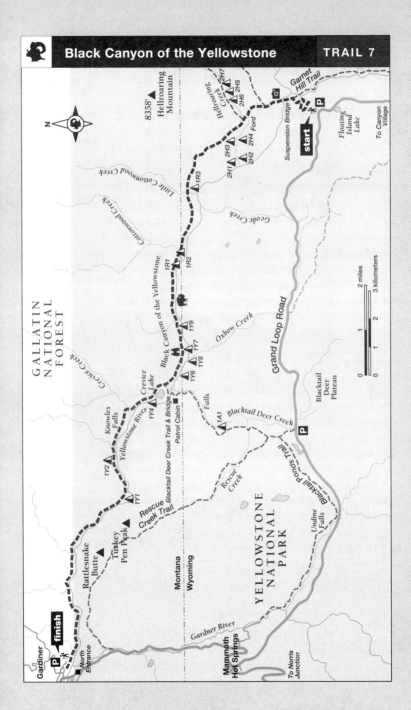

Black Canyon of the Yellowstone

TRAIL 7

N

GALLATIN NATIONAL FOREST

8358' Hellroaring Mountain

Hellroaring Creek 2H7

2H6 2H5

2H4 Ford

2H3

2H1 2H2

Little Cottonwood Creek

Cottonwood Creek

Crevice Creek

Knowles Falls

Yellowstone River

1Y4

1Y2

1Y1

Crevice Lake

1Y6 1Y8 1Y7

1Y9

Black Canyon of the Yellowstone

1R1

1R2

1R3

Geode Creek

Oxbow Creek

Garnet Hill Trail

Suspension Bridge

start

P

Floating Island Lake

To Canyon Village

Grand Loop Road

Blacktail Deer Plateau

1A1

Blacktail Deer Creek

Falls

Patrol Cabin

Blacktail Deer Creek Trail & Bridge

Rescue Creek

Rescue Creek Trail

P

Blacktail Ponds Trail

Undine Falls

Rattlesnake Butte

Tunkey Pen Peak

Montana
Wyoming

YELLOWSTONE NATIONAL PARK

Gardner River

Mammoth Hot Springs

To Norris Junction

Gardiner

finish

P

North Entrance

2 miles

3 kilometers

Black Canyon of the Yellowstone

This classic downhill hike is an early- and late-season favorite of park employees, since the campsites are snow-free as soon as early May and as late as October. It's just far enough away from the road to start feeling like you're in the wilderness, and is a prime route for fishing and wildlife watching.

Best Time

The trail is typically dry enough for hiking by mid-May. The ford of Hellroaring Creek, however, can be waist-deep and tricky as late as August during years of high runoff. Ticks are a nuisance in spring and early summer. The route is hot at midday in summer and can be frosty in the early morning, but is bug- and snow-free early and late in the season, when many of the park's higher-elevation trails are in worse shape.

Finding the Trail

From the west, go 14.1 miles east from Mammoth Junction (toward Tower-Roosevelt Junction) on the Grand Loop Road and turn left into the signed Hellroaring Trailhead (2K8) parking area (labeled a "gravel pit" on some older maps), which is 0.3 mile down a good gravel road on the north side of the road. From the east, go 3.4 miles west (toward Mammoth) from Tower-Roosevelt Junction on Grand Loop Road and turn right into the parking area.

The exit (western) trailhead is just outside of the park in the town of Gardiner, Montana, behind the private Rocky Mountain Campground. From the

TRAIL USE
Hike, Backpack, Horse
LENGTH
18.5 miles, 1-4 days
VERTICAL FEET
+1000'/-1250'
DIFFICULTY
– 1 2 3 4 **5** +
TRAIL TYPE
Point-to-point
SURFACE TYPE
Dirt

FEATURES
Canyon
Steep
Stream
Waterfall
Autumn Colors
Wildflowers
Birds
Wildlife
Great Views
Photo Opportunity
Camping
Swimming
Secluded
Geologic Interest

FACILITIES
Horse Staging

park's North Entrance, pass through the Roosevelt Arch and turn right on Park St. After a couple of blocks, turn left on Second St. and cross the Yellowstone River Bridge. At the first intersection, turn right on Jardine Road and head uphill past the campground's main entrance. Just beyond the campground, turn right on White Lane, a dead-end gravel road. The small parking area is on the right, adjacent to a prominent trailhead sign, just before the church parking lot. Please be considerate of others by taking care not to occupy more than one parking space.

Logistics

Most people prefer to do this hike one-way in the downhill direction, which requires a car shuttle. If in doubt about the Hellroaring Creek ford, use the stock bridge crossing upstream. You really can't go wrong with any of the campsites along the route, all of which prohibit wood fires. Your selection will likely be determined by availability and how many nights you will be camping.

Trail Description

From the **Hellroaring trailhead ▶1** (2K8) parking lot, a single-track earthen trail that receives heavy horse use winds down through damp Douglas-fir forest to an overlook of the Yellowstone River, with Garnet Hill looming to the right across Elk Creek.

 Great Views

Starting at a small burn area, the trail switchbacks down steeply for a total of 600 feet over the first mile, past the **Garnet Hill Trail junction ▶2** after 0.7 mile, through open grasslands dotted with wildflowers to the brawny steel **Yellowstone River suspension bridge, ▶3** which is bookended by juniper trees and just wide enough for two skinny horses.

 Steep

After checking out the whitewater roaring far below, you climb away from the river through a rocky canyon and over a sagebrush plateau, past the **Buffalo Plateau/Coyote Creek Trail junction▶4** to **Hellroaring junction,▶5** at 2 miles from the trailhead, where **Hellroaring Mtn.** (8358'), the park's biggest exposed granite outcropping, looms in the background.

Hellroaring Creek was named by an early explorer who reported that it was a "real hell roarer."

Your next move depends on the season and your destination. Before August, you'll want to scout the condition of the potentially tricky **Hellroaring Creek ford,▶6** a few hundred yards beyond the junction and around the left side of the glacial lake basin (which is dry by late summer), to decide whether you would rather use the **stock bridge**, 1.5 miles upstream from the junction. All even-numbered campsites along Hellroaring Creek are on the south bank of the creek and odd-numbered sites are on the north bank. These sites are the obvious first-night choice if you are planning a three-day trip.

From the junction on the north side of **Hellroaring Creek,▶7** east-west trending trails lead off to more campsites. If you've crossed via the stock bridge, turn right at this intersection. Fronting the confluence of Hellroaring Creek and the Yellowstone River, the ideal **campsite, 2H1,▶8** is accessed either along the north bank of the creek, via the spur trail

 Camping

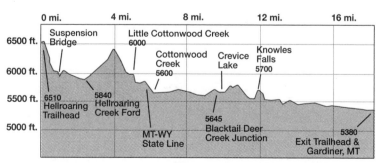

TRAIL 7 Black Canyon of the Yellowstone Elevation Profile

Yellowstone River suspension bridge: *A hiker contemplates the whitewater raging through the narrows far below.*

for **campsite 2H3**, or a few hundred yards later on via a cutoff from the main trail. Both these watercourses are blue-ribbon fishing spots for cutthroat trout after high waters recede, starting around mid-July.

⚠ **Camping**

The trail climbs away from the river, crossing a varied landscape of minor marshes, small glacial lakes, and open sagelands. As you switch back over

300 feet up a ridge, the impressive outline of **Electric Peak** (10,992') comes into view near the crest. The trail descends to the roomy **campsite 1R3, ▶9** perched high above the river 4.3 miles from the trailhead, before crossing **Little Cottonwood Creek.▶10** The views here down into the beginnings of the **Black Canyon of the Yellowstone** are stunning.

 Canyon

Appropriately, there's no signage announcing the **Wyoming-Montana state line,▶11** since this abstract political delineation 5.7 miles from the trailhead has no effect on your experience. A few hundred yards farther along, **campsites 1R2▶12** (hiker-only) and mixed-use **1R1▶13** are equally attractive, situated well off-trail on benches high above the river, with easy access to water around the mouth of Cottonwood Creek.

 Camping

Watch for elk antlers protruding from trees and ankle-busting badger burrows in the trail as it descends for a long, flat, forested stretch alongside the river. A couple of miles farther along, past trailside bison wallows, hiker-only **campsites 1Y9▶14** and **1Y7▶15** are 8.3 and 9 miles from the trailhead respectively. Both campsites are superb first-night riverfront options if you're making a two-day trip. Late in the season, sandy swimming beaches are exposed below the towering outcroppings of columnar basalt.

 Swimming

Just before the **Blacktail Bridge** and 9.8 miles from the trailhead, hiker-only **campsite 1Y5▶16** enjoys a secluded riverfront setting. If you've opted for the **Blacktail Deer Creek Trail** shortcut (described in Trail 8, page 87), you'll join the Yellowstone River Trail at the junction,**▶17** several hundred yards ahead on the north side of the bridge. The hiker-only **campsites 1Y6** and **1Y8** are across the bridge, to the east of the **Lower Blacktail Patrol Cabin**, 0.4 and 0.8 mile respectively down a spur trail along the south bank of the river.

 Camping

The trail skirts the northern shore of the fishless, aquamarine **Crevice Lake,▶18** which has no inlet or outlet but is a nice spot for a cool dip on a hot day. Due to the steep banks and lack of shade around the lake, the best spots for breaking your daylong hike in half with a picnic lunch are just before the lake, or a few hundred yards beyond it, near the river-front, hiker-only **campsite 1Y4,▶19** a total of 10.6 miles from the trailhead.

The trail leaves the river again to cross **Crevice Creek▶20** on a sturdy bridge 11.4 miles from the trailhead. This is a good place to tank up on water before the final bone-dry homestretch. Note: Most maps incorrectly depict an abandoned trail here heading right up the creek to a patrol cabin and the park's northern boundary.

Beyond, the trail begins an alternating pattern of climbing up above the river and winding through massive fields of scree and lichen-encrusted glacial boulders, before switchbacking down steeply to the river. Beyond the first such climb and descent, a short spur trail leads down to the viewpoint for the 15-foot **Knowles Falls,▶21** 11.8 miles from the trailhead, where the cascade is more impressive due to its volume than height.

�★◣ Waterfall

Next you reach flats leading to the hiker-only **campsites 1Y2▶22** (12.4 miles from the trailhead) and **1Y1,▶23** which is beyond an impressive narrows, 13.5 miles from the trailhead. Both these sites front the river but are not entirely secluded from the trail. Beyond the campsites, keep an eye out for snakes on the trail and bald eagles perched in the cottonwoods. As the river calms below the falls and changes color from jade green to an ashy gray, you'll see more willows along the shore and cacti near the trail. This change in flora ushers in the final hot and dry 5-mile stretch, which some hikers opt to skip by exiting via the **Blacktail Deer Creek trailhead** (1N5).

▲ Camping

The trail slaloms through park boundary markers en route to a sturdy old wooden bridge over the appealing **Bear Creek**. Nearby, a large, dormant thermal terrace is visible on the hillside to your right. The home stretch leads through a stark mud and rock garden—be especially careful of spiny trailside cacti here.

A sign announces your exit from the park and entry into the final, 0.5-mile stretch of **private land**, which begins just beyond an NPS Mammoth Area Trails notice board. This leafy tunnel of trail is a favorite local fishing access route and, around the autumnal equinox, can actually be one of the most visually appealing stretches on the entire route.

Obey all posted signs regarding private property to reach the **Yellowstone River trailhead** (1N1), above the Gardner River confluence in the whimsical park gateway town of **Gardiner, Montana**. ▶24

OPTIONS

Blacktail Deer Creek Shortcut

This hike is described from the uphill end, from east to west. It would be an extremely long, strenuous dayhike, but spreading it over two to four days will allow ample time for fishing, easygoing hiking, and plenty of relaxing. By starting at the Blacktail Deer Creek trailhead, you can shorten the route by about 5 miles. Another short alternative is to make an out-and-back jaunt to the Yellowstone River bridge—an easy but steep dayhike, with a 1600-foot total elevation change and a length of 2 miles round-trip.

Gardiner's Best Burger

After a grueling hike, the only thing better than a soak in the Boiling River (see Trail 2, page 43) is a half-pound buffalo cheeseburger and thick huckleberry shake at **Helen's Corral Drive-In**, on the western end of the main drag in Gardiner. Call (406) 848-7627; W. Scott St.; closed Tuesday.

▶1   0.0 Start at Hellroaring trailhead parking lot

▶2   0.7 Left at Garnet Hill Trail junction

▶3   1.0 Yellowstone River suspension bridge

▶4   1.6 Left at Buffalo Plateau/Coyote Creek Trail junction

▶5   2.0 Left at Hellroaring junction for low-water Hellroaring Creek ford
       and campsites 2H2 and 2H4; right for high-water stock bridge
       crossing and campsites 2H6, 2H8 and 2H9

▶6   2.2 Hellroaring Creek ford

▶7   2.3 Straight at junction; left for campsites 2H3 and 2H1;
       right for campsites 2H5 and 2H7

▶8   2.6 Campsite 2H1 cutoff/spur trail

▶9   4.3 Campsite 1R3 spur trail

▶10 4.5 Little Cottonwood Creek

▶11 5.7 Wyoming-Montana state line (no sign)

▶12 5.9 Campsite 1R2 spur trail

▶13 6.0 Campsite 1R1; Cottonwood Creek

▶14 8.3 Campsite 1Y9 spur trail

▶15 9.0 Campsite 1Y7 spur trail

▶16 9.8 Campsite 1Y5 spur trail

▶17 10.0 Right at Blacktail Deer Creek Trail junction;
       left for bridge, patrol cabin, and campsites 1Y6 and 1Y8

▶18 10.3 Crevice Lake

▶19 10.6 Campsite 1Y4 spur trail

▶20 11.4 Crevice Creek bridge

▶21 11.8 Knowles Falls

▶22 12.4 Campsite 1Y2 spur trail

▶23 13.5 Campsite 1Y1 spur trail

▶24 18.5 Arrive in Gardiner, Montana; Yellowstone River trailhead

Elk antlers: *Yellowstone's wildlife-rich Northern Range is an important overwintering refuge for elk and other large mammals.*

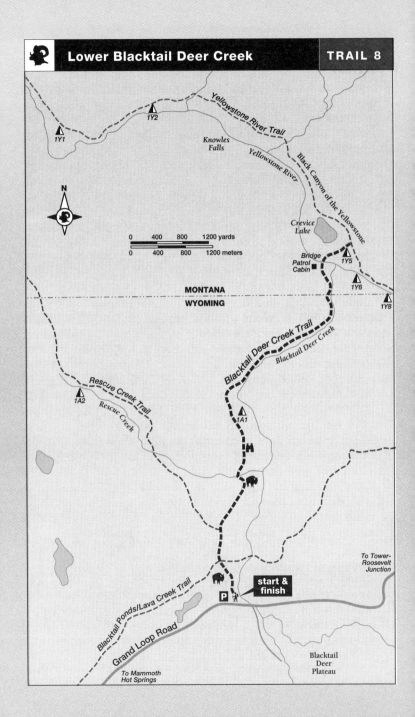

1Y1

1Y2

Yellowstone River Trail

Knowles Falls

Yellowstone River

Black Canyon of the Yellowstone

N

0   400   800   1200 yards
0   400   800   1200 meters

Crevice Lake

Bridge Patrol Cabin

1Y5

1Y6

MONTANA

WYOMING

1Y8

Blacktail Deer Creek Trail

Blacktail Deer Creek

Rescue Creek Trail

1A2

Rescue Creek

1A1

To Tower-Roosevelt Junction

start & finish

P

Blacktail Ponds/Lava Creek Trail

Grand Loop Road

To Mammoth Hot Springs

Blacktail Deer Plateau

Lower Blacktail Deer Creek

This athletic dayhike is a popular shortcut to the camping and abundant fishing opportunities in the lower reaches of the stunning Black Canyon of the Yellowstone. It's easily extended into a relaxing overnight trip.

Best Time

The trail and campsites become snow-free as soon as early May and usually remain so through October. Conversely, the route can be very hot and dry at midday and in summer due to its relatively low elevation.

Finding the Trail

From the west, go 6.5 miles east from Mammoth Junction (toward Tower-Roosevelt Junction) on Grand Loop Road and turn left into the small signed gravel Blacktail Deer Creek trailhead (1N5) parking area on the north side of the road. From the east, go 11 miles west (toward Mammoth) from Tower-Roosevelt Junction on Grand Loop Road and turn right into the parking area.

Trail Description

From the trailhead parking area, ▶1 the **Blacktail Deer Creek Trail** heads out across a sagebrush meadow where wildflowers flourish thanks to the 1988 fires, though little evidence of the fires remain. Soon, the trail skirts the east side of one of the three glacial **Blacktail Ponds,** ▶2 which are sensitive

TRAIL USE
Hike, Horse
LENGTH
8.0 miles, 4-5 hours
VERTICAL FEET
±1300'
DIFFICULTY
– 1 2 3 **4** 5 +
TRAIL TYPE
Out & Back
SURFACE TYPE
Dirt

FEATURES
Canyon
Steep
Stream
Autumn Colors
Birds
Wildflowers
Wildlife
Great Views
Photo Opportunity
Camping
Swimming
Geologic Interest

FACILITIES
Horse Staging

Birds

nesting grounds for numerous waterfowl, including sandhill cranes.

Beyond the **Lava Creek Trail junction,▶3** several fenced-in wildlife "exclosures" near the trail atop a small rise are used by NPS scientists to study the effects of browsing by elk on native plant species. The surrounding open, rolling sagelands are fine bison and elk habitat. Watch for deer, pronghorn antelope, and bighorn sheep between the

Wildlife

Rescue Creek Trail junction,▶4 0.7 mile beyond the trailhead, and the spur trail for the trailside **campsite 1A1▶5** (campfires allowed), at 1.8 miles.

After a plunge of nearly 1000 feet over the next 2 miles, the trail emerges near the head of the dramatic **Black Canyon of the Yellowstone** at the

Canyon

Lower Blacktail Patrol Cabin.▶6 A spur trail leads 0.4 and 0.8 mile respectively to the riverfront, hiker-only **campsites 1Y6** and more-desirable **1Y8**.

The substantial steel **Blacktail Bridge▶7** spans the Yellowstone River, with the **Yellowstone River**

Camping

Trail ▶8 junction a few hundred yards farther along, 4 miles from the trailhead. Here, you can either continue exploring along the river along the Black Canyon of the Yellowstone route, or retrace your steps to the trailhead parking area.▶9

TRAIL 8 Lower Blacktail Deer Creek Elevation Profile

MILESTONES

►1   0.0 Start at Blacktail Deer Creek trailhead

►2   0.2 Blacktail Ponds overlook

►3   0.4 Right at Blacktail Ponds/Lava Creek Trail junction

►4   0.7 Right at Rescue Creek Trail junction

►5   1.8 Campsite 1A1 spur trail

►6   3.7 Lower Blacktail Patrol Cabin; campsites 1Y6 and 1Y8 spur trail

►7   3.8 Blacktail Bridge

►8   4.0 Yellowstone River Trail junction

►9   8.0 Return to Blacktail Deer Creek parking area

Dayhike and Overnight Options

OPTIONS

For a longer dayhike, continue 0.3 mile downstream (west) on the Yellowstone River Trail to Crevice Lake, or 1.8 miles to Knowles Falls. Any of the 1Y-group campsites upstream or downstream make for a nice overnight trip, with the possibility of hiking upstream a total of 10 extra miles to exit at the Hellroaring trailhead. Campsite 1A1 is an easy destination for a first-time family trip into the backcountry.

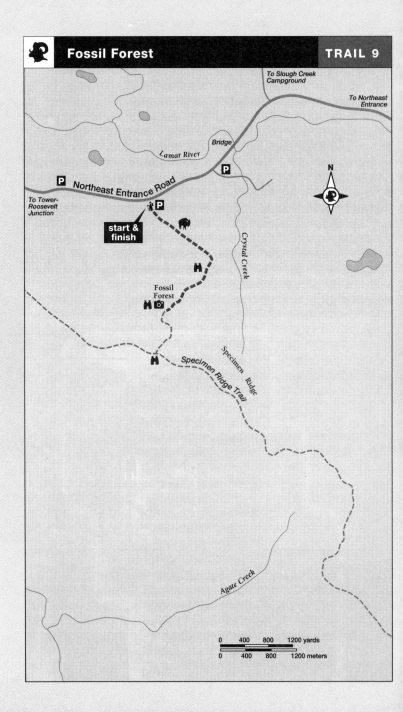

Fossil Forest

TRAIL 9

To Slough Creek Campground

To Northeast Entrance

Bridge

Lamar River

P

Northeast Entrance Road

P

To Tower-Roosevelt Junction

start & finish

P

N

Fossil Forest

Crystal Creek

Specimen Ridge

Specimen Ridge Trail

Agate Creek

| 0 | 400 | 800 | 1200 yards |
| 0 | 400 | 800 | 1200 meters |

Fossil Forest

This short but steep and challenging ascent is the most direct of several unmarked routes that end up at Yellowstone's most fascinating and significant petrified forest, located high up a ridge, with amazing, endless views.

Best Time

There is neither shade nor water at the trailhead or along the route, so early morning or later in the afternoon are best. The primary hiking season is June through October. Wildflowers are abundant after the snowmelt in July and August.

Finding the Trail

Finding the unsigned trailhead takes a bit of extra attention. From the west, head 4.1 miles east on the Grand Loop Road from Tower-Roosevelt Junction—1.2 miles past the signed Specimen Ridge trailhead parking area—and watch for a small, unsigned, paved turnout on the south (right) side of the road. From the east, go past the turnoff for Slough Creek Campground on Grand Loop Road, then 0.5 mile past the bridge over the Lamar River. Don't confuse the parking turnout you want with another signed trailhead and parking area, which has a designated handicapped parking spot and is just 0.2 mile past the bridge, where an old service road heads south up the Crystal Creek drainage.

TRAIL USE
Hike

LENGTH
3.0 miles, 2-3 hours

VERTICAL FEET
±1350'

DIFFICULTY
− 1 2 3 **4 5** +

TRAIL TYPE
Out & Back

SURFACE TYPE
Dirt, Paved

FEATURES
Mountain
Summit
Autumn Colors
Wildflowers
Birds
Wildlife
Great Views
Photo Opportunity
Secluded
Geologic interest
Steep

FACILITIES
None

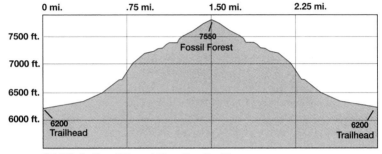

| 0 mi. | .75 mi. | 1.50 mi. | 2.25 mi. |

7500 ft.

7550
Fossil Forest

7000 ft.

6500 ft.

6000 ft.

6200
Trailhead

6200
Trailhead

TRAIL 9   Fossil Forest Elevation Profile

Logistics

The adjacent Crystal Creek drainage was used as an elk trapping site in the early 1950s, and was also home to one of three acclimatization pens during the wolf reintroduction in 1995.

If you have binoculars, before you head out, scan the ridge from the roadside turnouts to identify your destination: a pair of large, rocky outcroppings next to a forested patch below the crest of Specimen Ridge. Once you've found the correct parking area, you should be able to identify the trail heading up the ridge with the naked eye. Be aware that the temperature changes as fast as the elevation gain. Bring a jacket, as afternoon thundershowers are common, and it can get a bit brisk up top.

Trail Description

From the parking turnout,►1 an unsigned but well-beaten path heads south across the sagebrush foothills, through several bison wallows, toward a group of lichen-encrusted, granitic glacial erratic boulders►2 situated atop a small rise about 0.3 mile from the road. The ensuing steep beeline up the hillside will really get your calves and heart pumping. When tired, stop and smell the blossoms: The meadows here are usually bursting with wildflowers by July.

 Wildflowers

Watch closely as you climb, and you may begin to notice small fossilized shards. Trust me, you will be looking down at your feet a lot during this ath-

letic climb. At times it feels like you are on a
Stairmaster set at 10-plus.

You will begin to notice small, upright fossilized
stumps off to the left as spur trails branch off near
the top of the ridge. Fall colors peak here around the
end of September, a bit later than elsewhere in the
park. Behind you, views of the Northern Range are
unsurpassed.

 Steep

Literally acres are littered with small shards of
petrified material; you can hardly pitch a horseshoe
here off the various informal trails without hitting an
ossified stump: dogwoods, magnolias, oaks, walnuts,
maples, even avocado and breadfruit. As you crest
the ridge, the trail joins with another path trending
northwest-southeast along the ridgeline. Look back
north toward the trailhead, to see the footprint of glacial lakes and the Absaroka Range.

Follow the ridgeline, keeping a burn area to your
left and a Douglas-fir forest to your right, ignoring all
the other unofficial "social" paths. Upon emerging
from a small patch of forest, a gigantic upright fossilized redwood stump▶3 and two smaller standing
pine trunks appear about 1.5 miles from the parking
area. Take care on the rocky slope if you descend to
inspect the redwood's exposed root structures. The
silica-induced petrification occurred during volcanic
phases over a 15-million-year period, starting perhaps as much as 55 million years ago.

 **Geologic Interest**

Specimen Ridge and Crystal Creek Trails

The Fossil Forest can also eventually be accessed off the much
longer but very scenic, 19-mile Specimen Ridge Trail, or via the old
service road that climbs up the Crystal Creek drainage. A car shuttle
can be set up at either of these alternative trailheads to turn the route
into a longer, point-to-point dayhike. Note that there are no campsites
along the Specimen Trail and that the ford of the Lamar River on the
eastern end of the trail can be very dangerous early in the season.

It goes without saying that the NPS strictly prohibits the collection of any fossilized materials; please leave this mind-boggling place as you found it. (For a sad example of what can result from illegal souvenir hunting, visit the greatly diminished Petrified Tree near Tower-Roosevelt Junction. If you must take a piece of geologic history home with you, the Gallatin National Forest issues permits for small-scale collection in the Tom Miner Basin).

 Geologic Interest

From here, you have three options: straight up, straight down, or retrace your steps back to the trailhead. If you have a reserve of energy, the brisk 400-foot climb up to the top of Specimen Ridge is highly recommended. You'll be rewarded by a scenic picnic spot with breathtaking views southwest across the Grand Canyon of the Yellowstone to Mt. Washburn (the lookout tower is barely visible to the naked eye). Less advisable are the steep, unstable social paths that plunge higgledy-piggledy down along the western edge of the forest. If you are feeling less spry, poke around a bit for more stumps, then retrace your steps for the gentlest way back down to the trailhead parking area. ▶4

Steep

大	MILESTONES

▶1 0.0 Start at unsigned parking turnout
▶2 0.3 Glacial boulders
▶3 1.5 Fossil Forest
▶4 3.0 Return to trailhead

Details of rings on fossilized tree stump (*above*).

Twin petrified pine trees, *some 50 million years old, stand upright in the fossil forest below Specimen Ridge (left).*

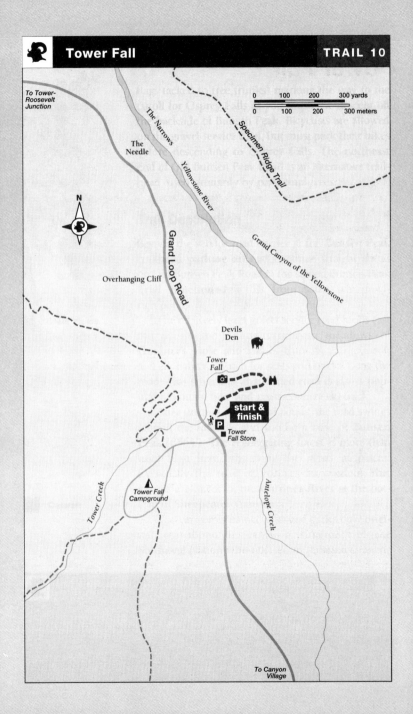

0 100 200 300 yards

0 100 200 300 meters

N

To Tower-
Roosevelt
Junction

The Narrows

The Needle

Specimen Ridge Trail

Yellowstone River

Grand Loop Road

Overhanging Cliff

Grand Canyon of the Yellowstone

Devils
Den

Tower
Fall

start &
finish

Tower
Fall Store

Tower Creek

Tower Fall
Campground

Antelope Creek

To Canyon
Village

Tower Fall

This easy jeans-and-tennis-shoes jaunt to an impressive waterfall is a perfect multigenerational affair, with something for the entire family. You can even leave the kids up top, at the general store, in the care of the jovial grandpas who will happily ply them with ice cream—and maybe even some fly-casting lessons in the parking lot.

Best Time

The trail is accessible from May through at least October. The water level of the falls is highest during spring runoff.

Finding the Trail

From the west, go 17.5 miles east on the Grand Loop Road from Mammoth Junction to Tower-Roosevelt Junction, then straight (south) for 2.3 miles to the parking area on the left-hand (north) side of the road. From the south, go 16.7 miles north on the Grand Loop Road over Dunraven Pass (8859') to the parking area on the right-hand side of the road. From the Northeast Entrance, head 29 miles southwest on the Northeast Entrance Road to Tower-Roosevelt Junction, then 2.3 miles south (left) on the Grand Loop Road.

Trail Description

The trailhead is accessed from the chaotic but ample parking area►1 opposite the Tower Fall Campground entrance. Stroll past the **general store** and

TRAIL USE
Hike
LENGTH
1.5 miles, 1 hour
VERTICAL FEET
±225'
DIFFICULTY
– **1** 2 3 4 5 +
TRAIL TYPE
Out & Back
SURFACE TYPE
Dirt & Paved

FEATURES
Child Friendly
Handicap Accessible
Canyon
Steep
Stream
Waterfall
Birds
Cool & Shady
Great Views
Photo Opportunity
Geologic Interest
Geothermal
Moonlight Hiking

FACILITIES
General Store
Restroom
Phone

Tower Fall *is at its most impressive during spring runoff.*

Morgan Konn

restrooms▶2 en route to the **Tower Fall Over-look**▶3 via a wide, paved, wheelchair-accessible path. Since the trees have grown in, you cannot get the same view here of the memorable 132-foot falls that artist Thomas Moran found in 1874, which inspired one of his most famous paintings.

 Waterfall

For the best views, continue downhill another 0.5 mile past the lookout on the wide, paved path via gentle switchbacks toward the **Yellowstone River** ▶4 to the base of **Tower Fall,**▶5 a total of 0.75 mile from the parking lot. The waterfall is just upstream from the impressive confluence of the river and Antelope and Tower creeks, in the most accessible stretch of the **Grand Canyon of the Yellowstone**. It's possible to escape the crowds here by following a network of fishermen's paths upstream along the Yellowstone, toward a small island near a bend in the river called Bannock Ford.

 Great Views

Retrace your steps back uphill to the parking area,▶6 after stopping by the general store for a Wilcoxson's Made-in-Montana ice cream bar.

 MILESTONES

▶1　0.0 Start at Tower Fall parking area

▶2　0.1 General store and restrooms

▶3　0.25 Tower Fall overlook (wheelchair accessible)

▶4　0.7 Left at Tower Creek/Yellowstone River confluence

▶5　0.75 Base of Tower Fall

▶6　1.5 Return to parking area

 Yellowstone River Trail

OPTIONS

At the bottom of the trail, it's possible to continue upstream along the south bank of the Yellowstone River through the Grand Canyon of the Yellowstone for up to 0.5 mile along well-beaten fishing trails. While you're at it, rig your fly rod and cast for some trout.

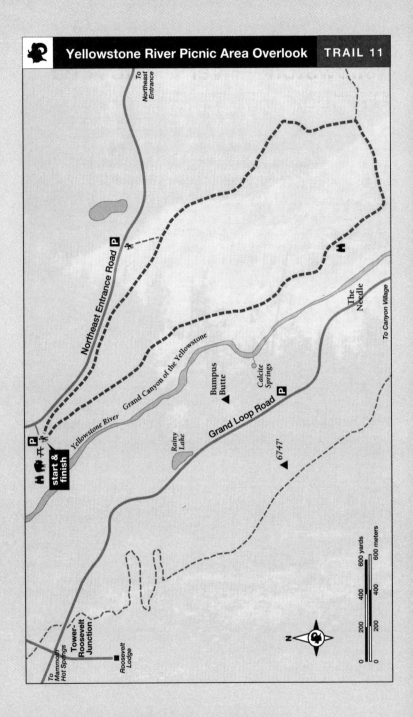

Yellowstone River Picnic Area Overlook

Bring your binoculars: this easy, family-friendly hike provides opportunities to spot wildlife and offers quick access to unobstructed views of both the Grand Canyon of the Yellowstone and the Absaroka Range. Turn around wherever you like, or complete the loop by following the start of the Specimen Ridge Trail.

Best Time

The exposed trail can get hot in the summer, but it's enjoyable whenever the weather is decent. The hiking season runs May to October, making it a good early- and late-season choice. Wildflower watchers are happiest here in spring.

Finding the Trail

From the west, go 17.5 miles east from Mammoth Hot Springs on the Grand Loop Road to the Tower-Roosevelt Junction. Turn left (northeast) on the Northeast Entrance Road and go 1.2 miles (0.5 mile past the Yellowstone River bridge) before turning right into the signed picnic area and trailhead parking lot on the south side of the road. From the Northeast Entrance, go 27.8 miles southwest on the Northeast Entrance Road and turn left into the parking lot. From the south, go 19 miles north over Dunraven Pass (8859') on the Grand Loop Road and turn right (northeast) at Tower-Roosevelt Junction, then continue 1.2 miles and turn right into the picnic area. In the parking area, ignore several unofficial social trails; the official (signed) trailhead is by the picnic table just to the left of the restroom.

TRAIL USE
Hike
LENGTH
4.0 miles, 1.5-2 hours
VERTICAL FEET
+200'
DIFFICULTY
– 1 **2** 3 4 5 +
TRAIL TYPE
Out & Back or Loop
SURFACE TYPE
Dirt

FEATURES
Child Friendly
Canyon
Wildflowers
Birds
Wildlife
Great Views
Photo Opportunity
Geologic Interest
Geothermal Activity

FACILITIES
Restrooms
Picnic Tables

Trail Description

In the **picnic area,** ►1 look for the trailhead on the east side of the parking lot. The earthen trail climbs 200 feet in the first few hundred yards for a breathtaking start to a breathtaking hike.

 Canyon

Once atop the hill, stop for a peek down into The Narrows of the **Grand Canyon of the Yellowstone** ►2 some 800 feet below. Can you hear the river roar? Take extra care with the kids near the precipitous canyon rim—there are no safety railings here in the backcountry. The Tower-Canyon road and overhanging cliffs of columnar basalt are visible across the canyon. Keep your eyes out for bighorn sheep scampering along the canyon's sheer walls.

 Wildlife

About halfway along the trail at 1.2 miles, you don't need an acute sense of smell to pick up on the sulfur odor wafting out of the active **Calcite Springs** ►3 thermal area on the opposite side of the canyon.

Geothermal

After 2 miles, the route reaches a viewpoint at a three-way junction with the **Specimen Ridge Trail.** ►4 Here, you can either retrace your steps to the trailhead or take the left fork toward the Specimen Ridge trailhead (2K4) to loop back to the picnic area and parking lot. ►5 Both return routes require approximately the same amount of time and effort. If opting for the loop, watch closely for an unsigned path heading off to the left just before you reach the road, to avoid having to finish up this otherwise scenic final stretch on the pavement.

𝗄 MILESTONES

► 1   0.0 Start at Yellowstone River Picnic Area trailhead

► 2   0.2 Grand Canyon of the Yellowstone overlook

► 3   1.2 Calcite Springs Overlook

► 4   2.0 Specimen Ridge Trail junction

► 5   4.0 Return to parking lot

Bannock Trail

HISTORY

The Bannock Trail was probably used off and on for centuries. Its current name comes from its frequent use in the 1800s by the Bannock, who crossed the Yellowstone Plateau when heading for the plains east of the park to hunt bison, after the totem animal had been exterminated from the Snake River Plains, the tribe's homeland. They crossed the Yellowstone River upstream from its confluence with Tower Creek, in the canyon far below the junction with the Specimen Ridge Trail. Many people have assumed this ford was an ancient crossing. However, archeological investigations have found no evidence of repeated, long-term use.

Female bighorn sheep *are frequently seen scampering down-canyon to the Yellowstone River (Trail 11).*

Central Yellowstone– Norris/Canyon Country

Central Yellowstone–Norris/Canyon Country

After the area around Old Faithful, Yellowstone's varied central core is the most heavily visited region of the park. The biggest crowds congregate around **Canyon Village**, since it is home to a concentration of visitor services, as well as the sprawling, motel-style Canyon Lodge & Cabins complex ($47-$147) and a forested, Xanterra-run campground.

If there were only one must-see attraction in the region, it would be the dramatic **Grand Canyon of the Yellowstone**. The canyon's scenic upper stretch is flush with huge waterfalls and is easily accessed from North and South Rim drives via several easy paths, scenic overlooks, and short spur trails.

The best place in the region to spot wildlife is the broad **Hadyen Valley**, a former arm of Yellowstone Lake between Canyon and Lake junctions, that attracts flocks of birds with its rich aquatic vegetation and hordes of charismatic megafauna with its vast grasslands. Some researchers have attributed the treeless valley's lack of typical aspens and cottonwood to the long-term absence of wolves, which allowed elk to heavily browse all the saplings. Others have suggested that flooding may have played an important role.

Legions of bison migrate in the fall across the infrequently visited **Central Plateau** via the **Nez Perce Creek/Mary Mtn. corridor** to the warmth of the **Firehole River Basin**, en route to the low-lying areas outside the park's western boundary, around West Yellowstone.

After the explosive Norris Geyser Basin, adjacent to the well-situated, NPS-run Norris Campground (open mid-May to late September), the region's second most dynamic thermal area is the fault-riddled Mud Volcano complex, where there's a short but worthwhile self-guided interpretive loop trail. The boardwalks afford a close-up whiff of several pungent, sulphur-stinking mudpots and some of the park's most acidic hydrothermal features, with a pH of 1-2, similar to stomach fluids or battery acid.

Adjacent to Madison Junction, the RV-friendly, Xanterra-run **Madison Campground** (open early May through October) is the closest camping option to Old Faithful (16 miles south), and a favorite with anglers thanks to its easy access to the world-famous **Madison River**. The closest showers are also in Old Faithful, but there are some nice tent-only campsites near the river, evening ranger programs, and lots of good wildlife watching and swimming nearby in the **Firehole River Canyon**.

During summer, rangers lead several outings around Norris and Canyon—including half-day wildlife—watching excursions in the Hayden Valley, shorter canyon rim walks focusing on geology and natural history, and a 45-minute evening talk daily at the outdoor Canyon Campground Amphitheater. Inquire at ranger stations about current schedules.

The 12-mile-long **Norris-Canyon Road** traverses the divide between the Central and Solfatara plateaus to connect Canyon (7734') and Norris (7484') junctions, via one of the park's least scenic stretches of road, locally known as "lodgepole alley."

Heading north from Canyon toward Tower-Roosevelt Junction, the Grand Loop Road and **Dunraven Pass (8859')** are scheduled to be closed year-round through at least the summer of 2005 due a major road-widening project. The road will remain open between Tower-Roosevelt Junction and Chittenden Road for access to the northern Mt. Washburn trailhead. Call (307) 344-2117 for Yellowstone road construction updates.

Permits and Maps

Except for the optional overnight add-on trip to Sevenmile Hole, none of the hikes in this chapter require backcountry permits.

Groundbreaking for a new **Canyon Visitor Education Center**, slated to include a 3-D map of the park and interactive displays about the Yellowstone Volcano Observatory and the park's geothermal features, was scheduled for the spring of 2005 at the time of research.

In the interim, there's a Yellowstone Association bookstore, backcountry office and **temporary visitor center** in a portable building facing Canyon Village's main parking lot. Call (307) 242-2550; open daily from 8 AM to 7 PM during the summer. At the entrance to the geyser basin, the **Norris Geyser Basin Museum and Information Station** also has helpful staff and a good bookstore. Call (307) 344-2812; open daily from 10 AM to 5 PM until October 10.

Overleaf: *Looking north from Mt. Washburn toward the Gallatin National Forest and Absaroka Range (Trail 17)*

Fourteen miles east of the park's **West Entrance** (open mid-April to mid-November), the **Madison Information Station** has a smaller bookstore and rangers on duty until October 10. Call (307) 344-2821; open daily from 9 AM to 5 PM during the summer. NPS rangers and USFS staff are also on duty year-round, just outside the park's West Entrance at the **West Yellowstone Chamber of Commerce Visitor Center**. Call (406) 646-4403; open daily from 8 AM to 8 PM during the summer; winter hours are shorter.

National Geographic's Trails Illustrated *Yellowstone National Park* map (no. 202, scale 1:126,720) depicts all the trails described in this chapter. In the same series, the individual 1:63,360 maps *Tower/Canyon* (no. 304), *Mammoth Hot Springs* (no. 303) and *Old Faithful* (no. 302) show the trails in greater detail, and include trailheads and backcountry campsites. All of the trails are covered by single maps, with the exception of the Mary Mtn. trail, which appears on portions of all three.

Morgan Konn

Dead trees in Mt. Washburn burn area *Vegetation has regenerated since the 1988 fire, including legendary displays of summer wildflowers.*

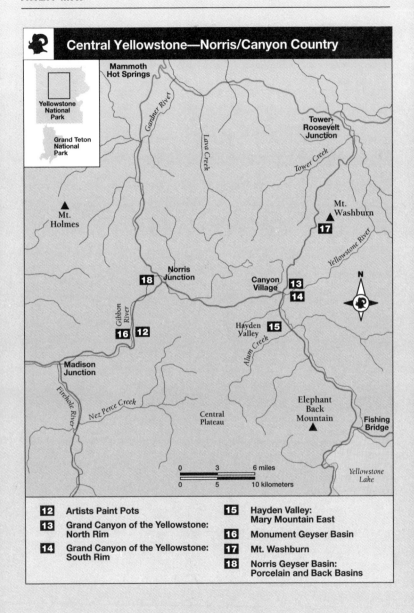

Central Yellowstone—Norris/Canyon Country

Yellowstone National Park

Grand Teton National Park

Mammoth Hot Springs

Gardner River

Lava Creek

Tower-Roosevelt Junction

Tower Creek

Mt. Holmes

Mt. Washburn

17

Yellowstone River

Norris Junction

18

Canyon Village

13

14

N

Gibbon River

Hayden Valley

15

16 **12**

Alum Creek

Madison Junction

Firehole River

Nez Perce Creek

Central Plateau

Elephant Back Mountain

Fishing Bridge

| 0 | 3 | 6 miles |
| 0 | 5 | 10 kilometers |

Yellowstone Lake

12	Artists Paint Pots	**15**	Hayden Valley: Mary Mountain East
13	Grand Canyon of the Yellowstone: North Rim	**16**	Monument Geyser Basin
14	Grand Canyon of the Yellowstone: South Rim	**17**	Mt. Washburn
		18	Norris Geyser Basin: Porcelain and Back Basins

Central Yellowstone—Norris/Canyon Country

TRAIL	Difficulty	Length	Type	USES & ACCESS	TERRAIN	FLORA & FAUNA	OTHER
12	1	1.2	Loop	Hiking, Child Friendly			Photo Opportunity, Swimming, Moonlight Hiking
13	2	3.8	Point-to-point	Hiking, Handicap Access, Child Friendly	Canyon, Stream, Waterfall	Birds	Great Views, Photo Opportunity, Historic, Geologic Interest, Swimming, Moonlight Hiking
14	2	3.2	Point-to-point	Hiking, Handicap Access, Child Friendly	Canyon, Stream, Waterfall	Birds	Great Views, Photo Opportunity, Historic, Geologic Interest, Swimming, Moonlight Hiking
15	4	10.0	Point-to-point	Hiking	Stream	Wildflowers, Birds, Wildlife	Great Views, Photo Opportunity, Geologic Interest, Swimming
16	3	3.0	Point-to-point	Hiking			Great Views, Photo Opportunity, Secluded, Swimming, Geothermal
17	4	6.0	Point-to-point	Hiking, Bicycling	Mountain, Summit	Wildflowers, Birds, Wildlife	Great Views, Photo Opportunity, Camping, Historic
18	2	2.0	Loop	Hiking, Handicap Access, Child Friendly			Photo Opportunity, Geologic Interest, Swimming, Moonlight Hiking

USES & ACCESS
- Hiking
- Bicycling
- Horses
- Backpacking
- Child Friendly
- Handicap Access
- Backcountry Permit Required
- Camping

TERRAIN
- Canyon
- Mountain
- Summit
- Stream
- Waterfall
- Lake
- Geothermal

FLORA & FAUNA
- Autumn Colors
- Wildflowers
- Birds
- Wildlife

DIFFICULTY
- 1 2 3 4 5 +
less   more

OTHER
- Cool & Shady
- Great Views
- Photo Opportunity
- Swimming
- Secluded
- Historic
- Geologic Interest
- Moonlight Hiking
- Steep

Central Yellowstone–Norris/Canyon Country

Canada geese

Morgan Konn

Hayden Valley: Mary Mountain East .129

Though it is possible to complete the entire Mary Mtn. Trail in a strenuous, daylong outing, the route is most often enjoyed as a more leisurely, out-and-back dayhike from either end of the trail. Bird-watching is especially good in the wildlife-rich western section, and in the summer, spotting bison and coyotes is almost guaranteed in the Hayden Valley.

TRAIL 15

Hike
10.0 miles, Out & Back
Difficulty: 1 2 3 **4** 5

Monument Geyser Basin 135

Aficionados of unique thermal areas will enjoy this stiff but scenic and straightforward ascent through a regenerating burn area to a seldom-visited geyser basin. Others may suspect that the lack of switch-backs on the trail is aimed at discouraging visitors.

TRAIL 16

Hike
3.0 miles, Out & Back
Difficulty: 1 2 **3** 4 5

Mt. Washburn .139

One of the park's most popular and rewarding day-hikes features great views, a gradual climb, loads of wildlife and wildflowers, plus panoramic views from a working fire lookout atop the northern end of the gigantic caldera created by the last eruption of Yellowstone's supervolcano.

TRAIL 17

Hike, Bike
6.0 miles, Out & Back
Difficulty: 1 2 3 **4** 5

Norris Geyser Basin 145

Boardwalks offer an up-close look at Yellowstone's hottest and most volatile hydrothermal area. The basin is home to Steamboat Geyser, the world's largest active geyser, as well as rare acidic geysers and a fascinating assortment of other dynamic thermal features.

TRAIL 18

Hike
2.0 miles, Loop
Difficulty: 1 **2** 3 4 5

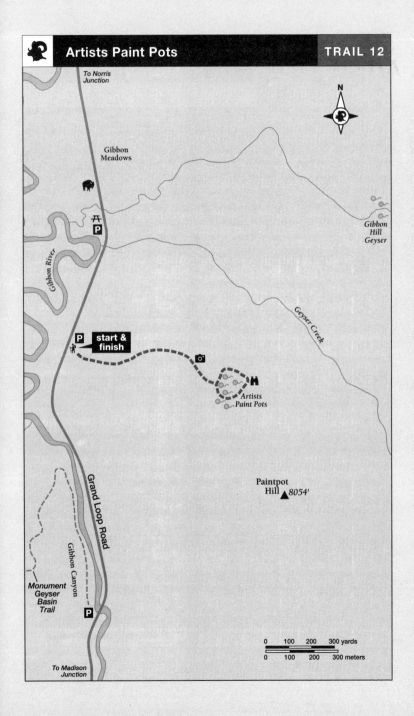

Artists Paint Pots

TRAIL 12

To Norris
Junction

Gibbon
Meadows

Gibbon River

Gibbon Hill
Geyser

Geyser Creek

P start &
finish

Artists
Paint Pots

Grand Loop Road

Paintpot
Hill ▲ 8054'

Gibbon Canyon

Monument
Geyser
Basin
Trail

| 0 | 100 | 200 | 300 yards |

| 0 | 100 | 200 | 300 meters |

To Madison
Junction

Artists Paint Pots

Interpretive signs are lacking, but this easy loop provides an intimate overview of several types of hydrothermal features. If thermal areas pique your interest, the hike combines nicely with the steep ramble up to the nearby Monument Geyser Basin.

Best Time

The shadeless route is usually passable as soon as the park opens in spring through October. Visit early in the morning to beat the tour bus crowds. Many of the paint pots' vibrant colors get washed out after heavy precipitation.

Finding the Trail

From the north, go 3.5 miles south of Norris Junction on Grand Loop Road and turn left into the well-signed parking area on the east side of the road. From the south, go 9.5 miles northwest on Grand Loop Road from Madison Junction and turn right into the parking area (which is 1 mile past the Gibbon River bridge).

Trail Description

From the east side of the large parking area,▶1 look for the wooden footbridge▶2 that leads to a wide, flat gravel trail, which passes through a regenerating patch of burned lodgepole pines. Steam plumes emanating from vents in the paint pot basin are visible against the hillside in the background.

TRAIL USE
Hike
LENGTH
1.2 miles, up to 1 hour
VERTICAL FEET
±100'
DIFFICULTY
– **1** 2 3 4 5 +
TRAIL TYPE
Loop
SURFACE TYPE
Mixed

FEATURES
Child Friendly
Photo Opportunity
Geothermal
Moonlight Hiking

FACILITIES
Picnic Tables

115

Paint pots (also known as mudpots when less colorful) form where sulfuric acid in the groundwater and heat-loving microorganisms conspire to break down rocks. Dissolved minerals then lend the varied range of reds, greens, and blues to the gloppy sort of clay.

 Great Views

 Geothermal

As the trail opens up and cuts right under some power lines, steam from the stark, white Monument Geyser Basin is visible high atop the ridge across the Grand Loop Road

The trail returns to a boardwalk just before reaching a junction▶3 for the loop portion of the trail, 0.4 mile from the trailhead at the edge of the thermal basin. Many folks walk in the clockwise direction and never make it up this far to see the highlight of the trail.

Heading in the counterclockwise direction, the trail winds around past an abandoned trail, up some stairs to the biggest and best of the mudpots for an onomatopoetic "bloop, blap, plop, ploop" symphony paired with a sulfurous beef jerky smell—a real feast of mixed messages for the senses.

Complete the full loop for a good overview of the entire basin. Gibbon Meadows and the thermal areas around Sylvan and Evening Primrose springs stretch out to the west, with Purple Mtn. (8391') in the background to the left and Mt. Holmes (10,336') to the far right. The geyser and other hydrothermal features down below are actually best viewed from above.

Loop down past some fumaroles, a steamy perpetual spouter and a connected roiling pool, to a bridge spanning the thermal outlet channel. Back at the first junction,▶4 retrace your steps to the parking area.▶5

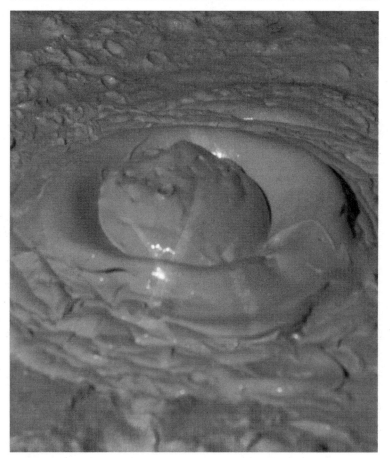

Mudpot *(also known as a paint pot) about to burp*

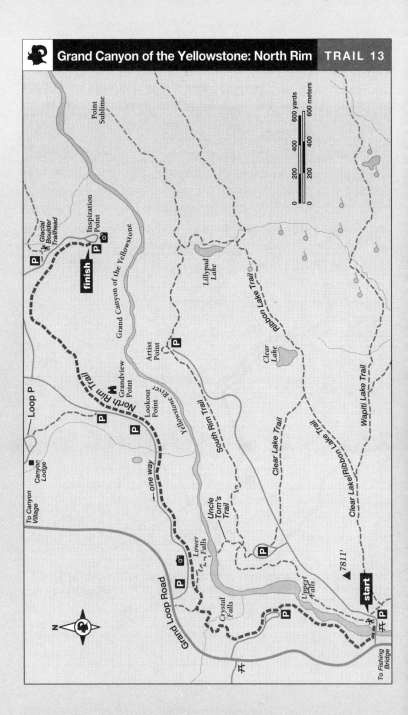

Point Sublime

600 yards
600 meters

Glacial Boulder Trailhead

Inspiration Point

finish

Grand Canyon of the Yellowstone

Lillypad Lake

Ribbon Lake Trail

Artist Point

Clear Lake

North Rim Trail

Grandview Point

Loop P

Lookout Point

Yellowstone River

South Rim Trail

Clear Lake Trail

Ribbon Lake Trail

Wapiti Lake Trail

To Canyon Village

Canyon Lodge

one way

Clear Lake/Ribbon Lake Trail

Uncle Tom's Trail

Lower Falls

7811'

start

Grand Loop Road

Crystal Falls

Upper Falls

To Canyon Village

To Fishing Bridge

N

Grand Canyon of the Yellowstone: North Rim

Although it often parallels a busy road, this popular route leads past a series of overlooks and scenic viewpoints, with a couple of opportunities to take steep detours below the canyon rim for close encounters with the impressive falls.

Best Time

The trails are most enjoyable in the early morning before the crowds descend, or around sunset. Most of the detours down to the falls can be icy in cold weather and are closed in winter. Check for seasonal closures at any visitor center.

Finding the Trail

From Canyon Village, go 2.2 miles south on the Grand Loop Road and turn left (east) on Artist Point Road. Cross over the Yellowstone River on Chittenden Bridge and park in the large lot on your right, signed for the Wapiti Lake trailhead and picnic area. From the south, go 13.8 miles north on the Grand Loop Road from the Fishing Bridge junction and turn right (east) at Artist Point Road.

Logistics

Set up a shuttle by leaving a vehicle in the parking loop at Inspiration Point, 1.6 miles southeast of Canyon Village at the end of a well-signed dead-end road, just past the smaller turnout for the Glacial Boulder trailhead. Otherwise, it's a 3-mile walk back

TRAIL USE
Hike

LENGTH
3.8 miles, 2-3 hours

VERTICAL FEET
±1200' including detours

DIFFICULTY
– 1 **2** 3 4 5 +

TRAIL TYPE
Point-to-point

SURFACE TYPE
Dirt and Paved

FEATURES
Child Friendly
Handicap Access
Canyon
Stream
Waterfall
Birds
Great Views
Photo Opportunity
Historic Interest
Geologic Interest
Geothermal
Moonlight Hiking

FACILITIES
Visitor Center
Restrooms
Picnic Tables
Phone

along the road or trail to Chittenden Bridge. From Loop P of the Canyon Lodge Cabins, a 0.5-mile paved trail leads from cabin P26 to Grandview Point.

You can make a leisurely full day of it by combining this hike with the canyon's equally impressive South Rim route (see Trail 14, page 125).

Trail Description

Ignore the Howard Eaton and Wapiti Lake trails that head out from the far (east) side of the parking area.▶1 Instead, walk back across **Chittenden Bridge**, and watch for traffic as you cross the road to the start of the **North Rim Trail.**▶2

Follow the old road as it traces the western bank of the Yellowstone River for 0.5 mile, to the signed turnoff on your right for the overlook of the gushing **Brink of the Upper Falls.**▶3 A short set of steps lead down and around to the actual brink,▶4 where the **Yellowstone River** plummets 109 feet— stop before you get to the bottom to look for rainbows and to listen to the roar. Afterward, retrace your steps to the large parking lot at the top of the staircase.▶5

Continue to your right through the parking lot and past the restrooms for a few hundred yards, then turn right on the signed continuation of the North Rim Trail.▶6 After the trail approaches the canyon rim, detour to your right on a short path to an overlook of the much smaller, three-stage **Crystal Falls,**▶7 the graceful tail end of Cascade Creek. It's best viewed from across the canyon at Uncle Tom's Point.

Photo Opportunity

Waterfall

Waterfall

Follow the trail away from the canyon rim and turn right at the signed path to the viewpoint for the **Brink of the Lower Falls,**►8 where a series of switchbacks drops down 600 feet toward the base of the stupendous, 308-foot cataract. Not far down the 0.5 mile side trail►9 (closed in winter), you'll see the brink and can catch a glimpse of the Upper Falls upstream. Even if you aren't inclined to hike all the way down to the bottom to look for rainbows and feel the spray,►10 it's worth at least a short detour.

If you haven't set up a shuttle, the Lower Falls overlook is a logical point to retrace your steps to the trailhead parking lot.

Back up top, turn right and walk against traffic, alongside the one-way road paralleling the canyon rim for a few hundred yards past some restrooms. Turn right on the paved trail at the parking turnout for **Lookout Point**►11 for the best views of the Lower Falls. Visible below to your right is the steep paved **Red Rock Trail,**►12 which drops 500 feet in 0.25 mile for yet another scenic and misty look upcanyon.

Back at the Lookout Point parking area,►13 turn right and follow the path alongside the road up to the parking area for **Grandview Point,**►14 where benches hewn from glacial boulders provide a nice picnic spot with views down the colorful canyon.

Here, the unpaved trail forks to the right, away from the road to end up at the **Inspiration Point**►15 parking loop. Steps (which are closed in the winter) lead down past inviting benches (with views of birds and thermal features in the multicolored canyon) to yet another dramatic overlook.

Glacial melt water carved out the canyon some 14,000 years ago. The colorful patches of orange, green, and brown rocks in the canyon walls near the river indicate active thermal areas.

 Great Views

 Photo Opportunity

►1   0.0 Start at Wapiti Lake parking area

►2   0.1 Right at North Rim Trail

►3   0.5 Right at Brink of the Upper Falls overlook

►4   0.7 Brink of the Upper Falls

►5   0.9 Right at Upper Falls parking lot

►6   1.0 Right on North Rim Trail

►7   1.1 Right to Crystal Falls overlook

►8   1.3 Right at Brink of the Lower Falls overlook

►9   1.8 Brink of the Lower Falls

►10 2.3 Right on North Rim Trail

►11 2.5 Right at Lookout Point

►12 2.75 Viewpoint at end of Red Rock Trail

►13 3.0 Right on road

►14 3.2 Grandview Point

►15 3.8 Arrive at Inspiration Point parking area

Yellowstone's Tallest Waterfalls

NOTES

The Lower Falls are often referred to as Yellowstone's tallest waterfall—but the wispy **Silver Cord Cascade**, visible across the canyon a mile downstream from the Glacial Boulder trailhead, plunges well over 1000 feet before reaching the bottom of the canyon, as do other nearby seasonal cascades (none of them named).

Morgan Konn

Upper Falls *from Artist Point at the east end of the South Rim Trail (Trail 14)*

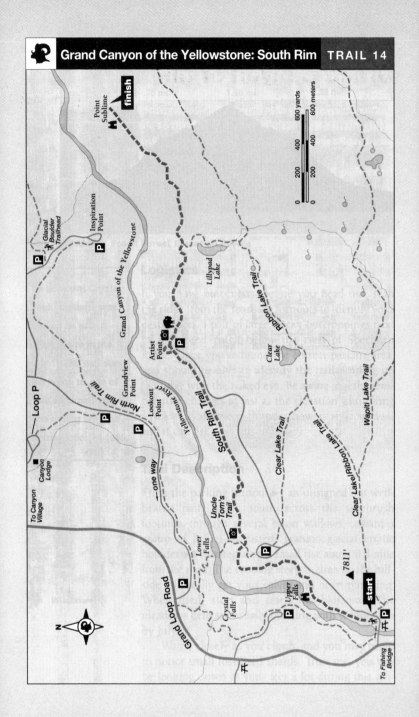

finish

Point Sublime

Glacial Boulder Trailhead

Inspiration Point

Loop P

Grand Canyon of the Yellowstone

Lillypad Lake

Ribbon Lake Trail

Artist Point

Clear Lake

North Rim Trail

Grandview Point

Yellowstone River

Lookout Point

Wapiti Lake Trail

Canyon Lodge

To Canyon Village

one way

South Rim Trail

Clear Lake Trail

Clear Lake/Ribbon Lake Trail

Uncle Tom's Trail

Lower Falls

7811'

Grand Loop Road

Crystal Falls

Upper Falls

start

P

To Fishing Bridge

N

600 yards

600 meters

0 200 400

Grand Canyon of the Yellowstone: South Rim

Although parts of this popular route parallel the busy South Rim Dr., the partially paved trail winds in and out of enough forests to provide some serenity. It's a great place to get out of the car to stretch your legs and lungs during a long drive around the Grand Loop.

Best Time

The colors in the canyon are most vibrant at sunrise and especially sunset, when crowds are thinnest. Uncle Tom's Trail is closed all winter, and also in spring and fall if icy. Check for seasonal closures at any visitor center.

Finding the Trail

From Canyon Village, go 2.2 miles south on the Grand Loop Road and turn left (east) on Artist Point Road. Cross over the Yellowstone River on Chittenden Bridge and park in the large lot on your right, signed for the Wapiti Lake trailhead and picnic area. From the south, go 13.8 miles north on the Grand Loop Road from the Fishing Bridge junction and turn right (east) at Artist Point Road.

Logistics

Arrange a shuttle by leaving a car at the busy Artist Point parking lot. Combining this hike with the canyon's equally impressive North Rim Trail, which starts at the same trailhead, makes for a leisurely full-day excursion (see Trail 13, page 119).

TRAIL USE
Hike
LENGTH
3.2 miles, 1.5-2.5 hours
VERTICAL FEET
±500' including
Uncle Tom's Trail
DIFFICULTY
– 1 **2** 3 4 5 +
TRAIL TYPE
Point-to-point
SURFACE TYPE
Dirt and Paved

FEATURES
Child Friendly
Handicap Access
Canyon
Stream
Waterfall
Birds
Great Views
Photo Opportunity
Historic Interest
Geologic Interest
Geothermal
Moonlight Hiking

FACILITIES
Restrooms
Picnic Tables

Trail Description

Ignore the Howard Eaton and Wapiti Lake trails that head out from the far (east) side of the parking area. ►1 Instead, walk back toward **Chittenden Bridge** and watch for traffic as you cross the road just before the bridge to the start of the **South Rim Trail.** ►2

The trail rises slightly, then drops down alongside the river after 0.6 miles for stellar views from the **Upper Falls overlook,** ►3 just before the restrooms and parking loop for **Uncle Tom's Trail.** ►4 When not closed in winter or due to icy conditions, the steep paved paths and hundreds of steel stairs, which descend 500 feet along a historic route, provide an unparalleled, close-up view of the **Lower Falls**. From the platform at the bottom, ►5 you not only see but also hear and feel the 308-foot falls' might. Not everyone can make this steep, vertigo-inspiring descent, but if you're able, it's worth every huff and puff on the return ascent.

Back up top, steer clear of the parking lot and continue to the left on the South Rim Trail, ►6 which traces the canyon rim out of sight of the road for 0.8 mile. You rejoin the road just before the parking loop for **Artist Point,** ►7 where a set of stunning overlooks attracts photographers by the busload.

Landscape painter Thomas Moran observed that "the canyon's beautiful tints were beyond the reach of human art," but that doesn't seem to stop folks from trying to capture them. If you have binoculars, it's also a fine point to scan the canyon walls for the nests of raptors, ravens, and swallows.

Most people turn back here, but even more superlative views await 0.5 mile beyond the Lilypad Lake junction, ►8 and a total of 1 mile beyond the Artist Point/Ribbon Lake trailhead (4K8) at **Point Sublime,** ►9 a relatively flat, one hour round-trip from Artist Point.

Waterfall

Steep

Great Views

Photo Opportunity

MILESTONES

▶1　0.0 Start at Wapiti Lake parking area

▶2　0.1 Right at South Rim Trail

▶3　0.7 Upper Falls overlook

▶4　0.8 Left at Uncle Tom's Trail

▶5　1.0 Lower Falls viewing platform

▶6　1.2 Left on South Rim Trail

▶7　2.0 Artist Point

▶8　2.5 Straight at Lily Pad Lake cutoff

▶9　3.0 Arrive at Point Sublime

NOTES

Ribbon Lake Overnight

Ribbon Lake is great first-time overnight option, just over 2 miles (about an hour) from the Artist Point/Ribbon Lake trailhead. Take care with wandering kids along this trail—there's a refreshing lack of railings here.

Uncle Tom-foolery

Uncle Tom Richardson was a pioneering entrepreneurial guide who rigged up a Rube Goldberg-esque series of ropes, ladders, and stairs. He then charged tourists to scramble 500 feet down into the canyon to the base of the Lower Falls.

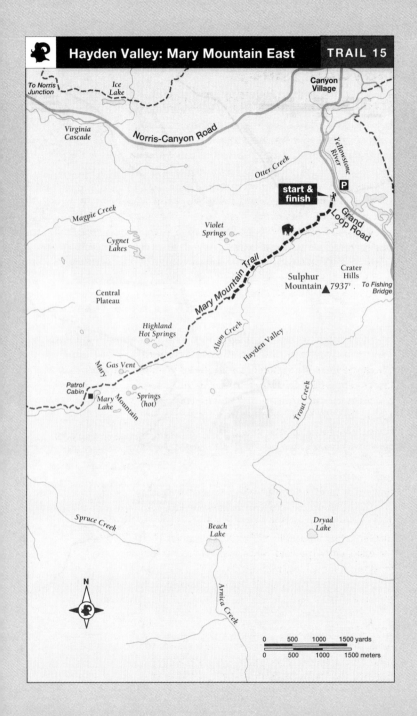

Hayden Valley: Mary Mountain East

TRAIL 15

To Norris
Junction

Ice
Lake

Canyon
Village

Virginia
Cascade

Norris-Canyon Road

Otter Creek

Yellowstone
River

Magpie Creek

**start &
finish**

P

Grand Loop Road

Violet
Springs

Mary Mountain Trail

Cygnet
Lakes

Central
Plateau

Sulphur
Mountain

Crater
Hills

7937'

To Fishing
Bridge

Highland
Hot Springs

Alum Creek

Hayden Valley

Mary.

Gas Vent

Patrol
Cabin

Mary Lake

Mary Mountain

Springs
(hot)

Trout Creek

Spruce Creek

Beach
Lake

Dryad
Lake

Arnica Creek

N

| 0 | 500 | 1000 | 1500 yards |
| 0 | 500 | 1000 | 1500 meters |

Hayden Valley:
Mary Mountain East

The first few miles of the eastern end of this often-overlooked trail meander along the forest northern edge of the wide-open Hayden Valley, through open sagelands and prime habitat for bison, coyote, and grizzly. Expect to see lots of birds and animals—and to get your feet wet—in one of the best places in the park to see a variety of wildlife. The optional day-long traverse of Mary Mtn. gets even less traffic.

Best Time

The low-lying portions of the trail are usually boggy: Check with a ranger station or visitor center for current conditions, especially early or late in the season. The western half of the trail is closed between March 10 and June 15 from Mary Lake to the western Nez Perce trailhead due to bear management restrictions.

Finding the Trail

From the north, go 4.5 miles south on the Grand Loop Road from Canyon Junction and turn left into the small Mary Mtn. trailhead parking turnout. The turnout is just north of the Alum Creek pullout on the east side of the road, and is sometimes referred to as the Alum Creek trailhead. From the south, go 11.5 miles north on Grand Loop Road from Fishing Bridge and turn right into the turnout.

Logistics

Aside from a possible dip in fishless Mary Lake, the trail's most interesting sections are within the first 5 miles of the trailhead. Since overnight camping is

TRAIL USE
Hike
LENGTH
10.0 miles, 5 hours
VERTICAL FEET
Negligible
DIFFICULTY
– 1 2 3 **4** 5 +
TRAIL TYPE
Out & Back
SURFACE TYPE
Dirt

FEATURES
Stream
Autumn Colors
Wildflowers
Birds
Wildlife
Great Views
Photo Opportunity
Geologic Interest
Geothermal

FACILITIES
None

banned en route due to heavy bear and bison activity, most everyone hikes this trail as an out-and-back route. When open, the Mary Mtn. traverse can be done one-way in one long day in either direction with a car shuttle; hiking from west to east adds 400 feet of elevation gain.

Check with the Canyon Ranger Station for updates on current wildlife activity, closures, and restrictions. A good topo map, compass, and route-finding skills are often necessary in the upper reaches of Hayden Valley, since bison like to use trail markers as scratching posts and knock them down faster than intrepid NPS trail crews can resurrect them. Whatever you do, do not attempt to walk through the middle of a bison herd. When in doubt, detour widely or turn around.

If at all possible, hike in a group. A seasonal park employee was mauled in June 2004 by two grizzlies while committing the three big no-nos—hiking alone, off-trail, and around dusk—at the northern end of the Hayden Valley.

Trail Description

Take care when crossing the busy Grand Loop Road to the **Mary Mtn. trailhead.▶1** Take a deep breath of fresh air and turn your bison and grizzly sensors on high alert, as you start out by skirting the forested northern edge of the wide-open **Hayden Valley**.

Wildlife

The perennially boggy trail wanders through rolling sagebrush and traces the treeline above the appealing, thermally fed **Alum Creek**. Keep your binoculars at the ready to avert potentially hazardous wildlife encounters, but also to scan the creek's mud flats for abundant raptors and water birds: including herons, American dippers, ducks, geese, pelicans, bald eagles, northern harriers, and nesting sandhill cranes.

Birds

Fortunately, the lack of trees in the valley, caused by the depositing of fine-grained glacial sediments some 13,000 or 14,000 years ago, mean the vistas are mostly open. Meadows outcompete trees in the resulting impermeable clay soils here, so the few lodgepole islands appear in outcroppings of volcanic rock. Grizzlies like to lurk around the valley's forest edges, however, especially in the spring and early summer, when they prey on newborn bison and elk calves. Mature bison are often hidden while they sleep behind large sagebrush bushes, and are most unpredictable during the fall mating season, which starts in late July or early August.

Most dayhikers take their time and only make it 4 miles from the trailhead, to the easy ford of **Violet Creek,▶2** where there are several interesting off-trail thermal areas. Over the next mile you'll climb a few hundred feet to reach a nice viewpoint▶3 above the western end of the Hayden Valley; it's a great place

Hayden Valley is named after geologist Ferdinand V. Hayden, who led three landmark US government surveys of Yellowstone, including the first official exploration of the region in 1871 that contributed to the creation of the park.

Mary Mtn. Patrol Cabin *Sorry, only for NPS use!*

to watch wildlife. Take care here to stick to the main trail: The orange-blazed posts are often toppled by itchy bison.

If you are not continuing on the optional extension to Mary Lake (see below), retrace your footsteps to return to the eastern Mary Mtn. trailhead.▶4

MILESTONES

▶1 0.0 Start at Mary Mtn. trailhead

▶2 4.0 Cross Violet Creek

▶3 5.0 Hayden Valley viewpoint

▶4 10.0 Return to Mary Mtn. trailhead

OPTIONS

Guided NPS Adventure Hikes

Rangers lead moderate-difficulty, four- to five-hour loop hikes (6 miles round-trip; $15 for adults, $5 for kids ages 7-15, free for kids ages 6 and younger) through the Hayden Valley on Tuesdays from July through mid-August. The hikes start at the Mary Mtn. trailhead and often venture off-trail to an unmapped backcountry thermal feature.

Mary Lake and Mary Mountain Traverse

Although camping is not allowed anywhere along the route, it's possible to traverse the vast, undeveloped Central Plateau by climbing a total of 500 feet in 21 miles; you'll end up in the Firehole River basin.

Seven miles beyond the eastern trailhead, the route enters an unburned alley of lodgepole pines—a veritable bison highway—atop the wild **Central Plateau**. The trail climbs gradually for 2 miles past dusty bison wallows and sulfurous gas vents to the barren **Highland Hot Springs** thermal area, beyond an easy ford of an unnamed creek.

Following the historic Mary Mtn. stagecoach route, the trail tops out near the western shore of the tranquil 20-acre **Mary Lake**. The fishless lake attracts lots of birds and is a nice spot for a shady picnic, or a refreshing quick dip in the middle of a long, hot day.

Monument Geyser *is also known as Thermos Bottle Geyser (Trail 16).*

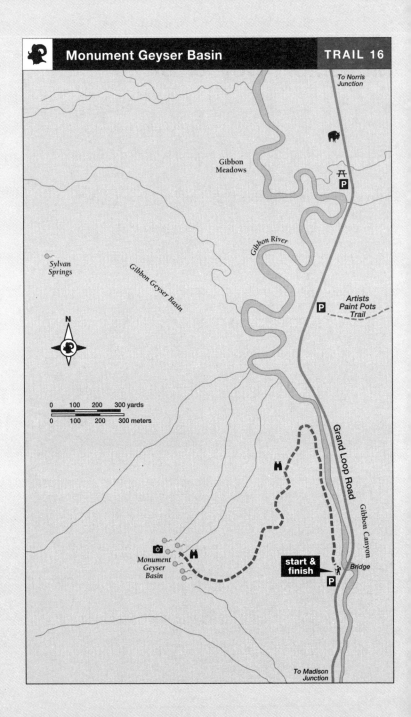

To Norris
Junction

Gibbon
Meadows

Gibbon River

Sylvan
Springs

Gibbon Geyser Basin

Artists
Paint Pots
Trail

N

| 0 | 100 | 200 | 300 yards |
| 0 | 100 | 200 | 300 meters |

Grand Loop Road

Gibbon Canyon

Monument
Geyser
Basin

**start &
finish**

Bridge

To Madison
Junction

Monument Geyser Basin

Since there are few switchbacks, you may get the feeling that this route to a seldom-visited geyser basin was designed to discourage visitors. If you are an aficionado of geothermal activity, however, the unique juice at the end of the stiff, shadeless climb is worth the squeeze.

Best Time

Because the remote basin tops out around 8000 feet, it's best to wait until snow has melted off the steep trail, usually by late June or early July. Check conditions with rangers before heading out in October. There is little shade and no water along the trail, so plan accordingly.

Finding the Trail

From the north, go 4.6 miles south of Norris Junction (a mile south of the Artists Paint Pots, just past the Gibbon River bridge) on the Grand Loop Road and turn right into the small gravel parking pullout on the west (right) side of the road. From the south, go 8.4 miles north of Madison Junction on Grand Loop Road and carefully turn left across oncoming traffic into the turnout just before the bridge. In fall 2004, the turnout was only signed from the south. Look for a trailhead register just off the road to confirm that you are on the right track.

TRAIL USE
Hike

LENGTH
3 miles, 1.5-2 hours

VERTICAL FEET
±650'

DIFFICULTY
– 1 2 **3** 4 5 +

TRAIL TYPE
Out & Back

SURFACE TYPE
Dirt

FEATURES
Steep
Great Views
Photo Opportunity
Secluded
Geothermal

FACILITIES
None

Trail Description

From the small parking turnout,►1 sign in at the trailhead register►2 and follow the single-track earthen trail upstream along the crystal-clear **Gibbon River**. The narrow trail is hemmed in by dense stands of lodgepole saplings that have enthusiastically sprouted since the 1988 North Fork fire.

After 0.3 mile,►3 the trail swings around the ridge and away from the river, and begins its short but stiff and unrelenting ascent. For a break, look for honking Canadian geese and browsing elk below, around the oxbows in the vast **Gibbon Meadows**. The small thermal areas visible along both banks of the Gibbon only hint at what awaits up top.

The straight-ahead climb lacks switchbacks and shade. Catch your breath in the shadow of one of the few remaining lodgepole pine snags, and enjoy the ever-expanding views to the north and south.

Whew: The trail finally tops out at an unsigned junction►4 near an overlook of Gibbon Canyon. Head right along the flat ridgetop and follow your nose to the sulphur smell and the most active part of the thought-provoking **Monument Geyser Basin.**►5

The highlight of the basin is the eponymous **Monument Geyser** (also known as Thermos Bottle Geyser): a steaming, 8-foot-tall spire on the far side of the basin that was created when silica precipitated out of water. Other visible thermal features include a variety of active and inactive geyser spires, steaming fumaroles (scalding steam vents), bubbling frying pans, turbid milky pools, and highly acidic mudpots. For a clue as to why you should not venture out into the basin, listen for hollow thumping sounds coming from beneath your feet.

When you've finished exploring, retrace your steps downhill to the trailhead—don't forget to sign out at the trail register—and parking area.►6

Steep

Birds

Great Views

Geothermal

MILESTONES

▶1   0.0 Start at Monument Geyser Basin parking turnout

▶2   0.1 Trailhead sign and trail register

▶3   0.3 Trail swings left above Gibbon Meadows; begin climb

▶4   1.4 Right at unsigned junction and Gibbon Canyon overlook

▶5   1.5 Monument Geyser Basin

▶6   3.0 Return to trailhead parking turnout

GEOLOGY

Stick to the Edges

The thin crust in the basin is extremely fragile, and the subsurface is superheated. Stay behind the downed limbs marking the solid edge of the basin and check things out from near the treeline. The shady areas here make a nice picnic spot.

Submerged Geyser Basin Spires

Geoscientists recently discovered that the profile of Monument Geyser Basin's spires closely resembles that of submerged spire fields beneath Yellowstone Lake. Researchers continue to study the complex of coalesced spires near Mary Bay with remotely operated underwater vehicles. Diatom fossils and lake sediments collected from Monument Geyser Basin suggest that the area was likely covered by a glacial lake more than 10,000 years ago.

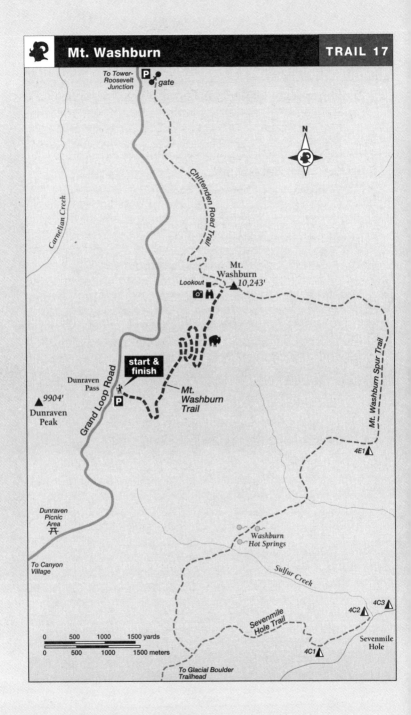

P

To Tower-
Roosevelt
Junction

gate

N

Chittenden Road Trail

Mt.
Washburn
▲ 10,243'

Camelian Creek

Lookout

start &
finish

Dunraven Pass

Grand Loop Road

▲ *9904'*
Dunraven
Peak

P

Mt.
Washburn
Trail

Mt. Washburn Spur Trail

4E1 ▲

Dunraven
Picnic
Area
⛺

To Canyon
Village

Washburn
Hot Springs

Sulfur Creek

4C3 ▲

4C2 ▲

*Sevenmile
Hole Trail*

Sevenmile
Hole

4C1 ▲

0	500	1000	1500 yards
0	500	1000	1500 meters

To Glacial Boulder
Trailhead

Mt. Washburn

One of the park's most popular and rewarding day-hikes starts out up high and continues climbing gradually along old roads and passes wildlife-rich wildflower meadows en route to a spectacular summit with panoramic views from a working fire lookout.

Best Time

The trail is hikable from May through October, with a good chance of encountering passable snow drifts at higher elevations early and late in the season. Frequent afternoon lightning and thundershowers mean it's best to head out as early as possible. Wildflower displays are legendary from around late July to early August, while elk, grizzlies, and bighorn sheep (don't feed them, and keep your distance!) can be spotted throughout the summer.

Bear management areas adjacent to Dunraven Pass and the Chittenden Road trail are off-limits for much of the year, so obey posted signs and don't stray from the trail.

Finding the Trail

From the south, go 4.5 miles north from Canyon Junction on the Grand Loop Road—a couple of miles past the Dunraven Picnic Area—and turn right into the to the frequently full Dunraven Pass trailhead parking area on the east side of the road. If there's no room to park here, continue 5 miles north, turn right, and double back uphill on an unpaved road to access the larger Chittenden Road trailhead parking area.

TRAIL USE
Hike, Bike
LENGTH
6.0 miles, 3-4 hours
VERTICAL FEET
±1400'
DIFFICULTY
– 1 2 3 **4** 5 +
TRAIL TYPE
Out & Back
SURFACE TYPE
Dirt & Paved

FEATURES
Mountain
Summit
Autumn Colors
Birds
Wildlife
Wildflowers
Great Views
Photo Opportunity
Camping
Historic
Geologic Interest
Steep

FACILITIES
Restrooms
Picnic Tables
Phone
Water

Logistics

Automobiles were first allowed into the park in 1915. Horse-drawn wagons were banned the following year. Since they lacked fuel pumps, early Model T Fords had to back up the mountain in reverse.

The Grand Loop Road is scheduled to be closed to all traffic between Canyon Junction and the Chittenden Road through 2005 while it's being widened to 24 feet to accommodate supersize RVs. Thus, until the project is completed the Chittenden parking area—which will remain accessible from Tower-Roosevelt Junction in the north—will provide the only access to Mt. Washburn trailheads.

The trails from Chittenden Road and Dunraven Pass are roughly the same length, but bicycles are only allowed on the marginally steeper Chittenden Road Trail, which is used by NPS vehicles to supply the fire lookout in summer.

Pack wind and rain gear in case of foul weather up top.

Trail Description

 Steep

From **Dunraven Pass**▶1 (8859'), a wide, abandoned road—originally engineered in 1905 for wagons and stagecoaches—climbs steadily and scenically through subalpine fir forest to a small gap, a nice stop for a short rest.

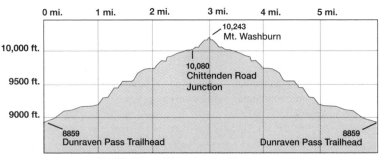

TRAIL17 Mt. Washburn Elevation Profile

About halfway up, as glimpses of the lookout atop the summit appear, broad switchbacks swing northeast up the ridge and views of the Grand Canyon and Yellowstone River drainage open up to the east (right). The higher up you go, the more likely you are to see stunted whitebark pines (a favorite grub source for grizzlies) as well as pikas, marmots, and Rocky Mountain bighorn sheep.

Some 10,000 people hike Mt. Washburn each year, making it the park's most popular trail.

Half a mile beyond the switchbacks, the road reaches a three-way junction▶**2** with the **Chittenden Road Trail** and **Mt. Washburn Spur Trail**. Follow the road uphill as it curves around to the left to arrive at the three-story **Mt. Washburn Lookout Tower** (10,243').▶**3**

Despite the presence of the working fire lookout (staffed only in summer), Mt. Washburn's slopes burned heavily during the 1988 fires. In addition to an outhouse, a pay phone (that only accepts credit cards), guest logbook, interpretive geology displays, and a powerful telescope in the sheltered ground-level observation room, the lookout offers incredible panoramas of most of the park from upstairs on the outdoor viewing platform.

 Wildlife

 Summit

On a clear day, the expansive views can stretch anywhere from 20 to 50 miles in all directions. The Absaroka Range extends beyond the park boundaries to the north and east. To the south is the Hayden Valley, Yellowstone Lake, and Mt. Sheridan—the southern end of the caldera that extends north to Mt. Washburn. To the west is the Gallatin Range. To the southwest you can often see vapor rising from the Norris, Upper, and Lower geyser basins; and sometimes you can even see all the way to the Tetons.

 Great Views

The descent from the summit back to the trailhead is easy, taking only 45 minutes to an hour. Retracing your steps, take a hard right at the Chittenden Road/Mt. Washburn Trail junction▶**4** to return to the Dunraven Pass parking area.▶**5**

MILESTONES

►1 0.0 Start at Dunraven Pass parking area

►2 2.6 Sharp left at Chittenden Road/Mt. Washburn Trail junction

►3 3.0 Mt. Washburn lookout tower

►4 3.4 Hard right at Chittenden Road/Mt. Washburn Trail junction

►5 6.0 Return to Dunraven Pass parking area

Washburn Spur and Sevenmile Hole

OPTIONS

You can make a full day of it by setting up a car shuttle at the Glacial Boulder trailhead near Canyon Village and descending from the summit down Mt. Washburn's steep, unburned eastern flank. The **Mt. Washburn Spur Trail** sees much less traffic than other two routes to the summit. It passes the **Washburn Hot Springs** mudpots, the Sevenmile Hole cutoff, and an unsigned overlook of the 1000-foot **Silver Cord Cascade** en route to the Glacial Boulder trailhead on Inspiration Point Road (11.5 miles and 6 to 8 hours total, one-way from Dunraven Pass).

The only overnight camping option along this challenging route is the decent, hiker-only **Washburn Meadow campsite 4E1,** in prime grizzly habitat 2.5 miles below the summit, with easy access to water.

The three riverfront, hiker-only 4C campsites (no wood fires allowed) in Sevenmile Hole are a worthy overnight detour, even though anglers often quip that it "feels like five miles in, seven miles out." All told, it's a stiff 11 miles round-trip and more than 1400 feet of elevation change from the Glacial Boulder.

Looking north from the summit *of Mt. Washburn*

Morgan Konn

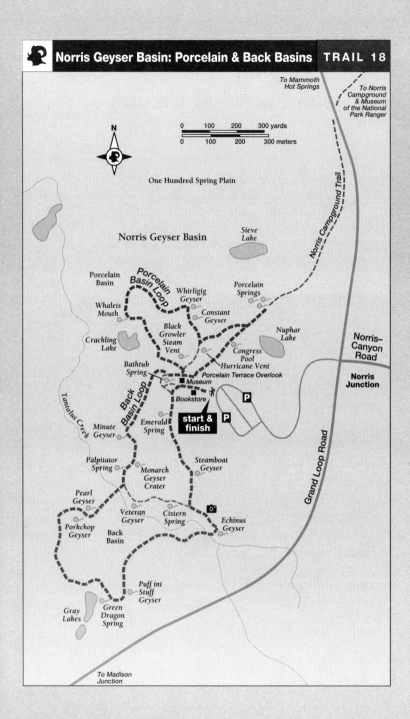

To Mammoth
Hot Springs

To Norris
Campground
& Museum
of the National
Park Ranger

N

| 0 | 100 | 200 | 300 yards |
| 0 | 100 | 200 | 300 meters |

One Hundred Spring Plain

Norris Campground Trail

Sieve
Lake

Norris Geyser Basin

Porcelain
Basin

Porcelain
Basin Loop

Whirligig
Geyser

Porcelain
Springs

Whaleis
Mouth

Constant
Geyser

Black
Growler
Steam
Vent

Nuphar
Lake

Crackling
Lake

Congress
Pool

Norris–
Canyon
Road

Bathtub
Spring

Hurricane Vent

Porcelain Terrace Overlook

Back
Basin Loop

Museum

Norris
Junction

Bookstore

P

Tantalus Creek

Minute
Geyser

Emerald
Spring

**start &
finish**

P

Palpitator
Spring

Monarch
Geyser
Crater

Steamboat
Geyser

Pearl
Geyser

Veteran
Geyser

Cistern
Spring

Echinus
Geyser

Porkchop
Geyser

Back
Basin

Grand Loop Road

Puff ini
Stuff
Geyser

Gray
Lakes

Green
Dragon
Spring

To Madison
Junction

Norris Geyser Basin: Porcelain & Back Basins

Yellowstone's most hyperactive and acidic hydrothermal area is home to many extremes. It's the park's hottest and most volatile basin, hosting the world's largest active geyser and rare acidic geysers. A leisurely stroll around the boardwalks provides an up-close look at the Earth at play, featuring a complete assortment of joyous geothermal exuberance.

Trying to describe the basin's ever-changing features is futile: Wander around to see what you discover, knowing that mysterious noises, new hot spots, and acrid smells await around every bend.

Best Time

There's little shade and no water in the basin. Boardwalks are subject to temporary closure due to thermal activity, but the basin is open whenever access roads are open. Overcast days are best for seeing the features at their steamiest.

Finding the Trail

From the north, go 21 miles south from Mammoth Junction on the Grand Loop Road to Norris Junction. Turn right (west) and continue 0.5 mile to the large Norris Geyser Basin parking loop. From the east, go 11.2 miles west on the Norris-Canyon Road from Canyon Junction and go straight through Norris Junction to enter the parking area. From the south, go 14 miles northeast from Madison Junction on Grand Loop Road and turn (west) left at Norris Junction. The boardwalk trails begin near the

TRAIL USE
Hike

LENGTH
2.0 miles, 1-2 hours

VERTICAL FEET
Negligible

DIFFICULTY
- 1 **2** 3 4 5 +

TRAIL TYPE
Loop

SURFACE TYPE
Boardwalk and Gravel

FEATURES
Child Friendly
Handicap Access
Photo Opportunity
Geologic Interest
Geothermal
Moonlight Hiking

FACILITIES
Bookstore
Information Station
Museum
Restrooms
Picnic Tables
Phone

bookstore and museum, near the northwest corner of the parking area.

Logistics

To hit the basin's highlights in an hour or less, walk clockwise around the Back Basin beginning from the bookstore (take the first left) and turn back when you've seen enough; for most folks, that's at the Echinus Geyser. Or you can cut the Back Basin loop in half by following the boardwalk that parallels Tantalus Creek and returning clockwise to the parking area.

Trail Description

From the parking loop,▶1 stop by the metal box between the Yellowstone Association bookstore and **Norris Museum**▶2 to pick up a self-guided trail map (50¢ donation requested). Check here with rangers for updates on recent thermal activity.

After checking out the exhibits about the origins of the world's geothermal features (half of which are in Yellowstone), begin the 0.5-mile **Porcelain Basin Loop** by turning right on the upper boardwalk. Pause at the **Porcelain Terrace**▶3 overlook for a bird's-eye preview of the hundreds of geothermal features packed into the wide-open, blindingly white basin.

After a short gravel stretch, the boardwalk resumes near a "solfatara," an unstable volcanic vent area yielding hot vapors and sulfur-rich gases like sulfuric acid. Nearby, roiling **Congress Pool**▶4 is often pale blue but sometimes brown and muddy. Straight ahead on the boardwalk, beyond a trail map sign at the junction, is the overlook of the milky **Porcelain Springs,**▶5 which is one of the most dynamic areas and was madly hissing steam at last look. The 1-mile trail to **Norris Campground** heads off to the northwest near the overlook.

Back at the boardwalk junction, follow the right fork down past an inviting bench and picnic overlook, then fork left at the junction near **Hurricane Vent.▶6** Past another bench on your right is **Whirligig Geyser,▶7** which has been dormant since 2000 but makes a rhythmic woosh-woosh sound similar to helicopter blades when it erupts. Nearby **Constant Geyser** erupts to 30 feet for only a few seconds at surprise intervals. The yellow-orange features and runoff channels here are some of the basin's most colorful.

Continue looping around the back side of the basin on a gravel trail. Near the **Whale's Mouth spring**, the boardwalk crosses a thermal runoff channel and the steamy, snap-pop **Crackling Lake ▶8** is to your right. Head up the stairs to the seriously stinky **Black Growler Steam Vent,▶9** which has been measured at up to 280°F and sounds like a factory when it's going off at full-tilt.

Up the short, steep hill at the four-way junction, turn right on the lower gravel path to begin the forested, 1.5-mile **Back Basin Loop,▶10** which was touched by the 1988 fires.

The main park road used to run very close to the once-mighty **Minute Geyser,▶11** which contributed to it getting clogged up in the early stagecoach days. Debris is still visible in the west vent, which used to spout up to 50 feet every 60 seconds. Today, the east vent sputters infrequently.

Continue straight ahead on the boardwalk past the trail sign at the next junction,**▶12** beyond **Monarch Geyser Crater** and **Palpitator Spring**. Ahead on your right is the colorful **Pearl Geyser,▶13** where the hissing and steaming sounds vaguely like a subway tunnel, and sporadic spouts reach up to 8 feet.

Here, the boardwalk was closed in 2003 and rerouted in 2004 after a surprise steam explosion destroyed the route beyond **Porchop Geyser**, now a calm spring within a huge blasted rocky hole;

Geologists are still trying to determine why sudden, intermittent "disturbances" (lasting up to a week) cause simultaneous dramatic behavioral changes in the basin's thermal features. It's believed that an underlying plumbing system connects most of the basin.

Steamboat Geyser's last major eruption was in October 2003. When active, it can soar two to three times as high as Old Faithful.

 Photo Opportunity

interpretive signs near the viewpoint explain the sequence of events.

The new boardwalk loops around the back side of Porkchop for 0.2 mile past the huge Gray Lakes to the noxious Green Dragon Spring,▶14 where there's a bench, which few people use to meditate on the sulphur-lined cavern's murkiness. Nearby, **Puff 'n' Stuff Geyser** pulsates with steam but rarely erupts.

A combination of boardwalks and sand and gravel paths winds around for 0.3 mile past several big, steaming pools; runoff channels; and an overlook of **Cistern Spring**—which is connected to Steamboat Geyser—to end up at a series of benches and viewing platforms around the crowd-pleasing **Echinus Geyser.**▶15 Pronounced *e-KI-nus*, it's the world's largest frequently active acid geyser (with a pH of 3.3-3.6, similar to vinegar). It erupts at intervals of one hour to four days and plays for three to five minutes.

Beyond the overlooks, turn right at the junction near **Cistern Spring**▶16 and climb the stairs alongside the runoff channel from **Steamboat Geyser,**▶17

Ranger-Led Programs

During the summer, ranger-led, 90-minute walks around Norris Geyser Basin depart daily except Thursday at 10 AM, starting at the museum. Rangers also give 20-minute talks daily at 2:30 PM. At the campground, there are 45-minute campfire talks nightly at 7:30 PM; check bulletin boards for program details.

Norris Campground Trail and Museum

If you are staying at the Norris Campground, a 1-mile trail to the geyser basin starts from near the **Museum of the National Park Ranger** (open daily 9 AM to 5 PM in summer), housed in the historic Norris Soldier Station log cabin. There's a video about the history of the Park Service, and it doesn't take much prodding to get retired rangers and volunteer docents to share stories about park history and lore.

the tallest active geyser in the world. From the lower viewing platform and upper overlook, patient geyser gazers await frequent, minor bursts of 10 to 70 feet. Its name comes from its powerful steam phase, which follows major eruptions for up to 24 hours.

  Geothermal

The last stop on the Back Basin loop is the vibrant **Emerald Spring,►18** a deep, clear-blue pool that's lined with yellow sulphur deposits and often appears green. Continue back up the hill and turn right at the museum and bookstore to return to the parking area.►19

🚶 MILESTONES

- ►1   0.0 Start at Norris Geyser Basin parking area
- ►2   0.1 Bookstore and Norris Museum
- ►3   0.15 Right at Porcelain Terrace Overlook
- ►4   0.2 Congress Pool
- ►5   0.3 Porcelain Springs overlook
- ►6   0.4 Right at junction near Hurricane Vent
- ►7   0.45 Whirligig Geyser
- ►8   0.6 Crackling Lake
- ►9   0.65 Black Growler Steam Vent
- ►10   0.7 Begin Back Basin Loop
- ►11   0.8 Minute Geyser
- ►12   0.9 Straight at junction near Tantalus Creek
- ►13   1.0 Pearl Geyser and Porkchop Geyser
- ►14   1.2 Gray Lakes and Green Dragon Spring
- ►15   1.5 Echinus Geyser
- ►16   1.6 Right up stairs near Cistern Spring
- ►17   1.65 Steamboat Geyser
- ►18   1.8 Emerald Spring
- ►19   2.0 Return to parking area

Southeast Yellowstone– Lake Country

Southeast Yellowstone– Lake Country

Visitor activity in the park's southeast quadrant concentrates around the impressive, 136-square-mile **Yellowstone Lake** (7733'), the largest natural freshwater alpine lake in North America. The region's dayhiking trails tend to be either short and flat, or steep and very scenic.

Even though it has well over a hundred miles of shoreline, Yellowstone Lake typically remains frozen from late December through early June. A thriving population of native cutthroat trout in the lake's tributaries attracts hordes of grizzlies in spring and anglers in summer. The lake's average temperature of 45°F precludes swimming year-round. As with most lakes, the water is calmest in the morning and becomes increasingly turbulent in the afternoon. More than 100 people have lost their lives while boating the park's lakes and streams.

When combined with adjacent USFS lands, the remote **Two Ocean Plateau** and **Thorofare region** in the park's southeastern corner compose the largest roadless wilderness in the Lower 48 US states, a veritable long-haul backpacker wonderland.

The **Buffalo Bill Scenic Highway** (US Hwys. 14/16/20), called "the most scenic 52 miles in the USA" by Teddy Roosevelt, links Cody to the park's **East Entrance** via the scenic Wapiti Valley. Seven miles inside the park, **Sylvan Pass** (8530') opens in early May and closes in early October, but reopens for winter snowcoach use from December through April. This is possible thanks to an NPS avalanche control program, which involves helicopters dropping explosive charges and howitzers launching 105mm artillery rounds into the hillside.

Xanterra manages three large, RV-dominated campgrounds around Yellowstone Lake. **Bridge Bay Campground** (open late May to mid-September) is near Bridge Bay Marina, 3 miles southwest of Lake Village. The drive-in sites mostly attract boaters and anglers, while the two tent-only loops have the most shade and good lake views. Due to frequent ursine visits, the controversial **Fishing Bridge RV Park** (open mid-May to early October), on the lake's north shore just east of Fishing Bridge Junction, only allows hard-sided vehicles—sorry, no pop-top campers.

On the lake's southwest shore, lakefront **Grant Village Campground** (opens around June 20 due to bears' use of nearby spawning streams, closes early October) has the most tent-only sites and the best shower and laundry facilities in the region. At 20 miles from Old Faithful, it's the second-closest frontcountry campground to the landmark; only the one near Madison Junction is closer.

The region's less developed, NPS-run alternative is forested **Lewis Lake Campground** (7779'; open mid-June to early November), 13 miles north of the park's **South Entrance** (open early May to early November). It's a favorite of Shoshone Lake-bound boaters. There are walk-in and tent-only sites, and generators are banned. An additional 40 boat-in and backcountry campsites are spread around the southern and eastern lakeshores.

The charming, 19th-century **Lake Yellowstone Hotel** (rates $104 to $444) is listed on the Register of Historic Places. Cabins at the nearby **Lake Lodge** come in two flavors: basic 1920s ($62) or motel-style ($125). Even if you aren't a guest, either place is an atmospheric spot to hang out and enjoy the lake views over a snack, meal, or drink.

The modern (circa 1984), cookie-cutter hotel rooms at **Grant Village** ($117) are hopelessly sterile but mostly wheelchair-accessible.

Overleaf: *Looking west from Avalanche Peak (Trail 19)*

Permits and Maps

The only trip in this chapter that requires a backcountry permit is if you take advantage of the appealing overnight options around Heart Lake. Fishing permits are available at all of the region's ranger stations, visitor centers, and general stores. Boating permits are issued at the South Entrance, Lewis Lake Campground, Grant Village Visitor Center, Bridge Bay Ranger Station, and Lake Ranger Station.

Near the outlet of Yellowstone Lake, on the lake's north shore, the **Fishing Bridge Visitor Center** has a bookstore and exhibits on birds and wildlife. Call (307) 242-2450; open daily from 8 AM to 7 PM in summer.

On the lake's southeast shore near West Thumb, the **Grant Village Visitor Center** also has a bookstore, natural history exhibits, and a video on the role fire has played in the park. Call (307) 242-2650; open daily from 8 AM to 7 PM in summer. The smaller **West Thumb Information Station** also has a good bookstore (open daily from 9 AM to 5 PM in summer).

The rustic, summer-only **Lake Ranger Station**, which occupies a 1923 log cabin, has good backcountry and boating info. It was styled after a trapper cabin and retains its octagonal community room and central stone fireplace. The station keeps a low profile, and the friendly rangers seem to prefer it that way. Last time I visited in 2004, bats were making themselves at home inside the roof! The seasonal **Lake Hospital** is near the Lake Hotel. Call (307) 242-7241; open daily from 8:30 AM to 8:30 PM, on call via 911 after hours, mid-May through September)

With the exception of the first few miles of the Heart Lake Trail—which barely appears on the *Old Faithful* map (no. 302)—it's in the bottom-right corner of the north side—all trails described in this chapter appear on National Geographic's Trails Illustrated *Yellowstone Lake* map (no. 305, scale 1:63,360).

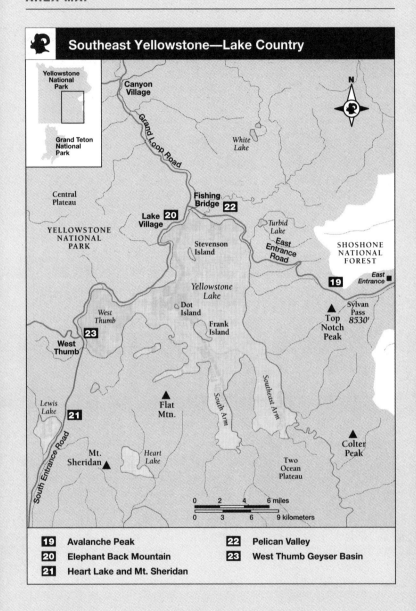

Southeast Yellowstone—Lake Country

Yellowstone National Park

Grand Teton National Park

Canyon Village

Grand Loop Road

White Lake

N

Central Plateau

Fishing Bridge **22**

Lake Village **20**

YELLOWSTONE NATIONAL PARK

Turbid Lake

East Entrance Road

SHOSHONE NATIONAL FOREST

Stevenson Island

East Entrance **19**

Yellowstone Lake

West Thumb

Dot Island

Frank Island

Sylvan Pass 8530'

Top Notch Peak

West Thumb **23**

Lewis Lake

Flat Mtn.

South Arm

Southeast Arm

Colter Peak

South Entrance Road

21

Mt. Sheridan

Heart Lake

Two Ocean Plateau

| 0 | 2 | 4 | 6 miles |
| 0 | 3 | 6 | 9 kilometers |

19	Avalanche Peak	**22**	Pelican Valley
20	Elephant Back Mountain	**23**	West Thumb Geyser Basin
21	Heart Lake and Mt. Sheridan		

Southeast Yellowstone—Lake Country

TRAIL	Difficulty	Length	Type	USES & ACCESS	TERRAIN	FLORA & FAUNA	OTHER
19	4	4.0	↗	🚶	⛰️△	✾	🏛️📷💧⛏️
20	3	3.5	↻	🚶👫	⛰️△	✿✾🐂	🌳🔭📷⛏️
21	5	15.0	↗	🚶🎒🛡️	⛰️△〰️🏳️	🐦🐂	🏛️📷△♨️
22	4	15.3	↻	🚶🐎	🏳️	✾🐦🐂	🏛️📷🏊♨️
23	1	0.6	↻	🚶♿👫	〰️	🐂	🔭📷♨️🌙

USES & ACCESS	TERRAIN	FLORA & FAUNA	OTHER
🚶 Hiking	Canyon	Autumn Colors	Cool & Shady
🚴 Bicycling	Mountain	Wildflowers	Great Views
🐎 Horses	Summit	Birds	Photo Opportunity
🎒 Backpacking	Stream	Wildlife	Swimming
👫 Child Friendly	Waterfall		Secluded
♿ Handicap Access	Lake		Historic
🛡️ Backcountry Permit Required	Geothermal		Geologic Interest
▲ Camping			Moonlight Hiking
		DIFFICULTY - 1 2 3 4 5 + less more	Steep

Southeast Yellowstone–Lake Country

Pelican Valley 173
The highlights are a few miles from the road, so this easygoing trail receives relatively light use as it loops around a wildlife-rich valley. Attractions include good fishing access, possible wolf sightings, and a close-up look at some of the best grizzly habitat in the Lower 48 states. Expect to get your feet wet— there are several unbridged creek crossings.

TRAIL 22

Hike, Horse
15.3 miles, Loop
Difficulty: 1 2 3 **4** 5

West Thumb Geyser Basin 179
Experience the meeting of hot and cold liquid during this boardwalk loop around a lakeside geyser basin. It's easily accessible and home to some of the park's deepest and most colorful hot springs.

TRAIL 23

Hike
0.6 mile, Loop
Difficulty: **1** 2 3 4 5

Morgan Konn

Leafy Indian paintbrush *bracts are most often scarlet, while the greenish-yellow flowers bloom from June to early September (Trail 30).*

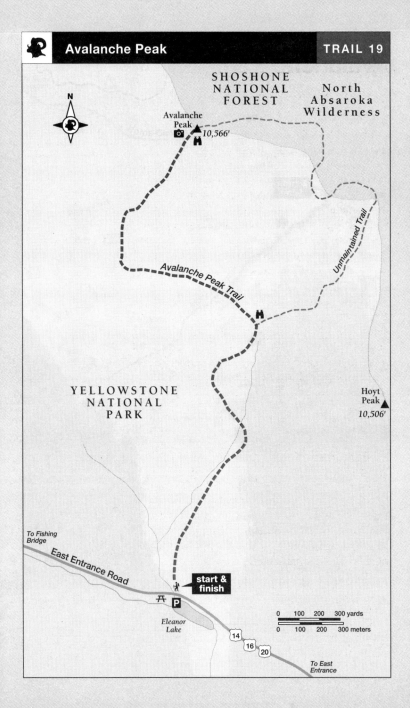

SHOSHONE
NATIONAL
FOREST

North
Absaroka
Wilderness

N

Avalanche
Peak
10,566'

Avalanche Peak Trail

Unmaintained Trail

YELLOWSTONE
NATIONAL
PARK

Hoyt
Peak
10,506'

To Fishing
Bridge

East Entrance Road

start &
finish

To East
Entrance

Eleanor
Lake

14
16
20

| 0 | 100 | 200 | 300 yards |
| 0 | 100 | 200 | 300 meters |

Avalanche Peak

This quick but steep and relentless ascent skips the switchbacks. The solitude and some of Yellowstone's best panoramic views are worth every ounce of exertion. The lightly traveled route traverses whitebark pine forest, old avalanche slides, and scree slopes adjacent to the North Absaroka Wilderness.

Best Time

Even on the steep south-facing slopes, snowfields persist above treeline well into July. Subalpine wildflowers peak soon after the late-spring snowmelt. Aside from seasonal snowmelt, there are no water sources above treeline. In the fall, grizzlies flock here to feed on whitebark pine nuts.

Finding the Trail

From the west, head 19 miles east from Fishing Bridge on the East Entrance Road and turn right into the paved parking area on the south side of the road, near the picnic area at the west end of Eleanor Lake. From the East Entrance, go 8 miles west, less than a mile past Sylvan Pass, and turn left into the parking area. The signed trailhead is across the road to the right (east) of the small creek.

Trail Description

From the signed trailhead (8470'),▶1 the unmarked but frequently blazed and well-maintained trail winds through unburned spruce-fir forest and

TRAIL USE
Hike
LENGTH
4 miles, 3-4 hours
ELEVATION GAIN/LOSS
±2100'
DIFFICULTY
– 1 2 3 **4** 5 +
TRAIL TYPE
Out & Back
SURFACE TYPE
Dirt

FEATURES
Mountain
Summit
Steep
Wildflowers
Great Views
Photo Opportunity
Secluded

FACILITIES
None

161

begins to climb steeply as it traces the drainage of an unnamed stream.

Steep

About a half-hour from the trailhead, the official trail cuts left across the stream▶2 and traverses west through an old avalanche chute. Avoid the temptation to follow the steeper route straight up the gulch: It's off-limits due to ongoing rehabilitation work. Next, the trail swings northeast and ducks back into mature whitebark pine stands; beware bears here in season.

Wildlife

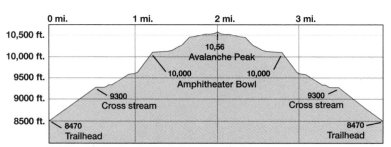

TRAIL 19 Avalanche Peak Elevation Profile

👟	MILESTONES

▶1   0.0 Start at Eleanor Lake parking area

▶2   0.5 Cross unnamed stream

▶3   1.2 Amphitheater bowl

▶4   2.0 Avalanche Peak

▶5   4.0 Return to parking area

A bit more than halfway up the mountain, the trail flattens out as it emerges from the forest at the base of a huge, amphitheater-like bowl▶3 where you get your first glimpse of **Avalanche Peak**. Above timberline, the main trail climbs to the left along an open scree slope to the shoulder of the peak's south ridge.

 Great Views

Take a break and savor the views back south and west over the Teton Wilderness and Yellowstone Lake before the final blustery ascent. The true **summit**▶4 (10,566') is along the narrow ridge to the northeast, beyond a series of talus wind shelters.

 Summit

From the peak, take in views of the Grand Tetons, Mt. Washburn, and Mt. Sheridan to the south, and the vast roadless North Absaroka Wilderness in the Shoshone National Forest directly to the east.

 **Photo Opportunity**

After enjoying a hard-earned picnic lunch, retrace your steps back to the parking area.▶5

Summit Loop Trail

OPTIONS

If you're up for a bit more of an adventure coming off the summit, look for an unmarked and unmaintained talus trail that drops precipitously down the peak's northeast arm to a saddle shared with **Hoyt Peak** (10,506'), on the park's eastern boundary. If you are comfortable negotiating this type of trail, you can descend through sparsely forested rolling hills to rejoin the main trail at foot of the southeast bowl.

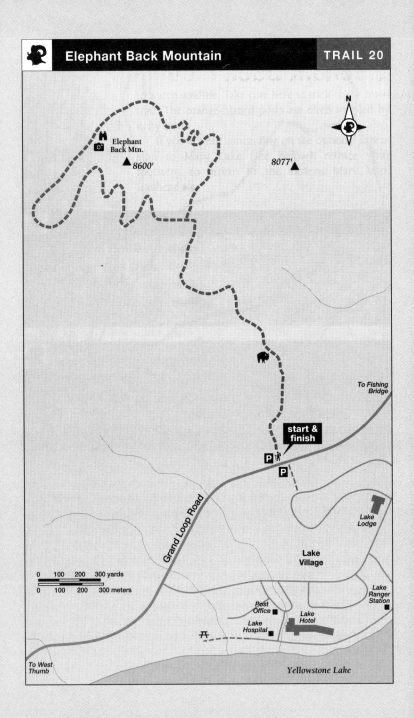

Elephant
Back Mtn.
▲ 8600'

▲ 8077'

To Fishing
Bridge

**start &
finish**

Grand Loop Road

Lake
Lodge

Lake
Village

0   100   200   300 yards

0   100   200   300 meters

Lake
Ranger
Station

Post
Office

Lake
Hotel

Lake
Hospital

To West
Thumb

Yellowstone Lake

Elephant Back Mountain

A popular family outing from Lake Village, this rewarding trail climbs gently through old-growth lodgepole pine forest, then loops around steeply to a picnic-worthy overlook with a sweeping panoramic view of Yellowstone Lake and beyond to the Absarokas.

Best Time

Bear activity is a possibility in spring due to the proximity to the lake's spawning streams. After snowmelt in June, any time of day is fine since most of the route is cool and shady.

Finding the Trail

If walking from Lake Village, follow signs and a paved path from the Lake Lodge through Section J of the cabins for 0.25 mile to the Grand Loop Road opposite the trailhead. If driving from the north, go 1 mile south of Fishing Bridge Junction on the Grand Loop Road and park in a turnout on either side of the road. From the south, go 20 miles north of West Thumb Junction, or 0.5 mile north (right) from Lake Junction.

Trail Description

From the parking turnout and signed trailhead (7800') on the north side of the road, ▶1 the well-maintained trail parallels the road to the south briefly before entering an impressive old-growth lodgepole pine forest.

TRAIL USE
Hike
LENGTH
3.5 miles, 1.5-2 hours
VERTICAL FEET
±800'
DIFFICULTY
– 1 2 **3** 4 5 +
TRAIL TYPE
Loop
SURFACE TYPE
Dirt

FEATURES
Child Friendly
Mountain
Summit
Steep
Autumn Colors
Wildflowers
Wildlife
Cool & Shady
Great Views
Photo Opportunity

FACILITIES
Ranger Station
Restrooms
Picnic Tables
Phone

Wildlife

Wildflowers

Great Views

Photo Opportunity

You soon pass by the former Lake Village waterworks and cross under a power line▶2 before starting an easy climb. Keep an eye out here for deer and moose—and grizzlies in the spring—browsing on the abundant mushrooms and wild berries that thrive on the unburned forest floor among the wildflowers.

After nearly a mile and 400 feet of gradual elevation gain, the trail forks at the loop junction.▶3 Take the slightly shorter and marginally steeper left-hand route for 0.8 mile via a short series of switchbacks to the **Elephant Back Mtn. overlook** (8600'),▶4 where wooden benches and pleasant picnic spots await in a clearing.

The impressive views to the east include the Yellowstone River outlet to the extreme left; the meadows of Pelican Valley and Storm Point to your left just beyond Fishing Bridge; Stevenson Island in the middle of Yellowstone Lake; the lake's South and Southeast Arms to your right; and the Absaroka Range defining the horizon in the background, beyond the park's rugged eastern boundary.

Return downhill via the gentler half of the loop for 0.9 mile to rejoin the main trail at the junction▶5 where the left-hand fork continues for 0.9 mile back to the parking area.▶6

🚶 MILESTONES

▶1 0.0 Parking area and trailhead
▶2 0.3 Old waterworks and power line
▶3 0.9 Left at loop junction
▶4 1.7 Elephant Back Mtn. overlook
▶5 2.6 Left at junction
▶6 3.5 Return to parking area

View from the Avalanche Peak Trail *(Trail 19)*

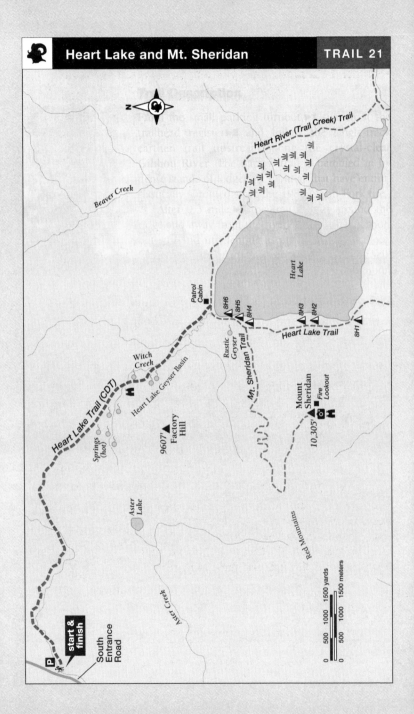

Heart River (Trail Creek) Trail

Beaver Creek

Heart Lake

Patrol Cabin

8H6
8H5
8H4
8H3
8H2
8H1

Heart Lake Trail

Witch Creek

Rustic Geyser

Mt. Sheridan Trail

Heart Lake Trail (CDT)

Heart Lake Geyser Basin

Mount Sheridan
10,305'
Fire Lookout

Springs (hot)

9607'
Factory Hill

Aster Lake

Red Mountains

Aster Creek

500 1000 1500 yards

500 1000 1500 meters

0

start & finish

P

South Entrance Road

Heart Lake and Mt. Sheridan

This demanding dayhike or more relaxed overnight trip is popular due to its wide range of attractions, including intriguing geysers and hot springs; the chance to bag a major peak; and inviting, lakefront, hiker-only campsites. It's also a well-maintained stretch of the Continental Divide National Scenic Trail.

Best Time

The Heart Lake Bear Management Area is closed from April 1 through at least June 30 due to heavy grizzly activity. Snowfields remain on the slopes of Mt. Sheridan until mid-July or later. Confirm current conditions with a ranger station or backcountry office before heading out; the closest rangers on duty are at the South Entrance and at Lake Village.

Finding the Trail

From the north, go 7 miles south on the South Entrance Road from West Thumb Junction (or 5.3 miles south of Grant Village) and turn left into the signed trailhead parking area on the east side of the road. From the park's South Entrance, go 15 miles north on the South Entrance Road, just beyond Lewis Lake, and turn right into the parking area.

Trail Description

From the trailhead parking area (7785'),▶1 the sandy, single-track route—a well-maintained part of the Continental Divide National Scenic Trail—

TRAIL USE
Hike, Backpack
LENGTH
15.0 miles, 1-2 days
VERTICAL FEET
±3500' including
Mt. Sheridan
DIFFICULTY
– 1 2 3 4 **5** +
TRAIL TYPE
Out & Back
SURFACE TYPE
Dirt

FEATURES
Backcountry Permit
Stream
Mountain
Summit
Lake
Birds
Wildlife
Great Views
Photo Opportunity
Geothermal
Camping

FACILITIES
Patrol Cabin
Restrooms

Mt. Sheridan and the
Red Mtns. mark the
approximate southern
boundary of Yellow-
stone's 600,000-year-
old volcanic caldera.

 Geothermal

 Lake

climbs subtly to the southeast through a patchwork
of rolling meadows and lodgepole pine forest.

Around 4.25 miles, after passing through a small
burn area left over from the 1988 fires, the trail crests
a minor rise and opens up near the head of the
hydrothermally fueled **Witch Creek** drainage.▶2
Below to your right are steaming fumaroles at the foot
of the bald-as-an-eagle **Factory Hill** (9607'). You also
get your first tantalizing view of the lake from here on
high, but it's still a couple of miles and 700 feet below.

The trail winds down along the creek through
the middle of a burn area and the animated **Heart
Lake Geyser Basin**, crossing the warm creek a couple of times via sturdy footbridges. Keep an eye out
for spouting thermal features on the creek's south
bank while you drop down toward the junction of
the **Heart Lake/Heart River Trail** junction▶3

The Heart River Trail along the north shore of
the lake, is often also called the **Trail Creek Trail**,
after its distant destination near the South Arm of
Yellowstone Lake. Nearby, the lakefront **Heart Lake
Patrol Cabin** is typically staffed all summer and
usually has the current weather and fishing report
for **Heart Lake** (7455').

If you're staying overnight at one of the six **8H
campsites**, turn right at the patrol cabin to follow

Heart Lake Patrol Cabin

the trail a few hundred yards across the Witch Creek inlet on a log bridge, then south along the lake's sandy western shore past the informal spur path to the thermal area around **Rustic Geyser.▶4** The **Mt. Sheridan Trail junction** and spur trails leading to campsites 8H4, 8H5, and 8H6 are a few hundred yards farther south.

 Camping

After watching for bald eagles fishing for cutthroat and lake trout and carefully exploring the fragile, marshy thermal areas, most dayhikers turn around here and retrace their steps to the trailhead parking area.▶5

 MILESTONES

▶1   0.0 Start at trailhead parking area

▶2   4.25 Witch Creek thermal area

▶3   7.25 Right at Heart Lake/Heart River Trail Junction

▶4   7.5 Spur route to Rustic Geyser

▶5   15.0 Return to trailhead parking area

Mt. Sheridan and Overnight Camping

The laborious, spiraling 2800-foot ascent of **Mt. Sheridan** (10,305'; 6 miles and 4 to 5 hours round-trip) is sometimes attempted as an add-on to the long Heart Lake dayhike, but it's much more enjoyable if you can score a reservation for a night or two at one of the six hiker-only **8H campsites**. Even if you're not climbing Mt. Sheridan, it's worth staying here just to see the sun rise over the lake. Only 8H2 and 8H3 (the most desirable sites) permit wood fires; all sites have a two-night-per-trip limit from July 1 to September 1 due to heavy demand. The 8H1 site is the farthest away and least desirable, a few hundred yards off the lake.

At Mt. Sheridan's talus-covered summit there's a **fire lookout** that's staffed in summer. The awesome panorama takes in the Pitchstone Plateau to the west, Shoshone Lake to the northwest, Yellowstone Lake to the northeast, and the jagged Tetons to the south. Carry extra water as there's only snowmelt along the trail.

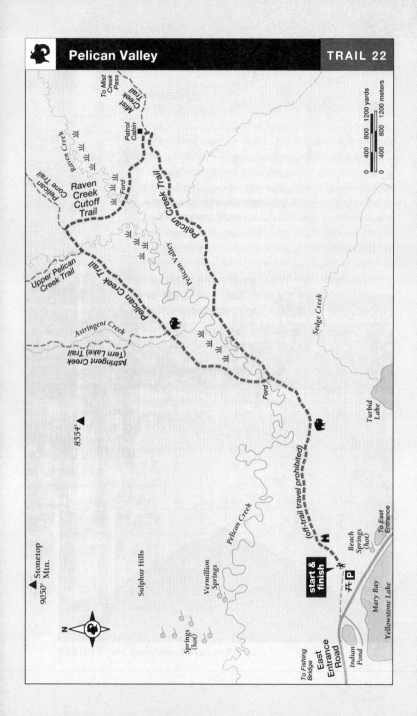

Pelican Valley

As it loops gently around the broad, wildlife-rich Pelican Valley, this lightly used trail provides good backcountry fishing access and a close-up look at some of the best grizzly habitat in the Lower 48 states. Herds of elk and bison have attracted a dynamic, denning wolf pack. Three creek fords can make completing the loop a challenge early in the season.

Best Time

Due to heavy grizzly bear activity, camping is prohibited year-round and the trail is off-limits from April 1 until July 3. From July 4 through November 10 the area is open for day use only between 9 AM and 7 PM. The opening holiday weekend is the busiest day in the valley and thus probably the least likely time to catch a glimpse of the big animals.

Due to the camping prohibition and time restrictions, there's no choice but to hike through the shadeless valley during the midday heat. Head out early, bring plenty of water, and—if you can—wait for an overcast, rainy, or even snowy day for the best chance at spotting wildlife.

Finding the Trail

From the west, go 3.5 miles east from Fishing Bridge Junction on the East Entrance Road. Turn left opposite the Storm Point trailhead and Indian (ex-Squaw) Pond onto an old gravel service road on the north side of the road, which leads 0.5 mile to the signed Pelican Valley trailhead (5K3) parking lot.

TRAIL USE
Hike, Horse

LENGTH
15.3 miles, 2.5 hours

VERTICAL FEET
±450'

DIFFICULTY
– 1 2 3 **4** 5 +

TRAIL TYPE
Loop

SURFACE TYPE
Dirt

FEATURES
Stream
Wildflowers
Birds
Wildlife
Great Views
Photo Opportunity
Swimming
Geothermal

FACILITIES
Horse Staging

173

From the east, go 23.5 miles west from the East Entrance on the East Entrance Road, past the Beach Springs picnic area, and turn right into the parking lot.

If you only want to do an easy 6-mile dayhike, turn around at Pelican Creek after a picnic lunch.

Logistics

Due to bear-management restrictions, the NPS recommends a minimum of four hikers per group. Off-trail travel is prohibited year-round along the first 2.5 miles of the Pelican Valley trail. The closest backcountry campsites are 3T3 and 3T2, east of Mist Creek Pass (8500'), 10 and 11 miles from the trailhead.

Trail Description

From the trailhead parking area (7800'),▶1 the abandoned Turbid Lake service road makes a beeline straight east for 0.5 mile. Where the old, off-limits road continues straight ahead, the trail forks▶2 to the north (left) to follow the forest edge to an overlook. Here you get your first tempting glimpse of the wide-open **Pelican Valley,**▶3 which is 1.5 miles beyond the trailhead.

The trail passes through several boggy sections—which are covered with wildflowers in midsummer—as it descends gently through open meadows to the valley floor. As you approach the usually unsigned (and off-limits) Turbid Lake Trail junction around 2 miles, make plenty of noise, keep alert, and monitor the forest edges—and the trail!—for signs of elk, bison, coyote and grizzly activity.

After 3.5 miles, you reach the south bank of Pelican Creek,▶4 near the deteriorating remains of an old fire-road bridge.

 **Photo Opportunity**

 Wildflowers

 Wildlife

Watch for fishing birds and cutthroat trout as you make the easy, ankle- to knee-high ford of the relatively warm, slow-moving creek. Here, the Pelican Creek Trail climbs gently up above the north bank of the meandering creek for 1.5 miles to an easy ford of **Astringent Creek.**▶5 Continue straight ahead to just beyond the creek, where the Astringent Creek Trail (also known as the Tern Lake Trail) forks north (left) up the Astringent Creek drainage to the closest backcountry campsites, beyond Fern Lake, in the Broad Creek drainage.

The trail contours along above some springs and minor marshy thermal areas: more good spots to survey the valley for wildlife. Keep one eye on the abundant clover patches here for signs of bear activity as you continue northeast along the forest edge for 1.7 miles, then drop down to another uncomplicated ford of Pelican Creek, just before the **Upper Pelican Creek Trail**▶6 junction. Keep in the open meadows to the right where the trail forks to the left (north) along the east side of Pelican Creek toward Wapiti Lake—more prime grizzly habitat.

A small, unnamed stream 0.4 mile farther along, just before the **Pelican Cone Trail**▶7 junction, provides the valley's best drinking water; it's cool and clear but purification is always advisable.

The ill-defined **Raven Creek Cutoff Trail** wends its way southeast across the rolling meadows in the middle of the Pelican Valley. Halfway across, it often requires a bit of scouting around to find a shallow ford amongst the meandering oxbows of **Raven Creek.**▶8 On the positive side, there are plenty of angling pools and waist-deep swimming holes here to cool off in the middle of a hot summer day.

Camping in and around the Pelican Valley has been prohibited since 1984, when a lone woman was killed during an unprovoked grizzly attack on her tent near White Lake.

 Wildlife

 Stream

Beyond Raven Creek, the faint trail can be difficult to follow as it continues through sagebrush-
interspersed meadows, past a pond that reeks of
sulfur and attracts flocks of waterfowl. Mt.
Chittenden (10,181') and other peaks visible in the
Absaroka Range define the park's rugged eastern
boundary.

The trail drops down to a dormant thermal area,
ducks into a patch of unburned forest, and roller-
coasters over some sagebrush rises en route to the
Pelican Springs Patrol Cabin,►9 where there's a
freshwater spring near the **Mist Creek Trail**
junction.

Turn right to loop back southwest along the
forested southern fringe of the valley towards the
trailhead. It's 4 miles of ups and downs along the
well-defined trail to reach the Pelican Bridge junction,**►10** then another 3 miles on the now-familiar
lollipop stretch of the loop to return to the trailhead
parking area.**►11**

⚐ MILESTONES

►1   0.0 Start at trailhead parking area

►2   0.5 Left at first fork

►3   1.5 Pelican Valley

►4   3.0 Pelican Creek ford and old bridge

►5   4.5 Ford Astringent Creek

►6   6.2 Right at Upper Pelican Creek Trail junction

►7   6.6 Right at Pelican Cone Trail junction

►8   7.3 Raven Creek ford

►9   8.3 Right on Mist Creek Trail junction at Pelican Springs Patrol Cabin

►10 12.3 Straight at Pelican Creek ford junction

►11 15.3 Return to trailhead parking area

NOTES

Mollie's Pack

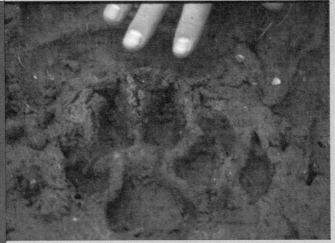

The bison- and elk-killing pack of **gray wolves** known as Mollie's Pack (originally the Crystal Creek pack) took up residence (known as "denning") and began reproducing within earshot of the Pelican Springs Patrol Cabin in 1999. In the summer of 2002, I observed them with binoculars from the trail around Raven Creek, every morning for a week.

As of 2004, NPS researchers continue to report intense wolf-bison and wolf-grizzly interactions in the valley and adjacent drainages. Please note that denning areas are strictly off-limits: If you are fortunate enough to encounter any wolves, watch them from a distance. Also look for wolf footprints in muddy areas of the trail (above).

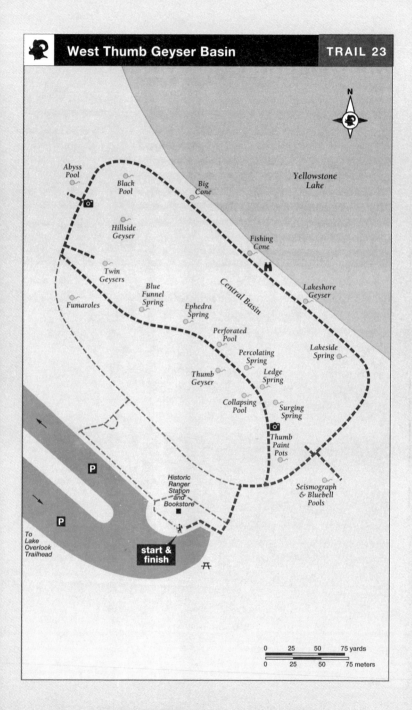

West Thumb Geyser Basin

TRAIL 23

N

Yellowstone Lake

Abyss Pool

Black Pool

Big Cone

Hillside Geyser

Fishing Cone

Twin Geysers

Central Basin

Lakeshore Geyser

Blue Funnel Spring

Fumaroles

Ephedra Spring

Perforated Pool

Percolating Spring

Lakeside Spring

Thumb Geyser

Ledge Spring

Collapsing Pool

Surging Spring

Thumb Paint Pots

Historic Ranger Station and Bookstore

Seismograph & Bluebell Pools

P

P

To Lake Overlook Trailhead

start & finish

| 0 | 25 | 50 | 75 yards |
| 0 | 25 | 50 | 75 meters |

West Thumb Geyser Basin

This relatively flat boardwalk loops around a varied geyser basin, a volcanic caldera within a caldera, and past some of the park's most colorful hot springs. Though they aren't the most volatile or dynamic attractions, it's an intimate and usually uncrowded look at some unique hydrothermal features. For the bigger picture, add a short climb to an overlook of the lake.

Best Time

Rain and snow tends to dilute the vibrant colors in many hydrothermal features. Therefore, the geyser basin is at its most brilliant in the middle of summer, especially July and August. It's also a popular winter destination. There's no shade, so it can get hot at midday. The overlook extension is only worth the effort on clear days.

Finding the Trail

From Old Faithful, drive west 17 miles on the Grand Loop Road over Craig Pass (8262'), turn left at West Thumb Junction, then immediately turn right into the Geyser Basin parking area on the southeast side of the road. From Lake Village, go 21 miles southeast along the lakeshore on the Grand Loop Road and turn left into the parking area. From the south, go north 22 miles on the South Entrance Road and turn right at West Thumb Junction. The Geyser Basin loop starts near the bookstore in the

TRAIL USE
Hike
LENGTH
0.6 mile, less than 1 hour
VERTICAL FEET
Negligible
DIFFICULTY
– **1** 2 3 4 5 +
TRAIL TYPE
Loop
SURFACE TYPE
Boardwalk

FEATURES
Child Friendly
Handicap Access
Lake
Wildlife
Great Views
Photo Opportunity
Geothermal
Moonlight Hiking

FACILITIES
Ranger Station
Bookstore
Restrooms
Picnic Tables
Phone

Watch for swirling patterns on the surface of Yellowstone Lake, which are evidence of submerged thermal vents.

 Geothermal

📷 **Photo Opportunity**

parking lot's southeast corner. The Lake Overlook trailhead is in the southwest corner.

Trail Description

Before leaving the parking lot,▶1 stop by the historic 1925 **Ranger Station**▶2 to browse some books, chat with the friendly Yellowstone Association staffers, and warm up in front of the woodstove. Head out counterclockwise (right) on the wheelchair-accessible boardwalk.▶3

Depending on the season, you may find the miniature acidic mud volcanoes known as the **Thumb Paint Pots**▶4 (called "mud puffs" by the 1871 Hayden Expedition) plopping and sputtering away; if there's been recent precipitation they might be washed out.

Nearby, the ultra-blue **Seismograph** and **Bluebell pools** receive runoff from the mudpots; the former is thought to perhaps have been altered by the 1959 Hebgen Lake earthquake, which registered 7.5 on the Richter scale.

Near the lakeshore, **Lakeside Spring** and **Lakeshore Geyser**▶5 contribute to the average of 3100 gallons of superheated water that overflows from the geyser basin into the lake every day. One of

OPTIONS

Yellowstone Lake Overlook

For a superb view of Yellowstone Lake and the park's entire eastern half, hike the **Lake Overlook Trail** loop (2 miles round-trip, 1 hour, 200-foot elevation gain). It starts from the southwest corner of the parking lot, and passes through meadows, a 1988 burn area, and regenerating forest before reaching the overlook. Highlights include a decent chance of spotting deer, elk, and bison—plus a minor possibility of encountering bears—and expansive views across the lake to the park's eastern boundary in the Absaroka Range. July is the best time for wildflowers.

Morgan Konn

Cookin' on the hook *is no longer allowed at Fishing Cone, on the edge of Yellowstone Lake.*

the geyser's vents usually remains submerged until the end of August. Though spouts of up to 50 feet were reported in the 1920s and 1930s, the last major eruption was in 1970.

The basin's most famous feature is **Fishing Cone,▶6** where tall tales grew out of the legends of mountain men "hooking and cooking" trout in one swift motion in the boiling natural stew pot. Today, fishing is not allowed here and the cone stays underwater until early summer.

 Great Views

Black Pool and **Abyss Pool▶7** are the basin's most striking, and most photographed, springs. Abyss, one of the park's deepest pools, is a real looker and is said to have a seemingly endless bottom; wait for a steam-free moment before snapping a photo. Black Pool is so named because it once harbored a thick, dark mat of thermophilic bacteria, but now it's kaleidoscopically colorful. The pool

 **Photo Opportunity**

Hikers *check out the Abyss Pool.*

erupted several times in 1991 and 1992, and subsequent rising water temperatures killed off the original black hue.

Turn left just before the inner boardwalk loop ▶8 to reach a spur platform out to the **Twin Geysers**. Though its eruptions are infrequent and unpredictable, when they last blew in 1999 the twin vents spouted in succession, 70 feet in the west, followed by over 100 feet in the east.

The highlights of the dynamic **Central Basin** ▶9 area between the two boardwalks are the brilliantly tinted **Blue Funnel Spring**, the overflowing, 167°F **Surging Spring,** ▶10 and the **Collapsing Pool**, which is constantly in flux.

Geothermal

Following the inner loop, you'll end up back where you started on the outer boardwalk, ▶11 a short distance from the Ranger Station and parking lot. ▶12

If you aren't ready to jump back on the road, cross the parking lot to pick up the **Lake Overlook Trail** near the exit for West Thumb Junction.

🚶 MILESTONES

▶1 0.0 Start at West Thumb Geyser Basin parking area

▶2 0.0 Historic Ranger Station: bookstore and warming hut

▶3 0.1 Right on outer boardwalk

▶4 0.15 Thumb Paint Pots and Seismograph and Bluebell pools

▶5 0.2 Lakeside Spring and Lakeshore Geyser

▶6 0.25 Fishing Cone

▶7 0.3 Black Pool and Abyss Pool

▶8 0.35 Left onto Twin Geysers platform just before inner boardwalk loop

▶9 0.4 Central Basin: Blue Funnel Spring, and Ephedra Spring

▶10 0.45 Thumb Geyser, Surging Spring, and Collapsing Pool

▶11 0.5 Right at outer boardwalk

▶12 0.6 Return to parking area

Hot Spring Organisms

NOTES

After five years of field research, University of Colorado scientists have theorized that the primary energy source for primitive organisms living in the park's hot springs at temperatures above 158°F (where photosynthesis isn't possible) is not sulfur (as is widely assumed) but hydrogen—the most abundant element in the universe.

The colors visible in hot springs are radiated by thermophilic (heat-loving) organisms; they correspond roughly to temperature ranges: Green and brown are the coolest; yellow and orange are hotter; and the whitish-blue of near-boiling waters indicates the hottest pools, where only the hardiest "extremophiles" can survive.

CHAPTER 5

Southwest Yellowstone–Cascade and Geyser Country

Southwest Yellowstone–Cascade and Geyser Country

Yellowstone's popular southwest corner exemplifies why one of the earliest nicknames for the park was America's Wonderland. Before the park was established in 1872, explorers queried respected periodicals back East about publishing their accounts of encounters with the region's astounding geysers, wildlife, and thermal features. The response was unanimous: "Sorry, we don't publish fiction."

Today, the region's iconic geothermal features are as active as ever and famous worldwide. The pilgrimage to the **Old Faithful Geyser** is obligatory for first-time visitors, and a wander through the gushing **Upper Geyser Basin** never fails to impress. Beyond the frontcountry boardwalks, several of the park's most spectacular geysers and waterfalls are only short distances from roadside trailheads.

For those with a few days to spare, overnight backpacking, stock trips (that is, using horses or pack animals), or boating around **Shoshone Lake** offer enticing escapes from the crowds. Accessing the relative solitude of the 200-square-mile **Bechler region** (also known as the **Cascade Corner** thanks to its many waterfalls) backcountry requires a long drive outside the park—from either West Yellowstone or the South Entrance. The Lamar Valley and Old Faithful aside, many frequent visitors claim that the Cascade Corner is Yellowstone's most captivating region.

There are no campgrounds near Old Faithful, but there are several easy overnight options at nearby backcountry campsites, most discussed in this chapter's trail descriptions. The closest options for tenting it in the frontcountry are at Madison Junction and in Grant Village, near the West Thumb of Yellowstone Lake.

The century-old **Old Faithful Inn** (doubles $82 to $195, suites $290 to $390), a National Historic Landmark, is worth a visit to see the spectacular architecture even if you aren't able to reserve a room or dine there. The west wing will be undergoing an $11 million restoration starting in 2005. Nearby, the less atmospheric **Old Faithful Lodge** has basic cabins ($58), with shared toilets, and motel-style units ($85), with private bathrooms. The shared showers ($3) in the lodge are available to nonguests; pick up a towel at the reception desk.

Larry Van Dyke

Old Faithful Inn *is a classic example of National Park Service architecture (or "parkitecture").*

In winter, the modern **Old Faithful Snow Lodge** (cabins $84 to $125, rooms $164) is a hive of activity. The **West Entrance Road** between West Yellowstone, Montana; Madison Junction; and Old Faithful typically opens for oversnow travel (including cross-country skiing, snowcoaches, and snowmobiles) the third week in December and is groomed until mid-March.

Depending on the weather, the vehicle-free period in early spring—before the road opens around the third week in April—can be a magical time to explore the Grand Loop Road. While park service crews perform spring road maintenance, visitors can bicycle, jog, inline skate, or explore via other nonmotorized means between the West Entrance and Mammoth, and sometimes between Norris and Canyon junctions. Contact the NPS at (307) 344-2109 to verify seasonal opening schedules.

Overleaf: *Backpacker crossing old Boundary Creek suspension bridge (Photo by Morgan Konn)*

Permits and Maps

The only permits required for the hikes in this chapter are for fishing, boating, and overnight stays at the region's numerous and popular backcountry campsites.

The **Old Faithful Visitor Center** is the park's busiest and most elaborate information center, receiving up to 25,000 visitors per day. Besides answering the million-dollar question (Q: "When is Old Faithful scheduled to erupt?" A: "There's no 'schedule.'"), rangers issue permits and lead free interpretive walks through the geyser basins. There's also a good bookstore and a theater that screens short films. A proposal to begin construction of a new, environmentally friendly, $11 million Visitor Education Center at the same location in the spring of 2006 was under review in early 2005. Call (307) 545-2750; open daily 8 AM to 8 PM in summer; hours are reduced in fall and winter.

The remote, summer-only **Bechler Ranger Station** also issues permits, but it's best to arrange for permits and campsite reservations at another backcountry office (see the Appendix, page 333, for a complete list) before trekking all the way out to the park's bottom left corner. For the Bechler Ranger Station, call (406) 581-7074; open 8 AM to 4:30 PM daily during the summer.

The Trails Illustrated *Old Faithful* (no. 302, scale 1:63,360) map shows all the hikes, trailheads, and campgrounds described in this chapter.

Southwest Yellowstone—Cascade & Geyser Country

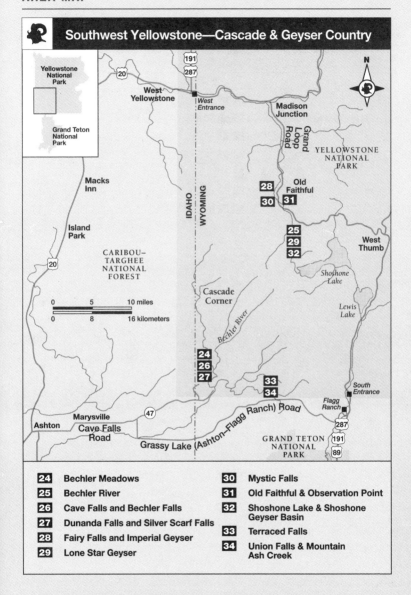

Yellowstone National Park

Grand Teton National Park

191
287

20

West Yellowstone

West Entrance

Madison Junction

Grand Loop Road

YELLOWSTONE NATIONAL PARK

Macks Inn

Island Park

20

CARIBOU–TARGHEE NATIONAL FOREST

28 **Old Faithful**
30 **31**

25
29
32

West Thumb

Shoshone Lake

Lewis Lake

Cascade Corner

Bechler River

0 5 10 miles
0 8 16 kilometers

24
26
27

33
34

South Entrance

Flagg Ranch

Ashton

Marysville

47

Cave Falls Road

Grassy Lake (Ashton–Flagg Ranch) Road

GRAND TETON NATIONAL PARK

287
191
89

IDAHO WYOMING

N

24	Bechler Meadows	**30**	Mystic Falls
25	Bechler River	**31**	Old Faithful & Observation Point
26	Cave Falls and Bechler Falls	**32**	Shoshone Lake & Shoshone Geyser Basin
27	Dunanda Falls and Silver Scarf Falls	**33**	Terraced Falls
28	Fairy Falls and Imperial Geyser	**34**	Union Falls & Mountain Ash Creek
29	Lone Star Geyser		

Southwest Yellowstone—Cascade and Geyser Country

TRAIL	Difficulty	Length	Type	USES & ACCESS	TERRAIN	FLORA & FAUNA	OTHER
24	3	7.8	loop	hiking, horses, backpacking	stream, waterfall	birds, wildlife	camping, swimming
25	5	29.7	out & back	hiking, horses, backpacking, permit	canyon, mountain, stream, waterfall	autumn colors, wildflowers, birds, wildlife	cool & shady, great views, photo, camping, swimming, steep
26	3	7.3	loop	hiking, horses, child friendly	stream, waterfall	autumn colors, birds, wildlife	photo, swimming
27	5	16.4	one way	hiking, horses, backpacking	stream, waterfall	autumn colors, birds, wildlife	photo, camping, steep, secluded
28	3	5/7	one way	hiking, bicycling, backpacking, child friendly	waterfall		photo, camping, steep, swimming
29	2	5.0	one way	hiking, bicycling, backpacking, child friendly, handicap access	stream	wildlife	cool & shady, photo, camping, geothermal, moonlight
30	3	4.0	loop	hiking, child friendly	canyon, stream, waterfall	wildflowers	great views, photo, steep
31	2	2.4	loop	hiking, handicap access, child friendly			great views, photo, steep, moonlight
32	5	17.0	one way	hiking, backpacking, permit	lake, stream	autumn colors, wildflowers, birds, wildlife	great views, photo, camping, geothermal
33	2	3.6	one way	hiking, horses, child friendly	canyon, stream, waterfall	autumn colors	cool & shady, great views, photo, secluded, moonlight
34	5	15.8	one way	hiking, horses, backpacking, permit	canyon, stream, waterfall	autumn colors	photo, camping, swimming, secluded, steep

USES & ACCESS
- Hiking
- Bicycling
- Horses
- Backpacking
- Child Friendly
- Handicap Access
- Backcountry Permit Required
- Camping

TERRAIN
- Canyon
- Mountain
- Summit
- Stream
- Waterfall
- Lake
- Geothermal

FLORA & FAUNA
- Autumn Colors
- Wildflowers
- Birds
- Wildlife

DIFFICULTY
- 1 2 3 4 5 +
less   more

OTHER
- Cool & Shady
- Great Views
- Photo Opportunity
- Swimming
- Secluded
- Historic
- Geologic Interest
- Moonlight Hiking
- Steep

Southwest Yellowstone– Cascade and Geyser Country

This easy, flat dayhike is designed to avoid river fords and provide a brief introduction to the wildlife-rich Bechler region, which was the least affected by the 1988 fires. Old Faithful aside, many frequent visitors claim that the Cascade Corner is Yellowstone's most captivating region.

The Cascade Corner comes as close as any region in Yellowstone to having it all - prime fishing, soakable hot springs, and lots of wildlife. This three- to five-day backcountry route passes by many of the region's highlights. And with a car shuttle, it's downhill most of the way.

This easy loop avoids river fords and provides a sample of what the remote Bechler region has to offer. It's not worth the drive by itself, but it is a nice easy hike if you already happen to be in the area.

This long but rewarding route offers a good sample of the Cascade Corner's varied delights: lush riparian zones; vast, wildlife-rich meadows; sublime hot pots; mesmerizing waterfalls; and invigorating stream crossings. And it is easily extended into a moderate overnight trip.

Old Faithful Geyser *viewed from Observation Point (Trail 31)*

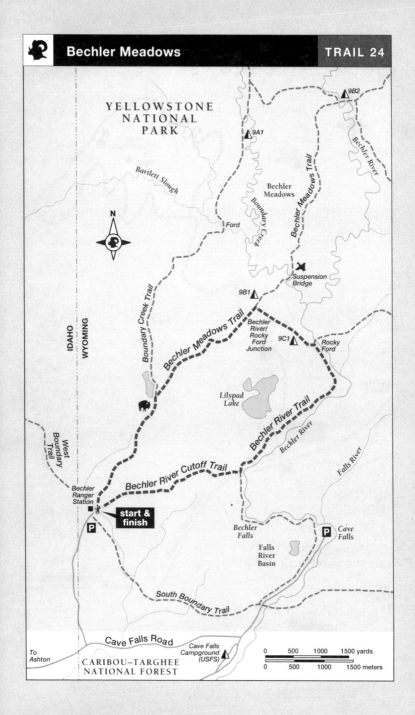

YELLOWSTONE
NATIONAL
PARK

Bartlett Slough

9B2

9A1

Bechler
Meadows

Bechler River

Boundary Creek

Bechler Meadows Trail

Ford

N

IDAHO

WYOMING

Suspension
Bridge

9B1

Boundary Creek Trail

Bechler Meadows Trail

Bechler
River/
Rocky
Ford
Junction

9C1

Rocky
Ford

Lilypad
Lake

Bechler River Trail

Bechler River

West
Boundary
Trail

Bechler River Cutoff Trail

Falls River

Bechler
Ranger
Station

P

start &
finish

P

Bechler
Falls

Cave
Falls

Falls
River
Basin

South Boundary Trail

Cave Falls Road

To
Ashton

Cave Falls
Campground
(USFS)

CARIBOU–TARGHEE
NATIONAL FOREST

| 0 | 500 | 1000 | 1500 yards |
| 0 | 500 | 1000 | 1500 meters |

Bechler Meadows

This easy, nearly flat dayhike is designed to provide a brief introduction to the wildlife-rich Bechler (pronounced *BECK-ler*) region, which was the least affected by the 1988 fires. Bechler is typically explored via multiday backpack trips. It's increasingly popular with anglers, scouting troops, and outfitters, and receives as many as 8000 visitors per year.

Best Time

The Bechler's meadows start drying out by mid-July, but low-lying areas can remain extremely boggy and buggy until early August. Rivers can run high through August as well, making fording challenging, and some areas are marshy year-round. Fishing improves as runoff levels subside. August is a busy month, while September is generally the best and most popular month for exploring. In October, every kind of condition is possible, from dry and gloriously sunny days to heavy early winter storms.

Finding the Trail

From Ashton, Idaho (60 miles and 1.5 hours south of West Yellowstone, Montana, via US Hwy. 20), drive 10 miles east past Marysville and jog left at the turnoff for Mesa Falls (Idaho Hwy. 47) to reach Cave Falls Road. Continue 10 miles on the graded gravel road past the Idaho-Wyoming state line, then turn left for the Bechler Ranger Station at the signed junction for Cave Falls.

From two miles south of Yellowstone's South Entrance at Flagg Ranch, it's possible to head 50

TRAIL USE
Hike, Backpack, Horse
LENGTH
7.8 miles, 4 hours
VERTICAL FEET
Negligible
DIFFICULTY
− 1 2 **3** 4 5 +
TRAIL TYPE
Loop
SURFACE TYPE
Dirt

FEATURES
Stream
Waterfall
Birds
Wildlife
Camping
Swimming

FACILITIES
Ranger Station
Restrooms
Water
Horse Staging

197

miles west on the unpaved Grassy Lake Road (variously called Ashton-Flagg Ranch Road, Reclamation Road, and USFS Road 261 on older maps) to reach a cutoff for Cave Falls Road. Unless you are fond of rough roads and your vehicle has high clearance, this route is not recommended. At the trailhead, park adjacent to the barn (if dayhiking) or in the horse staging area (if staying overnight). Check in at the Ranger Station—and pay your entrance fee, if you haven't yet elsewhere—before heading out. If camping, don't forget to post your permit stub on your dashboard.

Logistics

Contact the Bechler Ranger Station for an update on current weather, river-ford, and trail conditions.

Bechler's backcountry campsites aren't available for advance reservation until after July 20; some sites may be available earlier in July for in-person reservations, depending on weather conditions. Stock animals (llamas included) are not allowed on Bechler's trails until at least July 1.

During summer, it's a good idea to reserve Bechler's limited backcountry campsites as far in advance as possible. Most Bechler campsites may be reserved for only one or two nights. The only nearby frontcountry camping option is the primitive USFS Cave Falls Campground (with water and restrooms), 1 mile east of the turnoff for the Bechler Ranger station, in the Caribou-Targhee National Forest. There's also plenty of room for dispersed camping in the surrounding national forests.

 Camping

Trail Description

From the **Bechler Ranger Station**,▶1 the trailhead is just to the left of the barn on the north side of the parking area. After a hundred yards or so, turn left at the **Bechler Meadows Trail**▶2 junction.

After crossing a rotting boardwalk that has seen better days (which might well be replaced by the time you read this), the route strikes out to the north and winds through unburned lodgepole pine forest. As the trail opens up into some meadows at 1.7 miles, you reach the signed **Boundary Creek Trail** junction,▶3 opposite a couple large ponds that often attract moose and deer around dusk and dawn.

Proceed right here and continue for another 1.7 miles through islands of unburned forest to the **Bechler River/Rocky Ford cutoff** junction▶4 and the beginning of the vast seasonal wetlands of **Bechler Meadows**. Straight ahead and a hundred yards farther along is the trailside, hiker-only **campsite 9B1**, an easy overnight option for families and first-time campers. A few hundred yards beyond the campsite, a **suspension bridge** over meandering **Boundary Creek** provides easy access to the heart of the meadows, a nice spot for a picnic or some bird-watching for osprey, great blue herons, and sandhill cranes.

Turning right at the junction, the Rocky Ford cutoff trail skirts the southern fringes of the meadows. Soon after it begins to trace the west bank of the **Bechler River**, the trail passes the hiker-only **campsite 9C1**. Soon, at 4.2 miles, you pass by the

Bechler rangers live in a historic soldier station, built in 1911 to protect the region's abundant wildlife from poachers.

 Wildlife

 Camping

 Stream

Much More Than a Swamp

HISTORY

As recently as 1930, Idaho farmers lobbied the US Congress to build reservoirs within the park as part of irrigation schemes that would have dammed Yellowstone Lake and the Bechler River Valley—which they dismissed as a "swamp."

Historic

wide and slippery but relatively shallow **Rocky Ford** ▶5 crossing of the Bechler River on your left. The trail on the far side of the river follows part of the old Marysville wagon road to Jackson Hole, Wyoming, which was built by Mormons in the 1880s.

After a turn to the south and another pleasant 2-mile stretch along the river, turn right at the signed **Bechler River Cutoff Trail** ▶6 junction, where the trail swings away from the river. Or detour downstream for 0.5 mile to the rapids-like **Bechler Falls**, just upstream from the confluence with the Falls River. The broad, 15-foot cascade is impressive for being one of the Cascade Corner's most voluminous waterfalls.

Waterfall

Turning right at the junction, the cutoff trail makes a beeline back through unburned forest to a final junction, ▶7 where you turn left and continue a few hundred yards to arrive back at the Bechler Ranger Station parking area. ▶8

MILESTONES

▶1   0.0 Start at Bechler Ranger Station trailhead

▶2   0.1 Left at Bechler Meadows Trail junction

▶3   1.7 Right at Boundary Creek Trail junction

▶4   3.4 Right at Bechler River/Rocky Ford cutoff

▶5   4.2 Straight past Rocky Ford

▶6   6.2 Right at Bechler River Cutoff Trail junction

▶7   7.7 Left at junction to Bechler Ranger Station

▶8   7.8 Return to Bechler Ranger Station parking area

Bechler Falls and Cave Falls Detour

OPTIONS

If you are a falling water fanatic and were intrigued by the short detour to **Bechler Falls**, continue downstream another half-mile or so, past some rapids and the Bechler and Falls River confluence, to the 20-foot drop at **Cave Falls**. It's much wider than it is tall, and you can swim at its turbulent base. (Also see Trail 26, page 213).

The lower Bechler River Trail *is a riot of lush vegetation (Trail 25).*

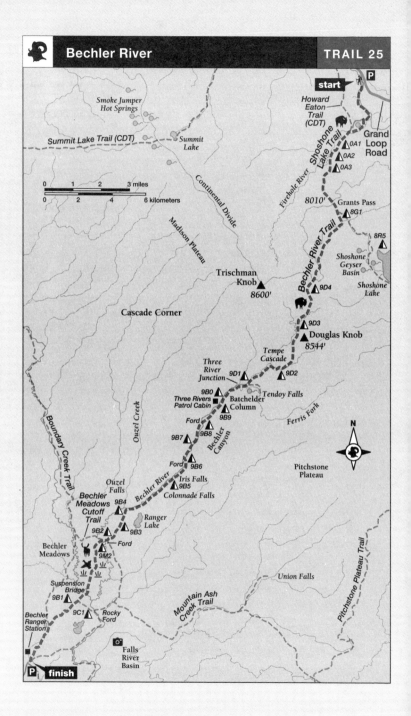

Bechler River

TRAIL 25

start

Howard
Eaton
Trail
(CDT)

Grand
Loop
Road

Smoke Jumper
Hot Springs

Summit Lake Trail (CDT)

Summit
Lake

Shoshone Lake Trail

0A1
0A2
0A3

8010'

Grants Pass

8G1

Firehole River

8R5

Continental Divide

Bechler River Trail

Shoshone
Geyser
Basin

Shoshone
Lake

Madison Plateau

Trischman
Knob
8600'

9D4

Cascade Corner

9D3

Douglas Knob
8544'

Tempe
Cascade

Three
River
Junction
9D1

9D2

Tendoy Falls

9B0

Three Rivers
Patrol Cabin

Batchelder
Column

9B9

Ferris Fork

Ford

9B7

9B8

Bechler
Canyon

Ouzel Creek

N

Ford

9B6

Pitchstone
Plateau

Boundary Creek Trail

Ouzel
Falls

Iris Falls

9B5

Bechler River

Colonnade Falls

Bechler
Meadows
Cutoff
Trail

9B4

9B2

Ranger
Lake

9B3

Ford

Bechler
Meadows

9M2

Union Falls

Pitchstone Plateau Trail

Suspension
Bridge

9B1

9C1

Rocky
Ford

Mountain Ash Creek Trail

Bechler
Ranger
Station

Falls
River
Basin

finish

0   1   2   3 miles
0   2   4   6 kilometers

Bechler River

The Cascade Corner comes as close as any part of Yellowstone to having it all. This three- to five-day route passes by many of the region's highlights. It's tough to argue with good catch-and-release fishing, soakable five-star hot pots, lovely backcountry campsites, and wildlife galore in the lower stretches—especially when the majority of the trail is downhill.

Best Time

Grants Pass (8010'), between Lone Star Geyser and the west end of Shoshone Lake, typically isn't free of snow until late June or early July. In Bechler Meadows, high water and pesky mosquitoes typically don't subside until late July or early August. For these reasons, this trip is most popular in August and September, when advance reservations are essential. October conditions can be glorious, but snaps of foul weather are also quite possible.

Finding the Trail

From the north, head south from Old Faithful for 2.7 miles on the Grand Loop Road. Turn right into the parking area just past the Kepler Cascades turnout, signed for the Lone Star trailhead, on the south side of the road. From Grant Village, go west on the Grand Loop Road from West Thumb Junction for 14.5 miles over Craig Pass (8262') and turn left into the trailhead parking area.

TRAIL USE
Hike, Backpack, Horse

LENGTH
29.7 miles, 3-5 days

VERTICAL FEET
+1300'/-2100'

DIFFICULTY
– 1 2 3 4 **5** +

TRAIL TYPE
Point-to-point

SURFACE TYPE
Dirt

FEATURES
Backcountry Permit
Canyon
Mountain
Stream
Waterfall
Autumn Colors
Wildflowers
Birds
Wildlife
Cool & Shady
Great Views
Camping
Swimming
Secluded
Geothermal

FACILITIES
None

Lone Star Geyser *(Trails 25, 29, and 32)*

Logistics

Check the predicted eruption schedule for Lone Star Geyser at the Old Faithful Ranger Station so you can plan your departure time accordingly. Seeing this impressive geyser in action is worth fitting into your trip schedule.

Bechler's backcountry campsites aren't available for advance reservation until after July 20; some sites may be available earlier for in-person reservations, depending on weather conditions.

A car shuttle is necessary for this hike, and be prepared for a long drive. From the Lone Star trailhead, the easiest way to reach the Bechler Ranger Station is via the West Entrance and West Yellowstone. The winding 105-mile drive takes at least four hours each way in favorable conditions. The alternative route, via the South Entrance and the unpaved Grassy Lake Road, is only slightly shorter but is much rougher and takes even longer.

Don't leave any valuables in your vehicles at the trailheads, display your backcountry permit inside your windshield, and register your plans with the Bechler Ranger Station. If you're concerned about the security of your vehicle, park at the nearby Kepler Cascades turnout, which sees less traffic.

Unless otherwise noted, campsites described here are hiker-only, allow wood campfires, and have a one-night limit.

Trail Description

From the **Lone Star trailhead,▶1** an abandoned service road heads south along the upper Firehole River. After passing the remains of an old water-works, the paved road traces the east bank of the river as it heads upstream.

After passing the **Spring Creek Trail▶2** junction at 1.6 miles, you may hear **Lone Star Geyser▶3** before you see it. During its steam phase, it can be heard up to a mile away. Major eruptions occur like clockwork, every three hours on average, with significant preplay in between active phases. Allow about an hour to reach the geyser on foot from the trailhead. (For details about Lone Star Geyser, see Trail 29, page 229.)

 Geothermal

A few hundred yards beyond the geyser basin, take a left at the well-signed **Shoshone Lake Trail▶4** junction, where bison are often spotted grazing and wallowing around thermal areas adjacent to the trail. If you are doing a five-day trip, you have three decent trailside options for first-night campsites in the next 1.5 miles.

 Wildlife

First up, the wide-open **campsite OA1▶5** is the only one which also allows stock parties. Watch out for bison barging through in the middle of the night! Four hundred yards down-trail, across the Upper Firehole River, **campsite OA2▶6** is your best choice. Almost a mile farther upstream, **campsite OA3▶7** is near Firehole Springs. Beyond here, the trail leaves the river and starts to climb up to cross the **Continental Divide**.

 Camping

If you choose not to linger here for fishing or geyser-gazing on your first day, you'll have to contend with a 300-foot climb through unburned forest to unsigned **Grants Pass** (8010'),**▶8** and a similar descent to the signed **Bechler River Trail junction,▶9** at 6.4 miles. The hiker- and llama-only **campsite 8G1** (no wood fires) is a hundred yards to

Camping

Wildlife

Waterfall

the left, off the Shoshone Lake Trail in Shoshone Meadows. If you can't reserve a spot here, it's a 2.5-mile detour down to the lovely **campsite 8R5** (no wood fires), fronting Basin Point Bay on the west the shore of **Shoshone Lake**. If you stay here, don't miss the opportunity to explore the Shoshone Geyser Basin, detailed in Trail 32, page 245.

If you have opted for the three-night plan, the absolute farthest you can comfortably go during your first day is 9.5 miles, crossing the Continental Divide (8500') again, to **campsite 9D4.▶10** The last first-night resort is the rocky **campsite 9D3,▶11** a popular stock-grazing site 1.2 miles farther along through meadows and prime moose habitat below **Douglas Knob▶12** (8544'). Neither of these sites allows wood fires.

It's all downhill beyond 9D4. Below 9D3, the trail drops into the **Littles Fork** drainage, then crosses the **Gregg Fork** of the Upper Bechler River just before **campsite 9D2,▶13** a decent overnight option at 13.5 miles. Just downstream is the 55-foot **Twister Falls** cascade, out of sight but visible from a short spur trail. From here on down, you're in the thick of the Waterfall Wonderland, first mapped in 1872 by the Hayden Survey's chief topographer, Gustavus R. Bechler.

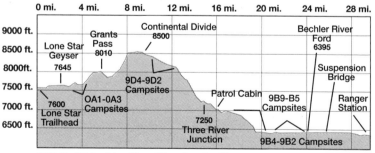

TRAIL 25 Bechler River Elevation Profile

The Ferris Fork *has plentiful waterfalls and intriguing thermal features.*

The trail descends gradually through lush unburned forest, along the east side of the Gregg Fork for another 1.5 miles to a typically unsigned (but well-beaten) half-mile side trail that heads east (left), past a hitch rail and upstream along the north bank of the **Ferris Fork**. The thermal features here defy description, but suffice it to say that it's well worth the detour, and your weary bones will thank you. Intrepid bushwhackers may discover several seldom-seen waterfalls upstream.

Back on the main route, the trail switchbacks down across the Gregg Fork, past 45-foot Ragged Falls to the ideal **campsite 9D1,▶14** (no wood fires) perched above **Three River Junction**, the captivating confluence of the Phillips, Gregg, and Ferris forks, forming the headwaters of the Bechler River. The **Three Rivers Patrol Cabin▶15** and stock-party **campsite 9B0** (two-night limit, no wood fires) are a mile below the junction, in a meadow riddled with algae-laden thermal features.

⚠ Camping

Albright Falls was
named in 1986 in
honor of Horace
Marden Albright, who
helped to found the
National Park Service
in 1916 and who
served as
Yellowstone's
superintendent from
1919 to 1929.

▲ Camping

🏳 Waterfall

The better overnight option, **campsite 9B9** (two-night limit, no wood fires), awaits a few hundred yards downstream, tucked away on the left-hand side of the trail below the towering **Batchelder Column.▶16** The impressive, roaring 260-foot **Albright Falls** cascade is visible (and audible!) from the stellar campsite. Fishing can be good below the falls.

A mile downstream, the trailside **campsite 9B8 ▶17** (with a pit toilet) is below a patch of burned forest, just before the first of two substantial fords of the Bechler River. Orange blazes usually mark the best places to cross, but don't hesitate to scout upstream and down-stream options if you don't like the looks of things where the trail hits the water.

Another mile down-canyon, just after a more serious 50-foot-wide ford (up to hip-deep in August), is **campsite 9B7,▶18** set back well off the trail, rumped up against the sheer canyon walls.

There's plenty more mud here, as cold feeder streams tumble across the trail. Less than a mile downstream is the nice trailside **campsite 9B6.▶19** The trail gets a bit steeper and rockier as it approaches the first of several cascades above the forested **Treasure Island** islet, in the middle of the river. To your left in the wet season, a series of unnamed cataracts plunge down from the Pitchstone Plateau.

The damp, less desirable **campsite 9B5▶20** is between the 40-foot, rainbow-producing **Iris Falls** and the spectacular, two-tiered **Colonnade Falls, ▶21** which is visible from a signed, 300-yard side trail that dead-ends at a nice viewpoint and picnic spot.

The lower stretch of trail alternates between meadows, fir-spruce forest, and boulder fields festooned with edible raspberries, huckleberries, and thimbleberries. Angler alert: A couple of miles down-stream, just before leaving the canyon, there's

Morgan Konn

Iris Falls

an opportunity to bushwhack up to your left—to **Ranger Lake**, where rainbow trout are rumored to lurk.

At the mouth of Bechler Canyon, trailside **campsite 9B4▶22** awaits below **Ouzel Falls**, which is a half-mile north of the trail and visible for miles around.

Less than a mile farther along, fronting the eastern edge of the vast meadows, **campsite 9B3▶23** (two-night limit) is reserved for stock parties. The popular trailside **campsite 9B2▶24** (two-night limit, no wood fires) is just before the knee- to thigh-high **Bechler River ford**, 5.7 miles from the exit trailhead.

Depending on the season and water level, you can opt to turn left here and stay on the east side of the Bechler River for a slightly longer but more scenic route back to the ranger station, via the wider but shallower **Rocky Ford**.

Our route continues straight ahead beyond the Bechler River ford. It passes the **9M2 stock campsite** (two-night limit, no wood fires) before crossing

> At 230 feet, Ouzel Falls is one of Yellowstone's tallest cascades, though it's hardly the most impressive. It's most striking early in the season, since it loses much of its oomph by the end of August.

a boggy section on a footbridge, just before the signed **Bechler Meadows Cutoff Trail** junction. ▶25

Again, depending on the season and prevailing conditions, it can be a soggy slog for the next 1.5 miles through the wildlife-rich meadows to the **Boundary Creek suspension bridge**. ▶26

Camping

Just beyond Boundary Creek is the exposed trailside **campsite 9B1**. ▶27 Keep heading straight on the Bechler Meadows Trail as the alternate River Trail rejoins in from the left, unless you have reserved the riverfront **campsite 9C1** (two-night limit) 0.5 mile down-stream (to your left at the junction). After a long stretch across a forested upland island, stay to the left at the **Boundary Creek Trail junction**. ▶28 From here, it's 1.6 miles to a signed junction ▶29 and, finally, the pit toilets and drinking water spigot near the **Bechler Ranger Station**. ▶30

Variations

OPTIONS

If you aren't driving, or want to avoid the pavement and crowds en route to Lone Star Geyser, you can start south from the **Howard Eaton trailhead**, 1 mile south of Old Faithful, on part of the Continental Divide National Scenic Trail.

If it's easier to arrange a shuttle to **Bechler Ranger Station**, the hike can be done in the uphill direction, but the northbound hike entails a total climb of more than 2000 feet.

🚶	**MILESTONES**

▶1 0.0 Start at Lone Star trailhead

▶2 1.6 Right at Spring Creek Trail junction

▶3 2.5 Lone Star Geyser

▶4 2.7 Left at Shoshone Lake Trail junction

▶5 2.9 Campsite OA1

▶6 3.3 Campsite OA2

▶7 4.1 Campsite OA3

▶8 6.0 Grants Pass

▶9 6.4 Right at Bechler River/Shoshone Lake Trail junction

▶10 9.5 Campsite 9D4

▶11 10.7 Campsite 9D3

▶12 12.0 Douglas Knob

▶13 13.5 Campsite 9D2

▶14 15.9 Three River Junction and campsite 9D1

▶15 16.8 Three Rivers Patrol Cabin and campsite 9B0

▶16 17.0 Campsite 9B9 and Batchelder Column

▶17 17.9 Campsite 9B8

▶18 18.9 Campsite 9B7

▶19 19.6 Campsite 9B6

▶20 20.8 Campsite 9B5

▶21 20.9 Colonnade Falls

▶22 22.6 Campsite 9B4

▶23 23.3 Campsite 9B3

▶24 24.0 Campsite 9B2 and Bechler River ford

▶25 24.5 Left at Bechler Meadows Cutoff Trail junction

▶26 26.0 Boundary Creek suspension bridge

▶27 26.3 Straight on Bechler Meadows Trail past campsite 9B1

▶28 28.0 Left at Boundary Creek Trail junction

P29 29.6 Straight to Bechler Ranger Station

P30 29.7 Arrive at Bechler Ranger Station parking area

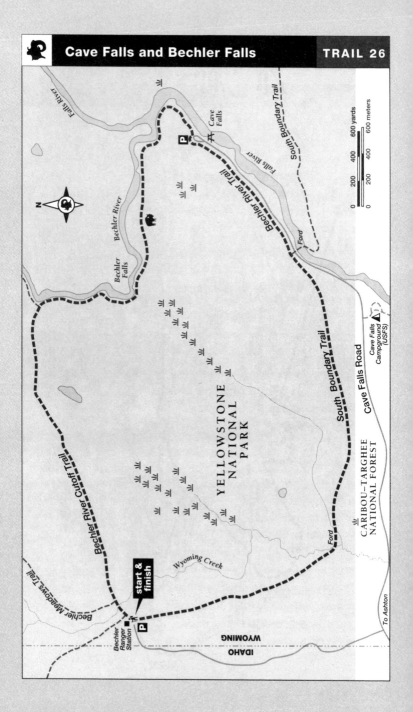

Cave Falls and Bechler Falls — TRAIL 26

Cave Falls and Bechler Falls

Wider than they are tall, Bechler and Cave falls are the most accessible cascades in the remote Bechler region. This easy loop provides a sample of what the area has to offer while avoiding river fords.

Best Time

Runoff is highest from May on, but access to the region is difficult and trails remain wet and muddy until mid-July. Of course, by the time the trails have dried out in August and September, the volume of the waterfalls is greatly diminished. Throughout October the weather can be good but is very unpredictable.

Finding the Trail

From the West Entrance at West Yellowstone, Montana, head south for 60 miles (1.5 hours) on US Hwy. 20 to Ashton, Idaho. Continue 10 miles east past Marysville and jog left at the turnoff for Mesa Falls (Idaho Hwy. 47) to reach Cave Falls Road. Continue 10 miles on the graded gravel road past the Idaho-Wyoming state line, then turn left for the Bechler Ranger Station at the signed junction for Cave Falls.

An alternate but very rough route from Yellowstone's South Entrance, heads 50 miles east from Flagg Ranch to a cutoff for the Bechler Ranger Station via the unpaved Grassy Lake Road (called Ashton-Flagg Ranch Road, Reclamation Road, or USFS Road 261 on some older maps).

TRAIL USE
Hike, Horse

LENGTH
7.3 miles, 2.5-3 hours

VERTICAL FEET
Negligible

DIFFICULTY
– 1 2 **3** 4 5 +

TRAIL TYPE
Loop

SURFACE TYPE
Dirt

FEATURES
Child Friendly
Stream
Waterfall
Autumn Colors
Birds
Wildlife
Photo Opportunity
Swimming

FACILITIES
Ranger Station
Restrooms
Picnic Tables
Horse Staging

213

Trail Description

South of the park, below the Cave Falls Campground, the Falls River features a 14-mile, class III whitewater kayak run through prime grizzly bear and bald eagle habitat.

 Waterfall

 Swimming

From the day-hiking parking area near the **Bechler Ranger Station,**▶1 look just south for the **South Boundary Trail trailhead.**▶2 The trail heads out southeast through lodgepole pines on a different route than the other trails that leave from the northwest side of the barn.

There's an easy ford of Wyoming Creek 0.5 mile from the trailhead, after which the trail parallels the park's southern boundary and paved **Cave Falls Road** for a mile. After passing the **USFS Cave Falls Campground** on the opposite side of the road,▶3 the trail enters the **Cave Falls** parking lot and picnic area at the end of the road, 3.8 miles from the trailhead.▶4

Cave Falls' name comes from the large cavern near its base on the river's west bank. Depending on the flow of the wide, two-tiered plunge, it's sometimes possible to wade upstream and swim near the base of the falls.

Save the Best for Last?

OPTIONS

The loop can be done in either direction with no change in difficulty. As described, the route leaves the best for the second half of the hike. You can cut out the part along the road by doing the trip clockwise and turning around at either Bechler or Cave Falls and retracing your steps.

Alternatively, you can start at the **Cave Falls trailhead** parking area and do an easy 2-mile, 1-hour out-and-back jaunt to Bechler Falls.

Beyond the falls, the trail continues upstream 0.2 mile along the west side of the Falls River past some rapids to the **Bechler River confluence.**▶5 Less than a mile farther upstream, **Bechler Falls**▶6 cascade over 15 feet. The understory vegetation here is a lush mix of mosses and ferns and thickets of berry bushes, beneath a crowded spruce-fir canopy. Monitor the banks above the river for moose, deer, and other berry-loving browsers.

The trail leaves the river a mile beyond the falls at the **Bechler River Cutoff Trail** junction,▶7 where it loops back around through unburned forest to the **Bechler Ranger Station** parking area.▶8

Above Cave Falls, the cutthroat and rainbow trout get bigger, and upstream the fishing gets better the farther you hike off-trail. Aquatic insects begin to hatch in July.

🚶	**MILESTONES**

▶1 0.0 Start at Bechler Ranger Station trailhead

▶2 0.1 Southeast on South Boundary Trail

▶3 2.8 Straight past Falls River ford parking area

▶4 3.8 Cave Falls overlook and picnic area

▶5 4.0 Bechler River/Falls River confluence

▶6 4.8 Bechler Falls

▶7 5.7 Left at Bechler River Cutoff Trail junction

▶8 7.3 Return to Bechler Ranger Station parking area

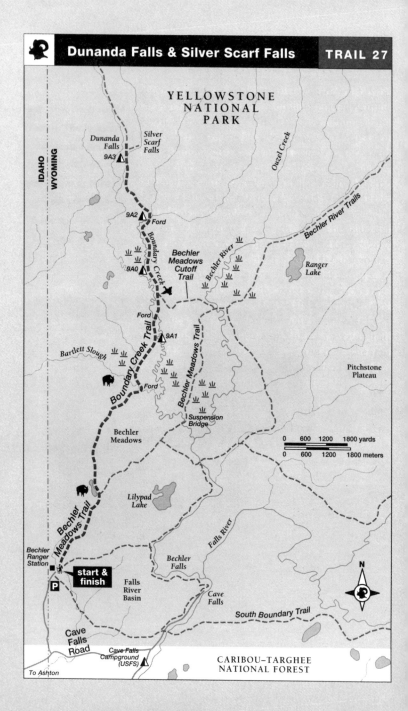

YELLOWSTONE
NATIONAL
PARK

Ouzel Creek

Dunanda
Falls
9A3

Silver
Scarf
Falls

IDAHO

WYOMING

9A2   Ford

Bechler River Trails

Boundary Creek

Bechler
Meadows
Cutoff
Trail

9A0

Bechler River

Ranger
Lake

Ford

9A1

Boundary Creek Trail

Bechler Meadows Trail

Bartlett Slough

Pitchstone
Plateau

Ford

Suspension
Bridge

Bechler
Meadows

0   600   1200   1800 yards
0   600   1200   1800 meters

Lilypad
Lake

Bechler
Meadows Trail

Bechler
Ranger
Station

start &
finish

P

Falls
River
Basin

Bechler
Falls

Falls River

Cave
Falls

South Boundary Trail

N

Cave
Falls
Road

Cave Falls
Campground
(USFS)

CARIBOU–TARGHEE
NATIONAL FOREST

To Ashton

Dunanda Falls and Silver Scarf Falls

For a sample of the Cascade Corner's varied delights, this rewarding daylong hike can't be beat. Highlights include lush riparian zones; vast, wildlife-rich meadows; sublime hot pots; invigorating stream crossings; and mesmerizing waterfalls. Since there are several good campsites en route, the trip is easily extended into a moderate overnighter.

Best Time

The Bechler is wet and buggy through the end of July. River fords can be tricky, and run high until mid-July, but waterfalls are at their most spectacular early in the season. August and September are the classic times to hike the Bechler. October is bug-free and can be glorious, or a real boondoggle if an early winter storm sweeps through. The lowest-lying parts of the trail can be swampy year-round. Definitely bring your hiking sandals or wading shoes, plus trekking poles for added stability.

Finding the Trail

From outside the park in Ashton, Idaho, (60 miles south of West Yellowstone, Montana, or 54 miles north of Victor, Idaho), go 10 miles east past Marysville and jog left at the turnoff for Mesa Falls (Idaho Hwy. 47) to reach Cave Falls Road. Continue 10 miles on the graded gravel road past the Idaho-Wyoming state line, then turn left for the Bechler Ranger Station at the signed junction for Cave Falls.

From Yellowstone's South Entrance, it's a rough 50 miles east from Flagg Ranch to a cutoff for the

TRAIL USE
Hike, Backpack, Horse

LENGTH
16.4 miles, 8-10 hours

VERTICAL FEET
±400'

DIFFICULTY
– 1 2 3 4 **5** +

TRAIL TYPE
Out & Back

SURFACE TYPE
Dirt

FEATURES
Stream
Waterfall
Autumn Colors
Birds
Wildlife
Photo Opportunity
Camping
Swimming
Secluded
Geothermal

FACILITIES
Ranger Station
Restrooms
Water
Horse Staging

217

Bechler Ranger Station via the unpaved Grassy Lake Road (called Ashton-Flagg Ranch Road, Reclamation Road, or USFS Road 261 on maps).

Trail Description

From **trailhead 9K1** between the barn and the **Bechler Ranger Station,▶1** head out north into unburned upland islands of lodgepole pine forest. Just beyond the **Bechler Meadows Trail** junction,▶2 the trail crosses a rotting boardwalk that has seen better days (and may have been replaced by the time you read this).

At 1.6 miles from the trailhead, fork left onto the **Boundary Creek Trail,▶3** which continues north past several ponds and through small marshy meadows. The forest thins out a bit as the trail crosses several boggy areas on logs.

As you approach the southern edge of the flat expanse of Bechler Meadows, you'll have to wade through the stagnant, murky **Bartlett Slough**. Early in the season it can be difficult to see the solid bottom, but by August it is usually a shallow crossing and, if you're lucky, may be bridged by logs. On the upside, there are good views of the Tetons in the background, and the surrounding territory is prime moose stomping grounds.

 Wildlife

Trailside **campsite 9A1**, situated in a mature island of lodgepole pine overlooking the meadows, receives heavy stock use and is a hundred yards before the **Boundary Creek** ford,▶4 5 miles from the trailhead. The crossing here can be knee- to thigh-high, even after the water level drops in July. Late in the season, the creek may be serendipitously bridged by deadfall. Things only get damper as you head upstream between the edge of the forest and the east bank of Boundary Creek. Scan the meadows for great blue herons and sandhill cranes.

Camping

At 6.4 miles, **campsite 9A0** is another popular stock site, on the opposite bank of a Boundary Creek tributary, just beyond the **Bechler Meadows Cutoff Trail junction.**▶5 You'll encounter several small, unbridged fords in the next mile—most should be crossable on fallen logs. Beyond a small ford and the nice, hiker-only **campsite 9A2**, in the middle of a large meadow, the trail traverses a decade-old burn area.

 Birds

A short spur trail to the hiker-only **campsite 9A3** joins the main trail just before the **Silver Scarf Falls junction,**▶6 8 miles from the trailhead. The campsite is within earshot of Dunanda Falls and is a great base camp for exploring nearby hydrothermal wonders.

The **Dunanda Falls** overlook▶7 is just beyond the final junction, a few hundred yards up the trail's left fork.

After exploring off-trail around the brink of the falls, it's a simple matter of pulling yourself away from the hot pots before retracing your steps back to the **Bechler Ranger Station.**▶8

👤 MILESTONES

▶1 0.0 Start at Bechler Ranger Station trailhead

▶2 0.1 Left at Bechler Meadows Trail junction

▶3 1.6 Left at Boundary Creek Trail junction

▶4 5.0 Campsite 9A1 and Boundary Creek ford

▶5 6.4 Left at Bechler Meadows Cutoff Trail; campsite 9AO

▶6 8.0 Left at Silver Scarf Falls spur trail junction

▶7 8.2 Dunanda Falls overlook

▶8 16.4 Return to Bechler Ranger Station parking area

OPTIONS

To Ford or Not to Ford?

By adding 0.6 mile in each direction, you can avoid the ford of
Boundary Creek: On your way to the falls, stay on the Bechler
Meadows Trail at the Boundary Creek Trail junction, then turn left on
the Bechler Meadows Cutoff Trail to rejoin the Boundary Creek Trail.
There's no guarantee, however, that the trail through Bechler
Meadows will be any less wet than the fords! It's always a good idea
to check current ford and trail conditions at the Bechler Ranger
Station before heading out.

Overnight Options

Few backpackers (and even fewer dayhikers) venture upstream
above Dunanda Falls on the **Boundary Creek Trail.** The trail traces
Boundary Creek as it climbs several hundred feet past solitary
campsite 9A4 and several intriguing thermal areas. Eventually, it
ends up at fishless **Buffalo Lake**, 1 mile east of the park's west
boundary.

    If you can score a campsite reservation, there are many good
options for extending the trip overnight.

View of **Dunanda Falls** *from the overlook*

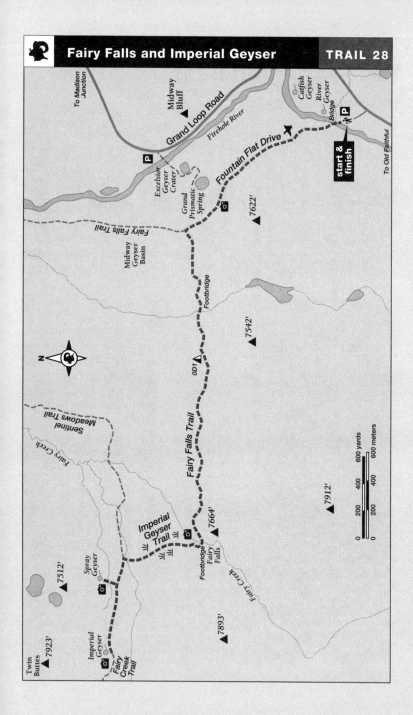

Fairy Falls and Imperial Geyser

TRAIL 28

To Madison Junction

Midway Bluff

Grand Loop Road

Catfish Geyser

River Geyser

Bridge

P

Firehole River

Fountain Flat Drive

start & finish

To Old Faithful

P

Excelsior Geyser Crater

Grand Prismatic Spring

7622'

Fairy Falls Trail

Midway Geyser Basin

Footbridge

7542'

7400'

Sentinel Meadows Trail

Fairy Creek

Fairy Falls Trail

7912'

0   200   400   600 yards

0   200   400   600 meters

Imperial Geyser Trail

Footbridge

7664'

Fairy Falls

Spray Geyser

7512'

Fairy Creek

7893'

Twin Buttes

7923'

Imperial Geyser

Fairy Creek Trail

Fairy Falls and Imperial Geyser

This family-friendly dayhike epitomizes what's so wonderful about the Yellowstone backcountry. Just a short distance off the road, you'll find one of the park's tallest waterfalls and a couple of intriguing, seldom-seen geothermal features. It's a jeans-and-tennis shoes sort of picnic outing.

Best Time

Fairy Falls is at its most spectacular in early spring, and the trail is normally hikable from May to October. There's little shade and no water along the trail, except for at the falls. Head out early to dodge the crowds and to avoid the midday heat. The entire surrounding Firehole area, including Firehole Freight Road and Firehole Lake Dr., is closed for bear management from March 10 through the Friday of Memorial Day weekend.

Finding the Trail

From the south, go 4.3 miles north from the Old Faithful overpass on the Grand Loop Road and turn left into the Fairy Falls (also known as Steel Bridge) trailhead parking area, on the west side of the road. From the north, head 11.2 miles south from Madison Junction on the Grand Loop Road, 1.4 miles past the Midway Geyser Basin turnoff, then turn right into the parking area.

TRAIL USE
Hike, Bike, Backpack

LENGTH
5.2 miles; 6.8 miles including Imperial Geyser; 2–3.5 hours

VERTICAL FEET
Negligible

DIFFICULTY
– 1 2 **3** 4 5 +

TRAIL TYPE
Out & Back

SURFACE TYPE
Dirt

FEATURES
Child Friendly
Waterfall
Photo Opportunity
Camping
Swimming
Geothermal

FACILITIES
None

223

Logistics

Ask about recent Imperial Geyser activity at the Old Faithful Visitor Center before heading out.

Trail Description

From the trailhead parking area,▶1 the wide, gravel **Fountain Flat Drive** (originally known as National Park Ave.) starts on the other side of an old **steel trestle bridge▶2** that spans the **Firehole River**. This stretch of the Firehole is a popular catch-and-release fishing access point. The first section of the trail skirts several riverside thermal features. The road itself is popular with bicyclists heading to the **Fountain Flats Drive trailhead**, 3.5 miles to the north.

As the trail swings away from the river, note the power lines on your left, and look for ducks and geese in the ponds and marshes to your right. Signs of the 1988 fires abound in the open meadows and on the denuded hillsides. Straight ahead, look for the steam rising from the Midway Geyser Basin.

Before you come level with **Grand Prismatic Spring** after 0.6 mile, you'll see its huge, marshy runoff field. Notice how the steam reflects the rainbow colors of the spring, which are especially visible with polarized sunglasses. You can get some idea of the vibrancy and immensity of the awe-inspiring spring as the trail skirts the **Midway Geyser Basin**, but the best views are from the hills to your left. For a better vantage point, as you pass under the second of three power lines,▶3 climb a few hundred feet on one of the unmaintained trails that snake their way uphill through charred deadfall.

After 1 mile, just beyond the geyser basin, the trail junctions with the **Fairy Falls Trail** (bicycles not allowed).▶4 Turning left, the trail enters an alley of regenerating lodgepole pines, already well over head height. You are also in the heart of the **Firehole**

Grand Prismatic Spring is one of the world's largest hot springs, comparable in size to Deildartunguhver in Iceland, but smaller than the geothermal complex in New Zealand's volcanic Waimangu Valley.

⚐ Birds

◉ Photo Opportunity

♨ Geothermal

Hikers walk around Grand Prismatic Spring *with fire-scarred hillsides beyond.*

Bear Management Area, so keep your wits about you and obey any posted signs.

You soon cross a wooden footbridge over a stream coming out of a small unnamed lake, before reaching the well-signed **OD1 campsite▶5** turnoff at 1.7 miles. The campsite is a few hundred yards north of the trail, in a small island of mature lodge-pole pines that survived the 1988 fires. It's also less than an hour from the trailhead, a good overnight option for families and first-time backpackers—but there's no water and sparse shade.

 Wildlife

Beyond the OD1 spur trail junction, the main trail does a few gentle ups and downs as it hugs the base of the ridge to your left. You soon start to see signs of forest diversification, including some wildflowers and quaking aspen saplings. Check out the twisted, gnarled branches on some of the remaining snags. Stop for a moment: Can you hear the falls reverberating off the base of the hills? Straight ahead, the **Twin Buttes** loom, bald as eagles.

 Camping

As you turn the corner to **Fairy Falls,**▶6 2.6 miles from the trailhead, you'll notice here how the mist from the falls makes the lush vegetation dramatically different. Estimated to drop nearly 200 feet, it's the tallest frontcountry waterfall in Greater Yellowstone. Since logjams no longer dam its outlet stream, the swimming hole at the base of the falls was a shallow puddle in October 2004. Fortunately, you can still catch a brisk shower. The area just downstream from the falls, where raspberries shoot up between the rocks, makes a nice picnic spot (shade or sun, take your pick).

From the falls, you can either retrace your steps to the trailhead, or forge ahead 0.9 mile to a couple of seldom-seen geysers for the unchoreographed antithesis of the Old Faithful experience. If you decide to press on, a trail sign for the **Imperial Geyser Trail,**▶7 just beyond the bridge points the way. It's 0.4 mile to a junction with the **Sentinel Meadows Trail,**▶8 then a few hundred yards more to the geyser basin.

Cross a couple of long, rickety old boardwalks (which may be replaced by the time you read this) that span damp meadows. These boardwalks may be closed to stock use. If the buffalo chips atop the walkway are any indication, apparently the bison are impervious to NPS management directives! From the middle of the second boardwalk, look for a steam plume off to your left. The broad trail wends its way

> Before the 1988 fires, only birds and helicopters could get a decent aerial view of Grand Prismatic Spring. Now, with some searching, you should be able to find an unobstructed photo-op viewpoint.

 Geothermal

Imperial Geyser and Twin Buttes

OPTIONS

The round-trip to **Imperial Geyser** adds 1.4 miles, negligible elevation gain, and from a half-hour to an hour, depending on how much of a geyser gazer you are. From the geyser basin, you can continue north off-trail for a half-mile to summit the **Twin Buttes** and get a good overview of the Lower and Midway Geyser basins.

past more aspen saplings as it heads toward the Twin Buttes. Watch here for black beetles and other winged insects that colonize burn areas after fires.

At the final unsigned junction,▶9 the right fork crosses a thermal runoff channel full of orange and green thermophilic strands and mats. If possible, please use the logs to cross and tread carefully to preserve the fragile microbiology. Solitary **Spray Geyser** is a near-perpetual spouter, erupting frequently to a height of 6 to 8 feet.

 Geothermal

Retrace your steps to a game trail that follows the runoff channel upstream through several bison wallows to reach **Imperial Geyser,**▶10 which was erupting frequently in the fall of 2004.

 **Photo Opportunity**

If you approach the sulfurous mudkettles around the back side of the geyser basin, take great care in the fragile area, and listen to the belching sounds for clues about how the basin's plumbing is connected.

Follow the trail downstream along the far side of the runoff channel to retrace your steps. Turn right at the Imperial Geyser Trail junction to return to the Fairy Falls trailhead parking area.▶11

🚶 MILESTONES

▶1   0.0 Start at Fairy Falls trailhead

▶2   0.1 Cross Firehole River on Solider Bridge

▶3   0.6 Cross under power lines

▶4   1.0 Left at Fairy Falls Trail junction

▶5   1.7 Straight past campsite 0D1 spur trail

▶6   2.6 Fairy Falls

▶7   2.8 Left at Imperial Geyser Trail junction

▶8   3.0 Left at Sentinel Meadows Trail junction

▶9   3.2 Right at unsigned fork to Spray Geyser

▶10 3.4 Right upstream to Imperial Geyser

▶11 6.8 Return to Fairy Falls parking area

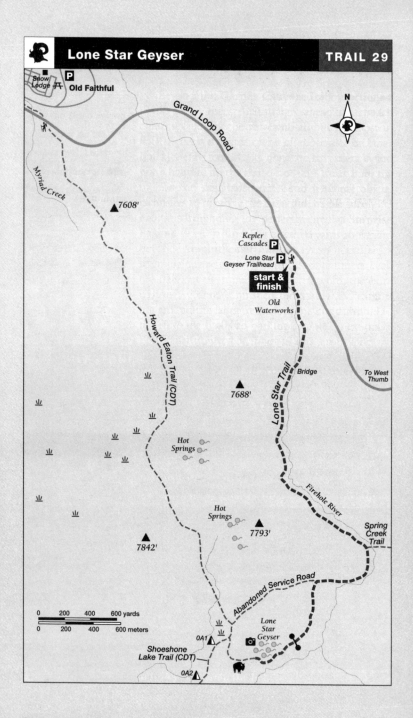

Snow
Lodge
P
Old Faithful

Grand Loop Road

N

Myriad Creek

▲7608'

Kepler
Cascades P

Lone Star P
Geyser Trailhead

**start &
finish**

Old
Waterworks

Howard Eaton Trail (CDT)

Bridge

To West
Thumb

Lone Star Trail

▲
7688'

Hot
Springs

Hot
Springs

Firehole River

▲
7793'

Spring
Creek
Trail

▲
7842'

Abandoned Service Road

0	200	400	600 yards
0	200	400	600 meters

Lone
Star
Geyser

0A1 ▲

Shoeshone
Lake Trail (CDT)

0A2 ▲

Lone Star Geyser

It's an easy stroll along an abandoned road to one of the park's most impressive and dependable geysers. The hike is justifiably popular with tour groups, and you might see a few backpackers heading out for the Bechler River Trail, which begins a day's hike down-trail, beyond Shoshone Lake. The geyser is a 10- to 15-minute bike ride from the trailhead. Allow at least an hour for the hike so you don't miss the eruption.

Best Time

Lone Star is a popular year-round destination, including in winter. The Old Faithful Visitor Center posts eruption predictions, and it's well worth timing your departure around the geyser's very regular cycles.

Finding the Trail

From the Old Faithful overpass, head 2.5 miles south on the Grand Loop Road and turn right into the trailhead parking lot on the south side of the road. From the southeast, go 14.5 miles west over Craig Pass (8262') from West Thumb Junction and turn left into the parking lot. The trailhead is just south of the Kepler Cascades turnout, which is a parking alternative if the Lone Star lot is full.

Logistics

Before heading out, check the predicted eruption schedule at the **Old Faithful Visitor Center**. Rangers occasionally lead 4.5-hour hikes here in the

TRAIL USE
Hike, Bike, Backpack
LENGTH
5.0 miles, 2.5–3 hours
VERTICAL FEET
Negligible
DIFFICULTY
– 1 **2** 3 4 5 +
TRAIL TYPE
Out & Back
SURFACE TYPE
Paved

FEATURES
Child Friendly
Handicap Accessible
Stream
Wildlife
Cool & Shady
Photo Opportunity
Camping
Geothermal
Moonlight Hiking

FACILITIES
None

summer and fall. Regular eruptions happen about every 3 hours, with minor eruptions around 30 minutes before the main event. Splashing preplay starts up to an hour before eruptions, and there's a noisy steam phase afterward.

Trail Description

From the parking lot,▶1 the trail starts out on a flat, abandoned service road just upstream from the **Kepler Cascades**. The traffic noise from the Grand Loop Road quickly fades as birds twittering, chipmunks chattering, and the rush of the **Firehole River** takes over. If you stop to listen and use your imagination, the wind here might sound like the ocean whistling through the trees.

After a few hundred yards, check out the old waterworks▶2 on the right-hand side, where the trail joins the Firehole River. The road becomes asphalt as the trail traces the east bank of the river upstream. Mature mixed conifer forest surrounds the route on all sides. There's a dampness in the air and green mosses in the understory as the river passes under a bridge and calms upstream. Watch for steaming thermal features off-trail in the woods to the right. Note the saplings growing up through the roadbed.

Stay on the road where the **Spring Creek Trail**▶3 joins in from the left after 1.6 miles. At 2 miles, follow the road as it jogs left at an abandoned service road.▶4

 Geothermal

You may hear **Lone Star Geyser** before you actually see it. During its steam phase between eruptions, it can be heard as far as a mile away. Less than a hundred yards after the road ends,▶5 you'll see the impressive 12-foot-tall geyserite cone.▶6 Major eruptions happen like clockwork, every three hours on average, with significant preplay in between. The eruptions can reach up to 45 feet and usually last

Larry Van Dyke

Lone Star Geyser *erupts roughly every three hours (Trails 25, 29, and 32).*

from 20 to 30 minutes. Check the NPS logbook near the bridge over the runoff channel to read reports of recent activity.

After the eruption, retrace your steps on the paved road back to the trailhead. ►7

 MILESTONES

►1 0.0 Start at Lone Star trailhead/Kepler Cascades parking lots
►2 0.2 Old Firehole River waterworks
►3 1.6 Keep right at Spring Creek Trail junction
►4 2.0 Keep left at abandoned service road
►5 2.4 End of paved road; bicycle parking area
►6 2.5 Lone Star Geyser
►7 5.0 Return to parking area

OPTIONS

Howard Eaton Trail

You can **avoid the crowds** en route to Lone Star Geyser by starting out from the Old Faithful area at the Howard Eaton trailhead. The route—part of the Continental Divide National Scenic Trail—is actually less scenic and a bit longer (5.8 miles round-trip), which is why you should have it all to yourself.

Backcountry Camping

The three campsites just beyond Lone Star Geyser on the Shoshone Lake Trail are perfect places for a family to spend a first night in the backcountry. **Campsite OA1** is 2.9 miles from the Lone Star trailhead; it allows stock parties. The hiker-only sites **OA2** and **OA3** are 0.4 and 1.2 miles farther along. All these sites allow campfires.

Spray Geyser *erupts even more frequently than its neighbor, Imperial Geyser, and is just as entertaining (Trail 28).*

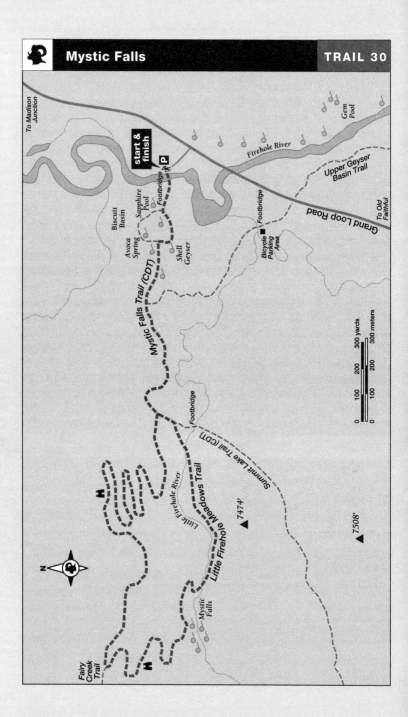

Mystic Falls

To Madison Junction

Gem Pool

start & finish

P

Firehole River

Upper Geyser Basin Trail

Footbridge

Grand Loop Road

To Old Faithful

Biscuit Basin

Sapphire Pool

Avoca Spring

Shell Geyser

Footbridge

Bicycle Parking Area

Mystic Falls Trail (CDT)

Footbridge

Summit Lake Trail (CDT)

300 yards
300 meters
0   100   200   300

Little Firehole River

Meadows Trail

Little Firehole

7474'

7508'

N

Fairy Creek Trail

Mystic Falls

Mystic Falls

This dayhike is popular thanks to its proximity to Old Faithful, and it offers easy access to a pretty backcountry cascade. Complete the full loop to leave the crowds behind and for an expansive overview of the Upper Geyser Basin.

Best Time

The flat, out-and-back option to the base of the falls is enjoyable anytime from May to October. Since there's a lack of shade, on sunny days the full loop should be done outside of midday hours.

Finding the Trail

From the south, go 2 miles north on the Grand Loop Road from the Old Faithful overpass and turn left into the Biscuit Basin Boardwalk parking area on the west side of the road. From the north, go 13.5 miles south from Madison Junction on the Grand Loop Road and turn right. The Mystic Falls trailhead is across the Firehole River Bridge, on the far side of the boardwalk loop, 0.3 mile west of the parking lot.

Logistics

Rangers offer free, guided, 90-minute walks daily during summer. The trips depart at 8 AM from the Firehole River Bridge, adjacent to the Biscuit Basin parking lot. You can also bicycle the 2 miles from Old Faithful to within 0.5 mile of the trailhead, via the Upper Geyser Basin Trail, but you'll have to walk the last stretch.

TRAIL USE
Hike
LENGTH
4.0 miles, 2–3 hours
VERTICAL FEET
±500 to falls,
±1000' for loop
DIFFICULTY
– 1 2 **3** 4 5 +
TRAIL TYPE
Loop
SURFACE TYPE
Boardwalk and Dirt

FEATURES
Child Friendly
Canyon
Stream
Waterfall
Wildflowers
Great Views
Photo Opportunity
Geothermal
Steep

FACILITIES
None

Trail Description

More than a quarter of the world's geysers are concentrated in the Upper Geyser Basin, which is home to about 150 spouting hydrothermal features.

From the **Biscuit Basin** parking lot,▶1 cross the Firehole River footbridge and follow the south side of the boardwalk loop▶2 clockwise (left) past several notable geysers and hot springs. Before you reach **Avoca Spring**, watch for a wide, sandy trail▶3 that heads off the boardwalk to your left, into the regenerating lodgepole pine forest. It's often unsigned, but usually marked by orange blazes. Wildflowers such as lupines, fireweed, and Indian paintbrush bloom prolifically here thanks to the 1988 fires.

Beyond the boardwalk, the nearly flat route—part of the Continental Divide National Scenic Trail—parallels the north side of the **Little Firehole River**. Stay to the left at 0.6 mile when the trail is met by the return loop of the **Mystic Falls Trail**.▶4 You will return here in about an hour if you opt for the full loop.

 Wildflowers

Soon after, head uphill (right) at the **Summit Lake/Little Firehole Meadows Trail junction**,▶5 near the mouth of the Little Firehole River canyon; you've missed the turnoff if you cross the river on the footbridge. The trail climbs gradually up into the canyon above the north side of the river for 0.5 mile to the base of **Mystic Falls**.▶6 Steam and orange algae blooms indicate abundant thermal seeps in the runoff.

 Waterfall

While the multitiered, 70-foot cascade is enchanting from below, it's best admired from above. You can either turn around here, making the

Out & Back Picnic Option

OPTIONS

The family-friendly, out-and-back option to the base of the falls involves 500 feet of elevation gain and takes a little over an hour round-trip. Figure on at least an extra half-hour for a picnic and short climb to the top of the falls.

hike an hour total, or continue the loop by climbing several hundred feet of switchbacks in a little less than a mile, to a worthwhile overlook of Old Faithful and the Upper Geyser Basin.

Steep

About 600 yards up the trail, there's a nice **overlook**▶7 near the top of the falls. The route continues climbing up through a regenerating lodgepole burn area to the **Fairy Creek/Little Firehole Meadows Trail junction.**▶8

Turn right, crest the ridge atop the Madison Plateau, and descend to the **Biscuit Basin Overlook**▶9 for an impressive overview of the aftermath of the 1988 fires and the entire Upper Geyser Basin. With decent binoculars, you can enjoy a good bird's-eye view of several major active geysers, including Old Faithful.

Great Views

From the overlook, the trail descends via switchbacks more than 500 feet over 0.9 mile to rejoin the **Mystic Falls Trail.**▶10 Fork left at the now-familiar junction and retrace your steps back through Biscuit Basin to the parking area.▶11

🚶 MILESTONES

▶1 0.0 Start at Biscuit Basin trailhead parking lot

▶2 0.2 Left at boardwalk loop junction

▶3 0.3 Left at unsigned Mystic Falls Trail junction

▶4 0.6 Left at Mystic Falls Trail loop junction

▶5 0.65 Right at Summit Lake/Little Firehole Meadows Trail junction

▶6 1.2 Mystic Falls

▶7 1.5 Mystic Falls Overlook

▶8 1.7 Right at Fairy Creek/Little Firehole Meadows Trail junction

▶9 2.5 Biscuit Basin Overlook

▶10 3.4 Mystic Falls Trail junction

▶11 4.0 Return to parking area

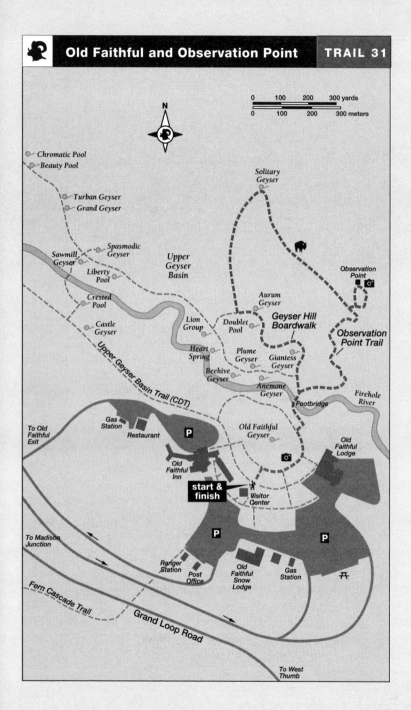

0   100   200   300 yards
0   100   200   300 meters

N

Chromatic Pool
Beauty Pool

Solitary
Geyser

Turban Geyser
Grand Geyser

Spasmodic
Geyser

Sawmill
Geyser

Liberty
Pool

Upper
Geyser
Basin

Observation
Point

Crested
Pool

Castle
Geyser

Lion
Group

Doublet
Pool

Aurum
Geyser

Geyser Hill
Boardwalk

Observation
Point Trail

Heart
Spring

Plume
Geyser

Giantess
Geyser

Beehive
Geyser

Anemone
Geyser

Firehole
River

Footbridge

Upper Geyser Basin Trail (CDT)

Gas
Station

Restaurant

P

Old Faithful
Geyser

Old
Faithful
Lodge

To Old
Faithful
Exit

Old
Faithful
Inn

start &
finish

Visitor
Center

P

To Madison
Junction

Ranger
Station

Post
Office

Old
Faithful
Snow
Lodge

Gas
Station

P

Fern Cascade Trail

Grand Loop Road

To West
Thumb

Old Faithful and Observation Point

For most folks, Old Faithful is a must-see. If you haven't seen the most famous geyser in the world's most active geyser basin, can you really say that you've been to Yellowstone? Here's how to gain an uncommon perspective on the iconic grand dame.

Best Time

Any time of day is a wonderful time to see her majesty in action. The boardwalks are accessible year-round, while the loop trail is typically hikable from May through October. Make sure to time your visit with an eruption (the average interval hovers around 90 minutes) by checking the predicted schedule with rangers at the Visitor Center.

Finding the Trail

From the north, go south from Madison Junction on the Grand Loop Road for 15.5 miles to the Old Faithful exit. From the east, go 17 miles west from West Thumb on the Grand Loop Road over Craig Pass (8262'). After exiting from either direction, follow signs from the overpass for about a mile to the Visitor Center and Old Faithful geyser parking areas.

Logistics

The **Old Faithful Visitor Center** posts eruption prediction schedules for five major geysers (Castle, Daisy, Grand, Old Faithful, and Riverside) in the Upper Geyser Basin. Predictions are also made for Great Fountain, 8 miles north of Old Faithful off

TRAIL USE
Hike
LENGTH
2.4 miles, 1.5 hours
VERTICAL FEET
±250'
DIFFICULTY
– 1 **2** 3 4 5 +
TRAIL TYPE
Loop
SURFACE TYPE
Dirt

FEATURES
Child Friendly
Handicap Accessible
Steep
Great Views
Photo Opportunity
Geothermal
Moonlight Hiking

FACILITIES
Visitor Center
Restrooms
Picnic Tables
Phone
Water

What To Do Before an Eruption?

If you've got time to burn before the next anticipated eruption, there are several intriguing options. The **Visitor Center** shows a film that gives a general introduction to the park, starting 30 minutes before an eruption is predicted. Another film about the inner workings of Old Faithful screens 15 minutes after each flare-up.

Morgan Konn

Or grab a drink from the bar or espresso cart on the mezzanine level of the **Old Faithful Inn** and—if you can stand the diesel fumes from the idling buses—sit out on the deck and watch the geyser warm up. In the captivating lobby, pick up a self-guiding brochure from the Inn's front desk, then check out the massive central fireplace and interior stylings of "parkitecture" pioneer Robert C. Reamer. Stairs in the rustic rafters shown above climb to the "Crows Nest."

Firehole Lake Drive, in the Lower Geyser Basin. These predictions are also posted at Old Faithful's lodgings and at the Madison Information Station.

All predictions are estimates; Old Faithful's performance intervals, for example, have varied historically from 45 to 120 minutes, with the current average time frame running 65 to 95 minutes.

Geothermal

If the next eruption is predicted (not scheduled!) for less than 30 minutes after you arrive, start the hike to Observation Point straight away. Otherwise, grab a snack or drink, and check out the lobby of the Inn or the Visitor Center's displays and short films. In any case, allow at least 20 to 30 minutes for the short but aerobic climb to the overlook.

Trail Description

From the northwest side of the parking lot, ▶1 follow signs to the **Visitor Center**, ▶2 and check the predicted eruption times so you can plan the best hiking strategy.

From the Visitor Center, find the plastic-lumber **boardwalk** ▶3 circling **Old Faithful**, and follow it counterclockwise (right) for a few hundred yards. Branch right to leave the boardwalk at the signed turnoff for the **Observation Point Trail**, ▶4 which soon crosses the **Firehole River** on a wooden footbridge. ▶5

Soon after the bridge, head uphill to your right on the dirt path ▶6 where the left fork leads to the **Geyser Hill** boardwalk loop. A bit of hard breathing and 0.5 mile later, take the signed right fork of the **Observation Point loop trail** ▶7 up to the overlook ▶8 for an expansive panorama of the Upper Geyser Basin. Catch your breath, check your

> Named for its predictability by the Washburn Expedition in 1870, Old Faithful's average interval between eruptions has lengthened due to earthquakes and vandalism, but it remains as predictable as it was over a century ago. Its outbursts last anywhere from 90 seconds to 5 minutes, reach heights of 106 to 184 feet, and expel 3700 to 8400 gallons of boiling water.

Geysers Galore

Unrepentant geyser gazers who can't get enough have plenty of exciting options for extending the hike from Old Faithful. It's possible to follow a network of boardwalks and paved bike paths—part of the **Continental Divide National Scenic Trail**—northwest for 2 miles, beyond **Geyser Hill** past the predictable **Grand** and **Riverside geysers** (90 minutes to 2 hours round-trip, including time for gazing), to the much-ogled **Morning Glory Pool**.

NOTES

Overheard on the
Geyser Hill boardwalk:
"Mom, are we done
with the hot stuff yet?"

watch, and find a comfortable spot with an unobstructed view of the activity below.

Heading back downhill, complete the Observation Point loop and turn right at the bottom of the hill. ▶9 Next, traverse 0.3 mile of mixed open forest—such good bear habitat that the trail is sometimes closed—to reach **Solitary Geyser**. ▶10 Solitary began its life as a hot spring, but morphed into a gusher after its water was diverted for use in a swimming pool in the 1940s. Today, the ex-spring spouts up to 15 feet every four to eight minutes.

Urban Legend

A group of bored seasonal employees once received a severe reprimand from the NPS after they engaged in a clever bit of street theater. A few minutes before Old Faithful was predicted to erupt, they rolled out a large red wagon wheel and pretended that they were cranking open the geyser's subterranean plumbing so that the crucial H_2O would appear, mocking visitors' expectations of timeliness.

On Demand?

In the height of summer, it's not uncommon to witness impatient crowds of spectators clapping in unison to urge the geyser on, while complaining that their bus might leave if the darn thing doesn't perform as scheduled.

Head 0.3 mile downhill to the **Geyser Hill boardwalk**▶11 junction. The level, wheelchair-accessible boardwalk winds past named and unnamed active geysers, including several near-perpetual spouters. Interpretive signs and self-guided trail brochures explain some of the intriguing hydrothermal phenomena.

When you're ready to conclude your hike, head back on the boardwalk toward Old Faithful. Where the Geyser Hill boardwalk ends, continue straight ahead on the paved walkway to return to the Firehole River footbridge.▶12 Retrace your steps clockwise on the boardwalk▶13 around Old Faithful—she may well be poised to erupt again—back to the Visitor Center▶14 and parking lot.▶15

Though probably Yellowstone's most famous, Old Faithful is neither the largest nor most regular geyser in the park. The largest active geyser in the world is Steamboat Geyser in the Norris Geyser Basin (see Trail 18).

🚶 MILESTONES

▶1   0.0 Start at Old Faithful parking lot

▶2   0.1 Visitor Center and restrooms

▶3   0.2 Counterclockwise (right) around Old Faithful boardwalk

▶4   0.3 Right onto Observation Point trail

▶5   0.35 Firehole River Bridge

▶6   0.4 Right at Geyser Hill Trail boardwalk junction

▶7   0.9 Right onto Observation Point loop trail

▶8   1.0 Observation Point overlook

▶9   1.1 Right at Geyser Hill Trail junction

▶10 1.4 Left (downhill) from Solitary Geyser

▶11 1.7 Left at Geyser Hill boardwalk junction

▶12 1.9 Straight at end of boardwalk to Firehole River footbridge

▶13 2.0 Left (clockwise) around Old Faithful boardwalk

▶14 2.3 Visitor Center

▶15 2.4 Return to parking lot

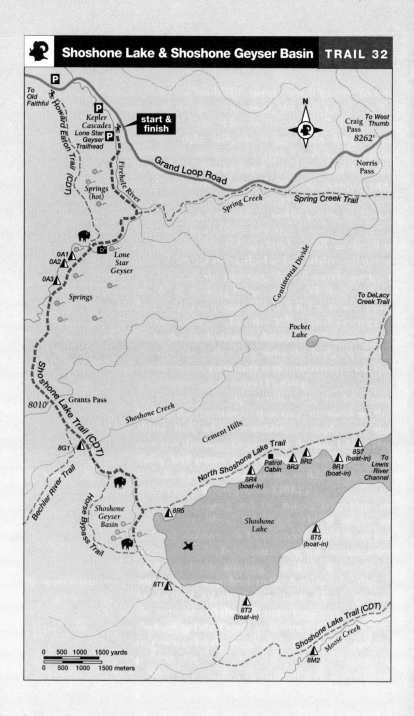

Shoshone Lake and Shoshone Geyser Basin

With no road access, forest-lined Shoshone Lake is the largest backcountry lake in the Lower 48 US states. An amazing geyser basin, good fishing, boat-in camping, and the possibility of extended backpacking and kayaking trips add to the allure. Nearly a third of all the park's backcountry use is concentrated around the lake.

Best Time

Lewis and Shoshone lakes are usually ice-free by the second or third week in June. Grant's Pass (8000'), between Lone Star Geyser and the west end of Shoshone Lake, typically isn't free of snow until late June or early July. Early-season flooding is common at some lakefront campsites, so many sites aren't available for reservation before July 1 or July 15. Contact a backcountry office for current conditions and for early-season walk-up permits. If you're planning a late-season trip, say for October, monitor the weather carefully.

Finding the Trail

From the north, head 2.5 miles south on the Grand Loop Road from the Old Faithful overpass, and turn right into the Lone Star Geyser parking lot on the south side of the road. From the southeast, go 14.5 miles west from West Thumb Junction over Craig Pass (8262') and turn left into the parking lot. The trailhead parking area is just south of the Kepler Cascades turnout, which is a parking alternative if the Lone Star lot is full.

TRAIL USE
Hike, Backpack
LENGTH
17.0 miles, 2–5 days
VERTICAL FEET
±600'
DIFFICULTY
– 1 2 3 4 **5** +
TRAIL TYPE
Out & Back
SURFACE TYPE
Dirt

FEATURES
Backcountry Permit
Stream
Lake
Autumn Colors
Birds
Wildflowers
Wildlife
Great Views
Photo Opportunity
Camping
Geothermal

FACILITIES
Patrol Cabin
Boat Launch

Logistics

The Shoshone Lake Trail is part of the Continental Divide Trail system, which links 3100 miles of America's most wild and dramatic back-country. Beyond Shoshone Lake, it continues southeast to Heart Lake, the Snake River head-waters, and into the Teton Wilderness.

Shoshone Lake has more boat-in campsites than hike-in sites. Wood fires are banned along the entire lakeshore; only campsite 8M2, well away from the lake, allows fires. All campsites have primitive toilets and a party limit of eight people, except 8T1, which is limited to one tent and four humans.

Boat access is via the boat dock at Lewis Lake Campground and the 3.5-mile Lewis River Channel, which enters Shoshone Lake at its southeast corner. This channel is very popular, since it's the only waterway in the park where motorized vessels are allowed. Mandatory boating permits ($5) are only available at the South Entrance, Grant Village, and Bridge Bay backcountry offices. See the appendix for locations and contact information of all the back-country offices.

Trail Description

From the **Lone Star trailhead,** **1** an abandoned service road heads south along the upper Firehole River. After passing the remains of an old water-works, the paved road traces the east bank of the river as it heads upstream.

 Geothermal

After passing the Spring Creek Trail junction ▶2 at 1.6 miles, you may hear **Lone Star Geyser** ▶3 before you see it. For a detailed description of the geyser and environs, see Trail 29, page 229.

Wildlife

A few hundred yards beyond the geyser basin, turn left after 2.7 miles at the well-signed **Shoshone Lake Trail junction,** ▶4 where bison are often spotted wallowing around thermal areas in view of the trail. If you are planning an extended trip, there are three decent first-night trailside campsites in the next 1.5 miles.

First up, the wide-open **campsite OA1** ▶5 is the only one which allows stock parties. Four hundred yards downtrail across the Upper Firehole River, campsite **OA2**▶6 is the best choice. Almost a mile farther upstream at 4.1 miles, **campsite OA3**▶7 is near Firehole Springs, the only site in this group that doesn't allow wood fires. Beyond here, the trail leaves the river and starts to climb up through unburned forest to the **Continental Divide**, reaching unsigned **Grants Pass** (8010') at the 6-mile mark.▶8

 Camping

Soon after the anticlimactic pass, you drop down along an upper fork of **Shoshone Creek** to the signed **Bechler River Trail junction**.▶9 The hiker- and llama-only **campsite 8G1**▶10 (no wood fires) is a hundred yards off-trail to the right, in Shoshone Meadows, 6.5 miles from the trailhead.

Watch for moose as you descend along and cross over Shoshone Creek on a footbridge. A mile downhill from the junction, keep to the main trail; don't take the signed **horse bypass trail** that forks off across a footbridge to the right (it loops 2.2 miles around to the south side of Shoshone Geyser Basin).▶11

 Wildlife

Continue down the pretty drainage for another mile to the **North Shoshone Lake Trail junction**,▶12

Birds

CAUTION

Boating Safety on Shoshone Lake

Frequent high winds and extremely cold water (which is often 40° to 50°F, and rarely warms above 60°F) pose serious challenges for canoeists and kayakers on the 8000-acre lake. Suitable bailing and personal flotation devices are required at all times. Avoid open-water crossings, and travel close to the shore and in the early morning and late afternoon when winds are calmer for maximum safety.

It's not possible to paddle upstream for the northernmost mile of the Lewis River channel. Instead, you must wade through up to 3 to 4 feet of cold water and drag your boat through the rocky-bottomed stream. Motors are allowed for crossing Lewis Lake, but must be left at the south end of the channel. Finally, the NPS suggests that boat-in campers select a site on the southern lakeshore for the first night of any trip.

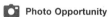
8.3 miles from the trailhead. The left fork, which contours above the lake's north shore and past the splendid hiker-only **campsite 8R5** fronting Basin Point Bay, is officially called the North Shoshone Lake Trail, but is known more casually as the North Shore Trail.

Following the right fork of the main Shoshone Lake Trail, you pass through a marshy area and soon arrive at the extraordinary and very volatile **Shoshone Geyser Basin.▶13** Unlike heavily visited frontcountry geyser basins, there's a notable absence of boardwalks, railings, and signage here. Please tread lightly through the fragile thermal areas: Help to keep the basin pristine by using common sense and keeping your wits about you as you explore the captivating thermal features rarely found so near the trail.

Besides the aforementioned campsite 8R5, trailside, hiker-only **campsite 8T1** (one tent and four person limit) is the closest to the basin, a few hun-

---

🚶 MILESTONES

▶1 0.0 Start at Kepler Cascades turnout/Lone Star trailhead parking lots

▶2 1.6 Right at Spring Creek Trail junction

▶3 2.5 Lone Star Geyser

▶4 2.7 Left at Shoshone Lake Trail junction

▶5 2.9 Campsite OA1

▶6 3.3 Campsite OA2

▶7 4.1 Campsite OA3

▶8 6.0 Grants Pass

▶9 6.4 Left at Bechler River/Shoshone Lake Trail junction

▶10 6.5 Campsite 8G1

▶11 7.4 Stay on main trail at Horse Bypass Trail junction

▶12 8.3 Right at North Shoshone Lake (North Shore) Trail

▶13 8.5 Shoshone Geyser Basin

▶14 17.0 Return to Lone Star trailhead parking lots

dred yards south of the junction of the horse bypass trail and the trail along the south shore. If you can't secure a reservation at one of these two popular sites, it's another 3 miles in either direction to the next options.

Lake

Our trail description ends here, but, depending on how many days you have to experience this fascinating area, your explorations should just be beginning. Once you've finished relaxing, fishing, watching the myriad wildlife and waterfowl, and enjoying the lake, retrace your steps to the northwest on the Shoshone Lake Trail, back to the Lone Star trailhead.▶14

Alternate Trailheads and Camping Options

A four- or five-day trip from the **Lone Star trailhead** allows for plenty of recreation time during an easygoing loop of the entire lake. You can cut the loop short with a car shuttle and an early exit via either the **DeLacy Creek** or **Dogshead trailheads**. A popular, longer point-to-point backpacking trip around the south side of the lake (3 to 5 days and 25 miles) involves a car shuttle between the Lone Star and DeLacy Creek trailheads.

The **DeLacy Creek trailhead**, about halfway between Old Faithful and West Thumb Junction, provides the most direct access to **Shoshone Lake**. The hike to the north lakeshore is 4 to 5 hours and 6 miles round-trip, with 200 feet of elevation loss on the way down.

There are a total of three trail-accessible, five boat-in, and two mixed hiking-boating campsites along the **north shore**. The **south shore** has eight boat-in sites, one tent-only site, and one two-party, hiking-boating site at the head of the Lewis River Channel. The remaining two trail-accessible sites (8M1 and 8M2) are well removed from the south shore and are shared with stock parties.

Guided DeLacy Creek Adventure Hike

During the summer, rangers occasionally lead popular half-day "adventure hikes" ($15 fee) to Shoshone Lake from the DeLacy Creek trailhead.

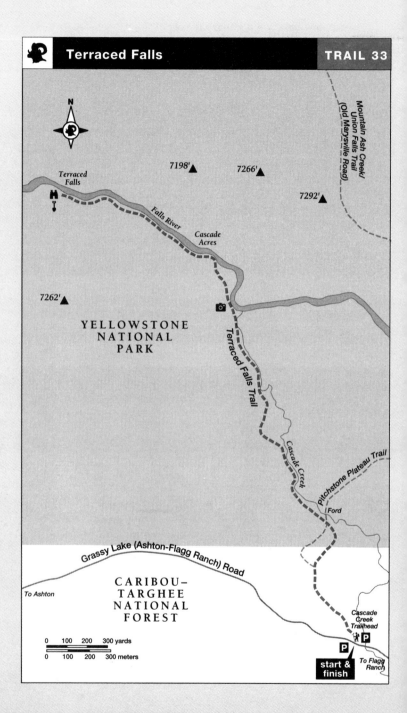

N

Terraced
Falls

7198' ▲   7266' ▲

Mountain Ash Creek/
Union Falls Trail
(Old Marysville Road)

7292' ▲

Falls River

Cascade
Acres

7262' ▲

YELLOWSTONE
NATIONAL
PARK

Terraced Falls Trail

Cascade Creek

Pitchstone Plateau Trail

Ford

Grassy Lake (Ashton-Flagg Ranch) Road

To Ashton

CARIBOU–
TARGHEE
NATIONAL
FOREST

0   100   200   300 yards
0   100   200   300 meters

Cascade
Creek
Trailhead

P   P

start &
finish

To Flagg
Ranch

Terraced Falls

This remote trail is difficult to access but once you're there, it's a fairly level, short hike and offers an up-close look at one of the Cascade Corner's bigger multitier waterfalls, set in a dramatic, volcano-forged canyon. If you're already in the area, it's a great late-season option and combines nicely with an overnight trip to Union Falls.

Best Time

There are no fords, so theoretically the trail can be hiked from about mid-June through October. In reality, the Grassy Lake access road is often rough going during the wet season, and like the rest of the Bechler region, it can be quite buggy until August. Grassy Lake Road closes for the winter as soon as snow levels make keeping the road open impractical. It's most enjoyable when fall colors peak, around the autumnal equinox.

Finding the Trail

From Yellowstone's South Entrance, go 2.5 miles south and turn right at Flagg Ranch. Follow the signs for Grassy Lake Road (called Ashton-Flagg Ranch Road, Reclamation Road, or USFS Road 261 on older maps). Drive west through the John D. Rockefeller Jr. Memorial Parkway (administered by Grand Teton National Park) along a decent graded gravel road, past eight free, primitive campgrounds. After 9 miles, without much fanfare, the road enters the Caribou-Targhee National Forest and rapidly deteriorates. Depending on the season, the stretch near the

TRAIL USE
Hike
LENGTH
3.6 miles, 1–2 hours
VERTICAL FEET
±250'
DIFFICULTY
– 1 **2** 3 4 5 +
TRAIL TYPE
Out & Back
SURFACE TYPE
Dirt

FEATURES
Child Friendly
Canyon
Stream
Waterfall
Autumn Colors
Cool & Shady
Great Views
Photo Opportunity
Secluded
Geologic

FACILITIES
None

251

Cascade Acres

reservoir can be easy going or a spine-jarring washboard and riddled with huge, tire-eating potholes.

Fortunately, the Cascade Creek trailhead is only 1.5 miles beyond the dam, on the northwest end of Grassy Lake Reservoir, on your right-hand (north) side. If the small trailhead parking area is full (not likely), there's a large parking area directly across the road, with free dispersed camping among the lodgepole pines.

From the west in Ashton, Idaho, it's an even rougher, 60-mile scramble over gravel Forest Service roads. Part of the route follows an old wagon trail and often it feels that way!

The Terraced Falls overlook sits atop the geographic limit of Yellowstone's Cascade Corner. It straddles the edge of lava flows that ended here approximately 70,000 years ago.

Trail Description

From the NPS-signed **Cascade Creek trailhead▶1** in the Caribou-Targhee National Forest, the little-used but well-maintained trail descends gently through lodgepole pine forest for 0.3 mile to the southern **Yellowstone National Park boundary.▶2** The boundary is indicated both by posted signs and an unexpected, 10-foot-wide clear-cut maintained by NPS boundary patrols.

Alternative Trailhead and Overnight Options

OPTIONS

This trip is easily combined with an overnight stay near **Union Falls** (see Trail 34), or added to the beginning or end of a long romp over the wild **Pitchstone Plateau**. Depending on the status of ongoing construction around Grassy Lake Reservoir, the **Grassy Lake trailhead**, 1.5 miles to the east, may be an alternative starting point. This last option would add 300 feet of elevation gain and 3.2 miles to the trip.

From the junction with the Terraced Falls Trail, the Pitchstone Plateau cutoff trail leads 0.8 mile to backcountry **campsite 9F2**, near the junction for the Mountain Ash Creek Trail to Union Falls.

A few hundred yards beyond a notice board—which posts NPS regulations, bear safety information, and useful details about the Bechler's tricky river fords—our route meets a **cutoff trail** to the Pitchstone Plateau,▶3 which begins across an easy ford of **Cascade Creek**.

No stock use is permitted on the **Terraced Falls Trail**, which begins here as the left fork of the junction just before Cascade Creek. The trail winds through mixed lodgepole pine stands as it traces the west bank of Cascade Creek, which joins the Falls River in 0.6 mile at a beautiful **confluence**.▶4

A little less than halfway to the overlook, stop to admire the long set of rapids known as **Cascade Acres**. Although the Falls River isn't always in view for the final 0.7 mile to the picture-perfect **Terraced Falls overlook**,▶5 it's almost always within earshot.

The maintained trail dead-ends at the overlook. The river continues flowing downstream through a rugged canyon to plunge over inaccessible Rainbow Falls and eventually meets the Bechler River just upstream from Cave Falls, near the Bechler Ranger Station.

After you've finished picnicking and exploring around the falls, retrace your steps to return to the trailhead parking area.▶6

📷 **Photo Opportunity**

🏔 **Waterfall**

🚶	MILESTONES

▶1 0.0 Start at Cascade Creek trailhead

▶2 0.3 Straight at Yellowstone National Park boundary

▶3 0.5 Left on Terraced Falls Trail just before Cascade Creek ford

▶4 1.1 Cascade Creek/Falls River confluence

▶5 1.8 Terraced Falls overlook

▶6 3.6 Return to trailhead parking area

Union Falls *is one of Yellowstone's tallest plunges and one of the most beautiful falls in the backcountry (Trail 34).*

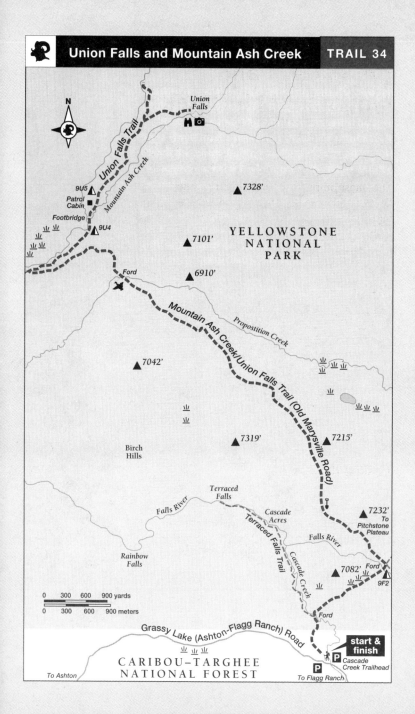

Union Falls and Mountain Ash Creek   TRAIL 34

Union Falls

YELLOWSTONE
NATIONAL
PARK

Union Falls Trail

9U5
Patrol Cabin
Footbridge
9U4

Mountain Ash Creek

▲ 7328'

▲ 7101'

Ford

▲ 6910'

Mountain Ash Creek/Union Falls Trail (Old Marysville Road)

Propostition Creek

▲ 7042'

▲ 7319'

▲ 7215'

Birch Hills

Terraced Falls

Falls River

Cascade Acres

Terraced Falls Trail

Rainbow Falls

Cascade Creek

Falls River

▲ 7232'
To Pitchstone Plateau

▲ 7082'   Ford
9F2

| 0 | 300 | 600 | 900 yards |
| 0 | 300 | 600 | 900 meters |

Grassy Lake (Ashton–Flagg Ranch) Road

Ford

start & finish
Cascade Creek Trailhead

CARIBOU–TARGHEE
NATIONAL FOREST

To Ashton

To Flagg Ranch

Union Falls and Mountain Ash Creek

The most impressive backcountry waterfall in Greater Yellowstone, along with a sublime swimming hole, await at the end of this hearty daylong hike. A couple of campsites near Union Falls allow for an easygoing overnight trip.

Best Time

Like most of the Cascade Corner, it's buggy and wet here until early August. Things dry out by late summer, but the falls are most impressive during the first half of July. The 9U group of campsites, all within five miles of the falls, don't dry out until early July. The heaviest trail usage happens before Labor Day, when scouting troops and day-trippers on horseback are out in force. Depending on the weather, October can be a wonderful time to hike here.

Finding the Trail

Getting to the trailhead is half the fun: From Yellowstone's South Entrance, go 2.5 miles south and turn right at Flagg Ranch. Follow the signs for Grassy Lake Road (called Ashton-Flagg Ranch Road, Reclamation Road, or USFS Road 261 on older maps).

Continue 9 miles west through the John D. Rockefeller Jr. Memorial Parkway area (administered by Grand Teton National Park) along the decent, graded gravel road past eight free primitive campgrounds. At 9 miles, without much fanfare, the road enters the Caribou-Targhee National Forest and begins to rapidly deteriorate. Depending on the

TRAIL USE
Hike, Backpack, Horse

LENGTH
15.8 miles, 8-10 hours

VERTICAL FEET
±1800'

DIFFICULTY
– 1 2 3 4 **5** +

TRAIL TYPE
Out & Back

SURFACE TYPE
Dirt

FEATURES
Backcountry Permit
Canyon
Stream
Waterfall
Autumn Colors
Photo Opportunity
Camping
Swimming
Secluded
Geothermal

FACILITIES
Horse Staging

season, the stretch around the reservoir can be easy going or a spine-jarring washboard and riddled with huge, tire-eating potholes.

Fortunately, the Cascade Creek trailhead is only 1.5 miles beyond the dam, on the northwest end of Grassy Lake Reservoir, on your right-hand (north) side. If the small trailhead parking area is full (not likely), there's a large parking area directly across the road, with free dispersed camping among the lodgepole pines.

From the west in Ashton, Idaho, it's an even rougher 60-mile scramble over gravel Forest Service roads. The road follows an old wagon route, and often it feels that way!

Logistics

The Yellowstone Park Foundation is working with the NPS and Montana Youth Conservation Corps to restore the tread of a flood-damaged section of trail a mile south of Union Falls. In addition to new drainage and erosion-control structures, some minor rerouting could occur.

Trail Description

Beyond the **Cascade Creek trailhead**▶1, the first 0.3 mile of trail descends gradually through the Caribou-Targhee National Forest to a sign for the south boundary of **Yellowstone National Park,**▶2 also indicated by an unexpected, 10-foot-wide clear-cut maintained by NPS boundary patrols.

A few hundred yards beyond a notice board—which post NPS regulations, bear safety information, and useful details about the Bechler's tricky river fords—our trail meets the **Terraced Falls Trail,**▶3 (see Trail 33, page 251). The **Cascade Creek ford** here is short and shallow, if ice-cold.

Beyond the ford, the trail crests a short, forested ridge then drops back down through willow-choked marshland to a junction with the **Mountain Ash Creek Trail**, above the **Falls River ford**.▶4 This ford, at 1.2 miles, is 50 feet wide and the thigh-high current can be quite swift through July. Later in the season, it's an easy, if slippery, less-than-knee-high crossing; bring wading shoes and a stick or trekking pole. By mid-September, it's barely calf-high.

The **Pitchstone Plateau Trail junction**,▶5 also the turnoff for **campsite 9F2**, is immediately beyond the ford. Forking left towards Union Falls, it's a steady climb several hundred feet away from the river, onto a forested plateau. As the sounds of the river fade, the trail levels off in a mature stand of mixed conifers.

 Camping

As a valley opens up to the left, watch for shiny black volcanic rock to start showing up under foot. It's a rocky descent down an open slope, along an old 1880s wagon road route, to **Proposition Creek**,▶6 at 4.9 miles from the trailhead. Blue jays flit about the fir-spruce forest around the two easy fords here. Don't be surprised by the chipmunks trawling the dense underbrush for mushrooms alongside the trail in the fall. After 0.8 mile, you arrive at another junction overlooking **Mountain Ash Creek**,▶7 where the trail doubles back and makes a hard right upstream along the creek.

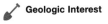 **Geologic Interest**

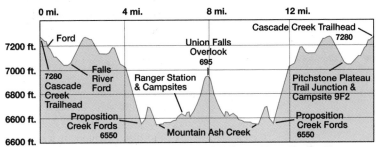

TRAIL 3 Union Falls and Mountain Ash Creek Elevation Profile

A half-mile along the south bank, look for a footbridge across the creek just before the signpost for the pleasant, hiker-only **campsite 9U4▶8** (wood fires allowed, two-night limit). The seasonal, **Union Falls Patrol Cabin▶9** is a few hundred yards beyond the bridge on the left-hand side, 6.4 miles from the trailhead. A spur trail heads several hundred yards off to the left to the equally pleasant **campsite 9U5 ▶10** (no wood fires, two-night limit), which is popular with stock parties. This site enjoys easy access to a shallow northern fork of Mountain Ash Creek that's warm enough for dipping in, and there's a large meadow out the front door; it's well worth the extra trek a few hundred yards off the trail.

Beyond the Ranger Station, it's a bit slow going on the sandy, horseworn trail for the next mile. Fortunately, only foot travel is allowed beyond the final unsigned fork▶11, where there's a horse hitching area.

The left fork, which deceptively appeared to be the main fork in late September 2004, dead-ends after 0.3 mile at an unnamed waterfall and sublime, lukewarm swimming hole known as **Ouzel Pool** (or **Scout Pool**, after the heavy use it receives by Boy Scout troops in midsummer). Carefully dog-paddle your way into a natural seat at the base of the falls to experience an indescribable natural whirlpool pummeling.

The unsigned right fork—which may still appear to be a mere runoff gully—winds around uphill for 0.5 mile to the **Union Falls▶12** overlook, 7.9 miles from the trailhead.

No doubt about it, the multifaceted 250-foot plunge is a real gusher. Just follow your ears toward the oceanlike sound: You'll hear it well before the falls come into view. Depending on the season, the precipitous, unmaintained path down to the base of the falls can be slick and treacherous, thanks to heavy mist from the falls.

Camping

Swimming

Waterfall

Photo Opportunity

If you can pull yourself away (it's getting late, no?) retrace your steps back to the Cascade Creek trailhead parking area. ▶13

MILESTONES

▶1 0.0 Cascade Creek trailhead

▶2 0.3 Yellowstone National Park boundary

▶3 0.4 Ford Cascade Creek at Terraced Falls trail junction

▶4 1.2 Falls River ford

▶5 1.3 Left at Pitchstone Plateau junction; campsite 9F2 turnoff

▶6 4.9 Proposition Creek fords

▶7 5.7 Right at Mountain Ash Creek Trail junction

▶8 6.2 Campsite 9U4

▶9 6.4 Union Falls Ranger Station

▶10 6.6 Campsite 9U5 spur trail

▶11 7.4 Right at unsigned horse-hitch junction

▶12 7.9 Union Falls

▶13 15.8 Return to Cascade Creek trailhead

Alternate Trailheads

OPTIONS

From the **Bechler Ranger Station trailhead**, it's 12.5 scenic, nearly flat miles one-way to Union Falls.

From the **Fish Lake trailhead**—0.5 miles down a very rough, high-clearance 4WD track off Grassy Lake Road—it's 7.8 level miles one-way to the falls, including a couple of significant river fords. The unmaintained track down to Fish Lake trailhead is mostly used by stock parties. The Fish Lake Trail itself passes by several pretty lakes and through a small but beautiful slice of the USFS-administered **Winegar Hole Wilderness** before entering Yellowstone NP. A couple of miles east of the **Cascade Creek trailhead** near Grassy Lake Reservoir, the **Grassy Lake trailhead** is a slightly longer and less scenic approach to the Union Falls Trail, which it joins at the Pitchstone Plateau Trail junction.

Grand Teton National Park

Grand Teton National Park

It's often said that the Teton Range is what mountains are supposed to look like. Indeed, the range is a textbook example of alpine topography and one of the most abrupt and iconic concentrations of rock and ice in the world, with its jagged peaks rising abruptly several thousand feet from Jackson Hole and the broad **Snake River Plain**.

As you traverse the sagebrush flats that dominate the valley floor, the trois **Tetons** appear to follow your eyes, like the **Mona Lisa**—a mesmerizing experience, no matter how many times you have laid eyes on them. In fact, the peaks' allure seems to grow with each new glimpse, as local climbers can attest.

If Yellowstone is primarily about spectacle (Old Faithful, bison photo-ops, dazzling thermal areas, charismatic megafauna, and so on), then the Teton experience is more active and participatory: In summer, it's all about hiking, climbing, fishing, floating, and mountaineering. In Yellowstone, it's easiest to observe wildlife alongside the roads, but in the Tetons your best bet is often to head for the backcountry. One distinct advantage is that the Tetons are blissfully bug free year-round, while Yellowstone can be quite the opposite in the early summer.

While the granitic peaks are the focal point of an international coterie of climbers, it's the lovely piedmont lakes and glacial canyons that attract legions of hikers to the park's 250 miles of trails each year. The hiking season runs from roughly May through October, depending on elevation and weather conditions. Snowfields usually disappear from valley trails by mid-June but linger on canyon trails and at higher elevations through the end of July. There's easily more than a summer's worth of world-class alpine and subalpine hiking and climbing here.

Since many more folks get out of their cars and hit the trails here than in Yellowstone, it pays to plan ahead, especially if you want to camp. During July and August, trailhead parking areas fill early, especially at South Jenny Lake, String Lake, Lupine Meadows, Death Canyon, and Granite Canyon. Get an early start and obey posted regulations to avoid parking tickets. Most trailheads don't have water or restrooms, so plan ahead.

265

The holy grail for hard-core backpackers is the high-altitude **Teton Crest Trail**, which traverses 40 exhilarating miles while straddling the range's rugged spine. The most popular stretch runs from **Rendezvous Mtn.** (10,450') in the south to **Paintbrush Divide** (10,720') and **String Lake** (6875') in the north. Due to the high elevation, the Crest Trail's short season runs from roughly mid-July to mid-September, with the first month or so being the best for wildflowers. Most people opt to do the hike in three to four nights, from south to north to take advantage of the high-level start and leave the most challenging sections for last. Even with a net 3575-foot elevation loss hiking south to north, there's still plenty of roller-coaster terrain along the way. For an even longer trip, it's possible to begin south of the park, on the eastern side of Teton Pass at the Ski Lake trailhead (7800'), in the Bridger-Teton National Forest.

The NPS administers an extensive system of primitive **backcountry campsites** in Grand Teton. Starting in the summer of 2005, the NPS will hand over management of the park's five developed, first-come, first-served **frontcountry campgrounds** ($15 per night, $5 per hiker/bicyclist site) to the Grand Teton Lodge Company and Signal Mountain Lodge. The contract calls for general site improvements, and future construction of badly needed shower and laundry facilities at the Gros Ventre and Signal Mountain campgrounds.

From most to least popular, frontcountry campgrounds include the tent-only **Jenny Lake** (50 sites, open mid-May to late September) popular with climbers; **Signal Mountain** (81 sites, open early May to mid-October) with an RV dump station and good views of Jackson Lake; chaotic **Colter Bay** (350 sites, open late May to late September), near services at Colter Village, with a separate RV park; secluded **Lizard Creek** (60 sites, open early June to early September), popular with boaters; and inconveniently located **Gros Ventre** (372 sites, open early May to mid-October), which has a dump station and is always the last to fill. The maximum stay in the park is 30 nights per year and 14 nights at each campground, except Jenny Lake, where it's 7 nights.

Just outside the park, the **Bridger-Teton National Forest** has some popular (but unreservable) camping options as well. These include free, primitive, dispersed sites north of the quaint settlement of Kelly on Shadow Mtn. (two-night limit); $12 sites in scenic Curtis Canyon, up a rough road 8 miles east of the National Elk Refuge; $5 primitive sites at Sheffield Creek just south of Flagg Ranch; and free, minimally developed sites spread out along the first 9 miles of the unpaved Grassy Lake Road, west of **Flagg Ranch.**

Overleaf: *Panorama of the Teton Range, looking west across Jackson Hole*

The best deal inside the park, hands down, are the unreservable dorm bunks ($10 per person) at the American Alpine Club's **Grand Teton Climbers' Ranch**, 4 miles north of the Moose Visitor Center off Teton Park Road. Call (307) 733-7271; www.americanalpineclub.org; open mid-June to mid-September.

See the Appendix for a summary of in-park lodging options (all non-smoking and without phones or TVs), most of which are open between May and October, weather depending.

Permits and Maps

All frontcountry campgrounds in Grand Teton National Park operate on a first-come, first-served basis (no reservations accepted); many campsites fill up by noon during the summer. None of the dayhikes in this chapter require permits.

All overnight trips require a **free backcountry camping permit**. One-third of the backcountry campsites are reservable in advance (applications accepted by mail, fax or in person from January 1 to May 15, for a non-refundable service fee of $15) while the rest are filled first come, first-served starting the first week of June at park permit offices. Download the park's Backcountry Camping brochure or contact the **Backcountry Permits Office** for details. Call (307) 739-3309 or (307) 739-3397.

The park headquarters are adjacent to the year-round **Moose Visitor Center**, where there's a 3-D relief map of the park and you can pick up permits, watch programs about the natural and cultural history of the park and buy a good range of books and maps. Phone (307) 739-3399; www.nps.gov/grte; open from 8 AM to 7 PM in summer, 8 AM to 5 PM the rest of the year. The **Jenny Lake Ranger Station** also issues permits and is the best place to get updates on backcountry hiking and climbing conditions. Phone (307) 739-3343; open daily from 8 AM to 7 PM in summer; with reduced spring and fall hours.

Nearby, the summer-only **Jenny Lake Visitor Center** has a bookstore, helpful staff, a 3-D map of Jackson Hole, and good interpretive geological displays. Phone (307) 739-3392; open daily from 8 AM to 7 PM, from June through September. On the east side of Jackson Lake, the **Colter Bay Visitor Center** also has a bookstore and issues permits. Phone (307) 739-3594; open daily from 8 AM to 7 PM in the summer, with reduced spring and fall hours. Next door is the worthwhile **Indian Arts Museum**.

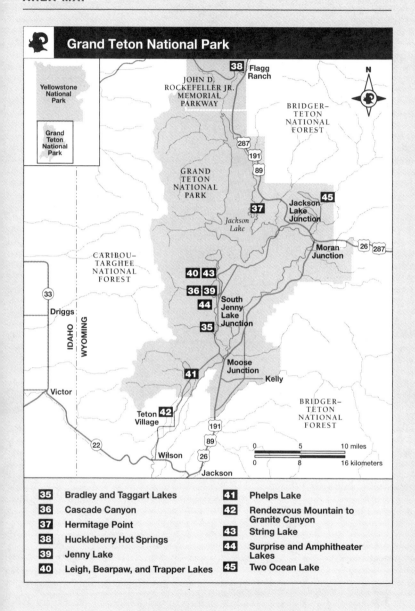

CHAPTER 6

Grand Teton National Park

35	Bradley and Taggart Lakes	41	Phelps Lake
36	Cascade Canyon	42	Rendezvous Mountain to Granite Canyon
37	Hermitage Point	43	String Lake
38	Huckleberry Hot Springs	44	Surprise and Amphitheater Lakes
39	Jenny Lake		
40	Leigh, Bearpaw, and Trapper Lakes	45	Two Ocean Lake

Grand Teton National Park

TRAIL	Difficulty	Length	Type	USES & ACCESS	TERRAIN	FLORA & FAUNA	OTHER
35	3	5.8		Hiking, Horses, Child Friendly	Lake	Autumn Colors, Wildflowers, Birds, Wildlife	Great Views, Moonlight Hiking
36	4	9.1		Hiking, Horses, Backpacking	Canyon, Lake, Stream, Waterfall	Autumn Colors, Wildflowers, Birds, Wildlife	Cool & Shady, Great Views, Photo Opportunity, Summit, Moonlight Hiking, Steep
37	4	9.4		Hiking, Horses, Backpacking, Child Friendly	Lake	Wildflowers, Birds, Wildlife	Cool & Shady, Great Views, Photo Opportunity, Summit
38	1	1.0		Hiking, Child Friendly	Stream	Birds, Wildlife	Swimming, Geothermal
39	3	7.0		Hiking, Horses, Handicap Access, Child Friendly	Canyon, Lake, Waterfall	Autumn Colors, Wildlife	Cool & Shady, Great Views, Photo Opportunity, Swimming
40	2/3	8.4		Hiking, Horses, Backpacking, Child Friendly	Lake	Autumn Colors, Wildflowers, Birds, Wildlife	Cool & Shady, Great Views, Photo Opportunity, Swimming
41	2/3	4.0		Hiking, Horses, Backpacking, Child Friendly	Lake, Stream	Autumn Colors, Wildflowers, Birds, Wildlife	Cool & Shady, Great Views, Photo Opportunity, Summit, Swimming
42	4/5	12.4		Hiking, Horses, Backpacking	Canyon, Mountain, Summit, Stream	Autumn Colors, Birds, Wildlife	Great Views, Photo Opportunity, Summit, Geologic Interest, Steep
43	2	3.4		Hiking, Horses, Handicap Access, Child Friendly	Lake, Stream	Autumn Colors, Wildflowers, Birds, Wildlife	Cool & Shady, Great Views, Photo Opportunity, Swimming, Geologic Interest
44	5	9.6		Hiking, Backpacking	Canyon, Mountain, Lake	Autumn Colors, Wildflowers, Birds, Wildlife	Great Views, Photo Opportunity, Summit, Geologic Interest, Steep
45	3/4	6.4		Hiking, Horses	Summit, Lake	Autumn Colors, Wildflowers, Birds, Wildlife	Great Views, Photo Opportunity, Secluded, Geologic Interest

USES & ACCESS
- Hiking
- Bicycling
- Horses
- Backpacking
- Child Friendly
- Handicap Access
- Backcountry Permit Required
- Camping

TERRAIN
- Canyon
- Mountain
- Summit
- Stream
- Waterfall
- Lake
- Geothermal

FLORA & FAUNA
- Autumn Colors
- Wildflowers
- Birds
- Wildlife

DIFFICULTY
- 1 2 3 4 5 +
less   more

OTHER
- Cool & Shady
- Great Views
- Photo Opportunity
- Swimming
- Secluded
- Historic
- Geologic Interest
- Moonlight Hiking
- Steep

Grand Teton National Park

This scenic, leisurely wander through regenerating lodgepole-pine forest is a great way to escape the crowds around Jenny Lake. Forested Bradley Lake provides a fine contrast to the burn areas around Taggart Lake, and the tranquil lakes teem with fish.

The confluence of several major climbing and back-packing trails, this challenging extension of the popular Jenny Lake and Hidden Falls route is the park's most popular and crowded canyon trail. Rightly so, since it's also one of the most beautiful and direct routes into the wild heart of the Tetons.

This rewarding lakefront jaunt is the perfect antidote to the crowds around Colter Bay Village. The forested habitat is varied, and the Teton views across Jackson Lake are superb. An overnight at the point, one of the park's best low-elevation campgrounds, makes a great first-time backcountry adventure.

One of Greater Yellowstone's worst kept secrets was once the site of a private campground. Thankfully, the undeveloped springs have reverted back to their natural state. They are a popular cross-country ski-ing destination in winter.

Jenny Lake 295

Yes, this must-see destination is the park's most popular dayhike—and it deserves all the attention it receives. The route is nearly flat, and you can catch an optional shuttle boat to Hidden Falls. Come at the right time, and the trail around the pretty lake might not even be crowded.

TRAIL 39

Hike, Horse
7.0 miles
Loop
Difficulty: 1 2 **3** 4 5

Leigh, Bearpaw, and Trapper Lakes .301

This family-friendly outing is easily extended into a stress-free overnighter. All three lakes are far away enough from the road to make you feel like you are in the backcountry. At midsummer, Leigh Lake is a favorite swimming hole and popular horseback-riding destination.

TRAIL 40

Hike, Backpack, Horse
8.4 miles, Out & Back
Difficulty: 1 **2** 3 4 5

Phelps Lake 305

This popular low-elevation outing climbs gently through shady, mature forest to a scenic overlook of a charming glacial lake. Fish and wildflowers are abundant, and the three lakefront campsites feel miles from the trailhead. Reserve ahead for an easy, family-friendly overnighter.

TRAIL 41

Hike, Backpack, Horse
4.0 miles, Out & Back
Difficulty: 1 **2** 3 4 5

Rendezvous Mountain to Granite Canyon 309

This route is spectacular—and 95 percent downhill—so it sees traffic whenever the weather is decent and the tram is in service. Lower Granite Canyon is a riot of vegetation and wildlife. With so many critters flitting about, it can feel busy even when no other hikers are around.

TRAIL 42

Hike, Backpack, Horse
12.4 miles, Loop
Difficulty: 1 2 3 **4 5**

Morgan Konn

Western thimbleberry *is a common riparian plant.*

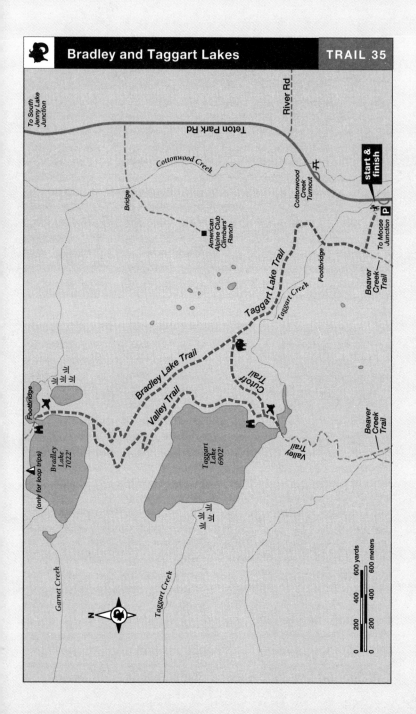

To South Jenny Lake Junction

River Rd

Teton Park Rd

Cottonwood Creek

start & finish

Bridge

Cottonwood Creek Turnout

American Alpine Club Climbers' Ranch

To Moose Junction

Footbridge

Beaver Creek Trail

Taggart Lake Trail

Taggart Creek

Bradley Lake Trail

Valley Trail

Cutoff Trail

Footbridge

Bradley Lake 7022'

Taggart Lake 6902'

Beaver Creek Trail

Valley Trail

(only for loop trips)

Garnet Creek

Taggart Creek

N

0   200   400   600 yards
0   200   400   600 meters

Bradley and Taggart Lakes

Escape the crowds at Jenny Lake with this scenic, leisurely wander through meadows and regenerating forest to a pair of glacial lakes. The untouched forests around Bradley Lake provide a vivid contrast to the Taggart Lake burn area. Both lakes teem with fish, but sorry, there's no swimming allowed.

Best Time

Almost any time between May and October is a good time to visit these low-elevation lakes. As elsewhere, you'll be the most comfortable and spot the most wildlife outside of the midday hours, since shade is in short supply in the burn areas.

Finding the Trail

From the south, head north out of Jackson for 8 miles on Hwys. 26/89/191 past the park's southern boundary, and turn left at Moose Junction. Continue 1 mile past the Visitor Center to the Moose Entrance Station. Go 2.3 miles north and turn left into the ample Taggart Lake trailhead parking area, on the west side of Teton Park Road. From the north, starting at Jackson Lake Junction, go 17.5 miles south on Teton Park Road, past the Jenny Lake Visitor Center, and turn right into the parking area.

Trail Description

From the parking area, ▶1 the wide trail heads west past some horse corrals, across a rolling sagebrush flat dotted with wildflowers. Halfway across the

TRAIL USE
Hike, Horse
LENGTH
5.8 miles, 3-4 hours
VERTICAL FEET
±550'
DIFFICULTY
– 1 2 **3** 4 5 +
TRAIL TYPE
Loop
SURFACE TYPE
Dirt

FEATURES
Child Friendly
Lake
Autumn Colors
Birds
Wildflowers
Wildlife
Great Views
Geologic Interest

FACILITIES
Restrooms
Picnic Tables

The timbered ridges that confine both lakes, known as lateral moraines, are composed of glacial debris; they give some of idea of how thick the glaciers once were.

 Wildflowers

 Great Views

 Lake

 Great Views

meadow, a footbridge spans a small stream. At the foot of the glacial moraine, the trail splits at a T-junction▶2 signed for the **Beaver Creek Trail**.

The right fork, the Taggart Lake Trail, heads northwest and crosses Taggart Creek on a wooden footbridges. After tracing the creek, the trail skirts the flank of the burned moraine. The Tetons appear and, if you're lucky, the delights of post-fire regeneration—busy birds, active wildlife, and blooming wildflowers—are very much in evidence.

Beyond the **Valley Trail** cutoff to Bradley Lake▶3 at 1.3 miles, the left fork of the trail traces the ridge of the moraine, then descends through stands of quaking baby aspens and thick-as-dog-hair lodgepole pines. After 1.3 miles, take a short detour south (left) at the Valley Trail junction▶4 along the south shore to the outlet of **Taggart Lake** (6902'). On a clear day, from the bridge over the outlet stream, you'll find unobstructed views of the remarkable Grand Teton (13,770').

Retrace your steps north along the lakeshore back to the junction,▶5 then continue north on the Valley Trail, which switchbacks steeply over the moraine dividing Taggart and Bradley lakes. The Valley Trail passes another junction for the Bradley Lake Trail just before it hits the well-forested southeast shore of **Bradley Lake** (7022').

Before turning tail for home, take time to explore the placid lakeshore. Or, if you're so inclined, detour▶6 0.3 miles north (left) along the lakeshore to the bridge spanning the lake's narrow neck for more stunning, up-close Teton views. Retrace your steps back to the Bradley Lake Trail▶7 for the final, 2.2-mile home stretch of the loop, over the moraine and through more burn area, and past the Bradley Lake Cutoff.▶8 Return to the now-familiar junction for the Taggart Lake trailhead▶9 and the parking area.▶10

MILESTONES

▶1   0.0 Start at Taggart Lake trailhead parking area

▶2   0.2 Right on Taggart Lake Trail at Beaver Creek Trail junction

▶3   1.3 Left on Valley Trail

▶4   1.8 Left along shore for optional detour to Taggart Lake outlet

▶5   1.9 North (straight ahead) on Valley Trail at Taggart Lake Trail junction

▶6   3.0 Left along shore at Bradley Lake Trail (optional detour)

▶7   3.6 Left on Bradley Lake Trail

▶8   4.5 Straight (southeast) at Cutoff Trail junction

▶9   5.6 Left at junction for Taggart Lake trailhead

▶10 5.8 Return to parking area

Early Season Access

NOTES

Early in the season—say, mid-May—the **Beaver Creek Trail** is a good alternative to reach Taggart Lake via the Valley Trail (4.2 miles round-trip), when the more northerly Bradley Lake route remains covered by snow. Either lake can be visited by itself as a loop hike, and any of these routes can be done in either direction without an increase in difficulty.

Bradley Lake Camping

The campsite on the north shore of Bradley Lake is a sweet spot reserved for backpackers doing multiday trips.

Regrowth

In 1985, a lightning-sparked fire burned more than 1000 acres of lodgepole pine forest around Taggart Lake. Among the charred tree trunks, signs of healthy regeneration are rampant: rapidly growing seedlings, lush grasses, and abundant wildflower displays.

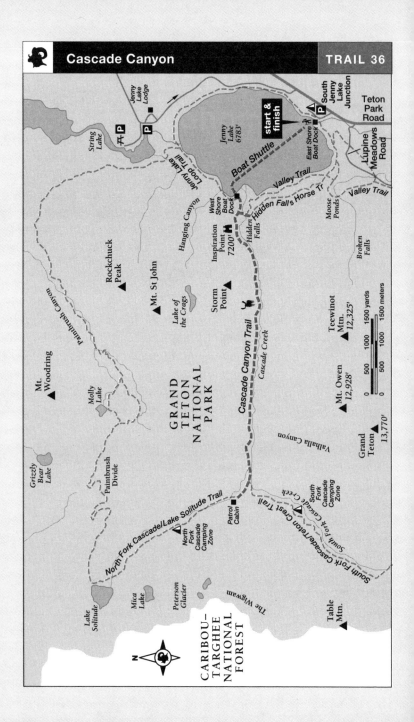

Cascade Canyon TRAIL 36

Jenny Lake Lodge

String Lake

P P

Jenny Lake Loop Trail

Jenny Lake 6783'

start & finish

Boat Shuttle

South Jenny Lake Junction

Teton Park Road

East Shore Boat Dock

Lupine Meadows Road

Valley Trail

Valley Trail

Hidden Falls Horse Tr.

West Shore Boat Dock

Hanging Canyon

Inspiration Point 7200'

Hidden Falls

Moose Ponds

Rockchuck Peak

Mt. St John

Lake of the Crags

Storm Point

Broken Falls

Cascade Canyon Trail

Cascade Creek

Teewinot Mtn. 12,325'

Mt. Woodring

Paintbrush Canyon

Molly Lake

GRAND TETON NATIONAL PARK

Mt. Owen 12,928'

Valhalla Canyon

Grand Teton 13,770'

Grizzly Bear Lake

Paintbrush Divide

0 500 1000 1500 yards
0 500 1000 1500 meters

North Fork Cascade/Lake Solitude Trail

Patrol Cabin

North Fork Cascade Camping Zone

South Fork Cascade Creek

South Fork/Teton Crest Trail

South Fork Cascade Camping Zone

Lake Solitude

Mica Lake

Peterson Glacier

The Wigwam

Table Mtn.

CARIBOU-TARGHEE NATIONAL FOREST

N

Cascade Canyon

This challenging extension of the popular Jenny Lake and Hidden Falls loop (see Trail 39, page 295) is the park's most popular and crowded canyon trail. In summer, it's a bottleneck of sorts, at the confluence of several major climbing and backpacking trails. Thanks to the scenic boat shuttle, it's also one of the most beautiful and direct routes into the wild heart of the Tetons.

Best Time

Snow can linger in the upper reaches of the canyon until early July. Since they are at relatively low elevation, the lower stretches of the canyon are accessible from June through October. Hidden Falls is at its most spectacular early in the season. Afternoon thunder showers, which appear with little warning, are common in the canyon.

Finding the Trail

From the south, follow Hwys. 26/89/191 north out of Jackson for 8 miles past the park's southern boundary, and turn left at Moose Junction. Continue 1 mile past the Visitor Center to the Moose Entrance Station. Go 7 miles north on Teton Park Road and turn left at the South Jenny Lake Junction. Follow the signs for the East Shore Boat Dock for another 0.5 mile (making a couple of right-hand turns) through the developed area around the Visitor Center/Ranger Station to arrive at the trailhead parking area. From the north, starting at Jackson Lake Junction, take Teton Park Road 12.5 miles south

TRAIL USE
Hike, Backpack, Horse
LENGTH
9.1 miles, 5-6 hours
VERTICAL FEET
±1100'
DIFFICULTY
– 1 2 3 **4** 5 +
TRAIL TYPE
Out & Back
SURFACE TYPE
Dirt

FEATURES
Canyon
Lake
Stream
Waterfall
Autumn Colors
Wildflowers
Wildlife
Cool & Shady
Camping
Geologic Interest

FACILITIES
Visitor Center
Ranger Station
Restrooms
Phone
Water
Horse Staging

(past North Jenny Lake Junction) and turn right into the South Jenny Lake parking area.

Logistics

Jenny Lake's parking lots often fill to capacity in mid-summer. Turn up as early as possible to find a space.

Taking a seasonal shuttle boat across Jenny Lake cuts out the first two miles of hiking in each direction. Catch the first boat to beat the crowds to the falls. **Jenny Lake Boating** shuttles depart Jenny Lake's East Shore Boat Dock for the Cascade Canyon trailhead dock every 15 minutes daily, weather permitting, between May 15 and September 30. From June 1 to September 15, hours of operation are 8 AM to 6 PM, with service reduced to 10 AM to 4 PM during May and the second half of Sept-ember. Fares are $5 or $7.50 (one-way or round-trip) for passengers 13 and older, and $4 or $5 for children older than six years old. Kids ages six and younger ride free. Call (307) 734-9227 for more information.

Trail Description

From the parking area near the **Visitor Center,**▶1 follow signs to the **East Shore Boat Dock**, on the southeast end of the lake.▶2 During the high season, you can catch a shuttle boat for the scenic, 12-minute ride across the lake to the **West Shore Boat**

 Lake

Dock,▶3 where there are no visitor services.

Once on the opposite side of the lake, follow signs to your left (south) for a couple hundred yards along the well-beaten paths to the signed **Jenny Lake Loop Trail junction.**▶4 Turn right (west) on the middle trail at the three-way intersection to follow a path that parallels the north side of **Cascade Creek** before crossing over it on a footbridge.

 Waterfall

Follow signs to the viewpoint of the 200-foot **Hidden Falls,**▶5 tucked away in a spruce-fir forest behind a split-rail fence.

Heading back toward the lake and away from the falls, turn left and follow signs across a bridge over Cascade Creek. Soon you start the 0.4-mile climb (also signed for Cascade Canyon) to **Inspiration Point** (7200')►6 for sweeping views east across the Snake River Valley to the Gros Ventre Range and back west to the Cathedral Group: Teewinot Mtn. (12,325'), the Grand Teton (13,770'), and Mt. Owen (12,928'), the second highest peak in the Teton Range.

Most casual visitors do not make it beyond Inspiration Point, so the farther you go up the canyon, the more peaceful things should become. Begin the gradual, gentle 0.6-mile climb—past the horse bypass trail intersection—to the mouth of the U-shaped Cascade Canyon,►7 where the majesty of the mile-high, glacially sculpted walls really begins to sink in.

Several large talus slopes—home to many vocal marmots, as well as pika—intersect the trail from the right as it follows the north side of Cascade Creek and traverses prime wild berry habitat. (Look for raspberries, huckleberries, thimbleberries and

Teewinot comes from the Shoshone word meaning "many pinnacles." The name is thought to have once applied to the entire Teton range.

 Great Views

 Canyon

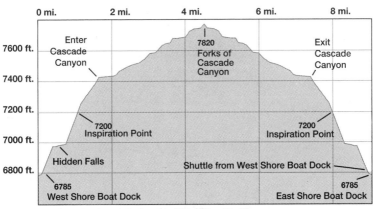

TRAIL 36 Cascade Canyon Elevation Profile

grouse whortleberries.) If you can properly identify them, you are welcome to pick small quantities for personal use, but leave some for the critters that frequent the area, too.

Thanks to the sheer canyon walls, you'll enjoy great views beyond the Douglas-fir canopy all the way up the canyon. Just before the **Forks of Cascade Canyon**▸8 junction (look for the huge limber pine specimen), the trail crosses over Cascade Creek on a footbridge and starts to climb more noticeably again. (See Options for a short description of the North and South Fork trails.)

About 0.3 miles up the North Fork Trail, the

大 MILESTONES

▸1   0.0 Start at south Jenny Lake parking area
▸2   0.1 Visitor Center and East Shore Boat Dock
▸3   0.1 Shuttle boat to West Shore Boat Dock
▸4   0.3 Jenny Lake Loop Trail junction
▸5   0.6 Hidden Falls
▸6   1.0 Inspiration Point
▸7   1.6 Enter Cascade Canyon
▸8   4.5 Forks of Cascade Canyon
▸9   9.0 Back at West Shore Boat Dock
▸10 9.0 Shuttle Boat to East Shore Boat Dock
▸11 9.1 Return to South Jenny Lake parking area

Cascade Patrol Cabin makes a nice picnic spot before you do a U-turn and retrace your steps down the canyon to the shuttle boat▶9 to the East Shore Boat Dock▶10 and the South Jenny Lake trailhead parking area.▶11

 Stream

OPTIONS

North and South Forks of Cascade Canyon

You can extend this hike into an overnight trip by getting a back-country permit for either the North Fork or South Fork Cascade Canyon camping zones, which start just beyond the trail fork near the head of the canyon.

The **South Fork**, usually snow-free by mid-July, gains 2600 feet over 5.1 scenic miles en route to **Hurricane Pass** (10,372') on the park's western boundary.

The **North Fork** climbs a gentler 1200 feet in 2.7 miles to the eastern shore of 50-acre **Lake Solitude** (9035'), a misnomer for this striking and extremely popular destination. If you plan on camping, you can take the two-day Cascade Canyon–Paintbrush Divide and Canyon route—the park's most popular high-country loop—which gains 3850 feet over 19.2 miles.

Skipping the Shuttle Boat

If the boats aren't running or you'd rather skip the shuttle, it's a straightforward, flat, and well-signed 2-mile walk around the southern and western lakeshore via the **Valley Trail** or **Hidden Falls Horse Trail** to reach **Hidden Falls** (see Trail 39, page 295). In summer, rangers lead interpretive hikes from the Jenny Lake Visitor Center to Hidden Falls, which can cause some crowding on the main trails. An infrequently used horse trail that starts north of the West Shore Boat Dock skips the crowded area around Hidden Falls and intersects with the Cascade Canyon Trail a few hundred yards above Inspiration Point.

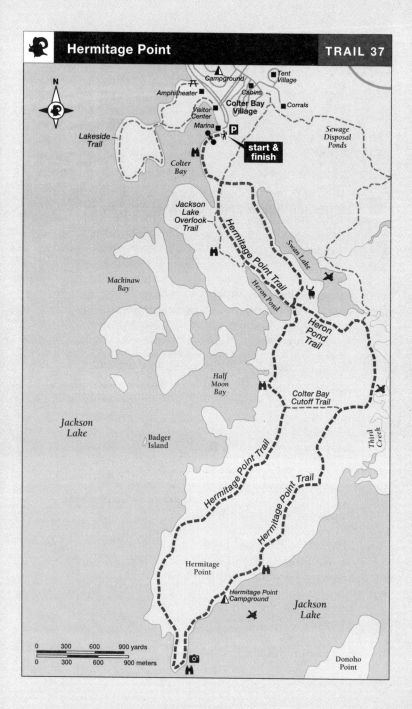

Hermitage Point

TRAIL 37

N

Campground

Tent Village

Amphitheater

Cabins

Colter Bay Village

Corrals

Visitor Center

Marina

P

start & finish

Sewage Disposal Ponds

Lakeside Trail

Colter Bay

Jackson Lake Overlook Trail

Hermitage Point Trail

Swan Lake

Heron Pond

Heron Pond Trail

Mackinaw Bay

Colter Bay Cutoff Trail

Half Moon Bay

Third Creek

Jackson Lake

Badger Island

Hermitage Point Trail

Hermitage Point Trail

Hermitage Point

Hermitage Point Campground

Jackson Lake

| 0 | 300 | 600 | 900 yards |
| 0 | 300 | 600 | 900 meters |

Donoho Point

Hermitage Point

This easygoing but rewarding shoreline jaunt leaves the crowds at Colter Bay behind. The forested habitat is ever-changing, and the views across Jackson Lake are amazing. It's a flexible route, too: Add an overnight at one of the park's best low-elevation campgrounds for the perfect first-time backcountry adventure.

Best Time

The trail is hikable from mid-May through October. In the hottest months of the summer, it's most enjoyable in early morning or late afternoon. Dawn and dusk are the best times for spotting wildlife. Sunset behind the Tetons is magical from Colter Bay.

Finding the Trail

From the south, head north out of Jackson on Hwy. 26/89/191 for 26 miles past the park's southern boundary. At Moran Junction, turn left onto Hwy. 26/287, go 4 miles past the park entrance station, and bear right at Jackson Lake Junction. Turn left into Colter Bay Village, 5.2 miles beyond Jackson Lake Junction. Follow the signs 1 mile to the Colter Bay Visitor Center. The Visitor Center is just to the right of the final T-junction; the marina and trailhead are to your left.

Park near the boat ramp at the marina. The trailhead is in the southeast corner of the large parking area, between the boat ramp and the nondescript brown pump-house building.

TRAIL USE
Hike, Backpack, Horse
LENGTH
9.4 miles, 4-6 hours
VERTICAL FEET
±150'
DIFFICULTY
– 1 2 3 **4** 5 +
TRAIL TYPE
Loop
SURFACE TYPE
Mixed

FEATURES
Child Friendly
Lake
Birds
Wildflowers
Wildlife
Cool & Shady
Great Views
Photo Opportunity
Camping

FACILITIES
Visitor Center
Restrooms
Picnic Tables
Phone
Water
Boat Launch
Horse Staging

Logistics

All the trail junctions described here are signed; ignore the numerous unmarked junctions with horse trails and unofficial trails. There are public restrooms near the trailhead at the Visitor Center and marina. Pick up a free trail map from the box at the service road entrance gate.

Trail Description

From the trailhead, ▶1 follow the wide gravel service road past the gate and along the shore overlooking the marina, while soaking up the views across **Colter Bay** to Mt. Moran (12,605'). At the end of the service road, stay right at the first trail junction. ▶2 The route turns into a single-track trail and enters a mixed lodgepole pine and fir forest.

 Great Views

A few hundred yards farther along, your next option is to turn right on the **Jackson Lake Overlook Trail,** ▶3 or forge ahead on the flat route. If you're in the mood and have the gumption, it's well worth the short, gentle ascent and the slightly longer loop to take in the breezy views from the sagebrush meadow atop the knoll. Jackson Lake is actually obscured by pines, but there's a nice panorama of the Teton Range. The overlook route rejoins the lower trail after 0.5 mile, just before the north end of lily-laden, yellow-green **Heron Pond.** ▶4

 Shore

After skirting the edge of the pond and passing several unmarked spurs leading down toward the shoreline, make a hard right 1.4 miles beyond the trailhead at four-way trail junction. ▶5 The trail hugs the pond's southern shore, bringing close enough to see beavers working on their lodges and to hear the ducks, pelicans, and Canada geese splashing about. Dense lodgepole stands obscure the lake from view until you reach the **Colter Bay cutoff trail** junction at 2.2 miles, ▶6 beyond which most of the horses and crowds disappear.

 Birds

Beavers are busy at Heron Pond; *Mt. Moran looms in the background (Trail 37).*

At the junction, follow the right fork along the peninsula and watch for tantalizing glimpses of the Teton Range across the lake to your right. A small grove of majestic, towering aspens appears on the left just before the views really open up. After what seems like much longer than a mile, the dense, dog-hair forest finally gives way to sagebrush meadows and, on clear days, truly grand views.

Great Views

The mercifully undeveloped **Hermitage Point▶7** is breezy, but when it's sunny it can be a wonderful place for a picnic amidst the fragrant sagebrush. Many unofficial trails lead to all manner of photo opportunities around the point.

Afterwards, proceed 0.5 mile from the sign on the far side of the point, past a short spur trail to the **Hermitage Point campground,▶8** one of the park's nicest low-elevation backcountry campsites. It's perfectly perched above the shoreline 4.9 miles from the trailhead, though a bit exposed; this gives it stunning, 180° views. The site fronts a placid bay that harbors tons of birdlife—bring your binoculars.

Camping

Immediately beyond the campground, the trail climbs away from the lake, straight up a moraine wall to an overlook, then drops through mixed fir forest and more sagebrush meadow to the east end of the previously seen Colter Bay cutoff trail.▶9

At this juncture, the cutoff saves no distance, so forge ahead on the main trail alongside Third Creek. Watch for moose lurking in the willows, and raptors soaring against the backdrop of the Teton Wilderness to the east.

 Birds

Just below the southeast arm of Swan Lake, turn left at the signed junction for the Heron Pond Trail.▶10 Crest a small forested rise, then drop down past a glimpse of Swan Lake to a now-familiar four-way junction at **Heron Pond.**▶11

OPTIONS

Kid-Friendly Shortcuts

If you've got little ones in tow, or want to opt out of the longer loop midway, there are three opportunities to cut the hike short, using signed cutoff trails to return to Colter Bay. You can loop back around at the north end of Heron Pond (2 miles round-trip via the Jackson Lake Overlook) or the south end of Heron Pond (2.6 miles round-trip), or turn around 0.8 miles beyond Heron Pond at the Colter Bay cutoff trail (5.4 miles round-trip).

Indian Arts Museum and Visitor Center

The free **Indian Arts Museum** at Colter Bay Visitor Center makes a nice pre- or post-hike stop to see artifacts recovered from Jackson Lake, plus a wide-ranging Plains Indian collection. Free, guided tours are offered around 4 PM daily in the summer. The **Visitor Center** has a good selection of books about Native American subjects, plus handicrafts demonstrations and videos on Native American arts and wildlife. The museum is open from 8 AM to 7 PM daily in summer, 8 AM to 5 PM in May and September.

Chuckwagon Fare

John Colter's Chuckwagon is a convenient if kitschy pre- or post-hike stop for a buffet breakfast or lunch ($10 or less) or cowboy-worthy dinner (entrees range from $10 to $20). They'll even fry up your trout for you, pardner, if you bring it in cleaned before 4 PM.

Take a hard right (not the path you followed previously along the shore of the pond), and head north over a gentle rise and 0.3 mile down to the west shore of **Swan Lake**. The lake is named after a pair of rare and endangered trumpeter swans who have abided here for two decades. The couple have yet to produce any offspring, but have been observed defending their nesting patch from other swans. Other creatures that share the lake's resources include beavers, moose, elk, deer, herons, cranes, and less showy birds.

 Birds

 Wildlife

After you travel north along the lakeshore for almost a mile and take in the lake and its gregarious inhabitants, make a soft (not hard) left toward Colter Bay at yet another well-signed four-way junction.▶**12** Merge right onto the service road▶**13** to finish the loop at the Colter Bay/Hermitage Point trailhead parking area.▶**14**

🚶 **MILESTONES**

▶**1**   0.0 Start at Hermitage Point trailhead

▶**2**   0.2 Right at first junction

▶**3**   0.4 Right at Jackson Lake Overlook trail (optional)

▶**4**   1.0 Right at north end of Heron Pond to rejoin main trail

▶**5**   1.4 Hard right at four-way trail junction

▶**6**   2.2 Right at Colter Bay cutoff trail junction

▶**7**   4.4 Left around Hermitage Point

▶**8**   4.9 Straight past Hermitage Point Campground

▶**9**   6.6 Right past cutoff trail junction

▶**10**   7.3 Left on Heron Pond trail at Swan Lake junction

▶**11**   7.8 Right Heron Pond four-way junction to Swan Lake

▶**12**   8.7 Soft (not hard) left at four-way junction to Colter Bay

▶**13**   Right on service road to Colter Bay/Hermitage Point trailhead

▶**14**   9.4 Return to parking area

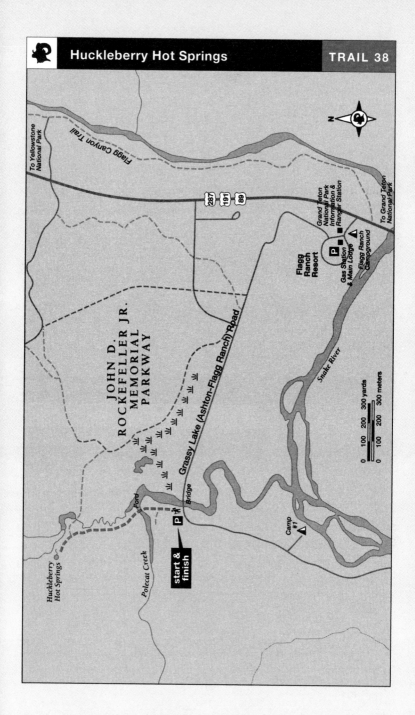

To Yellowstone National Park

Flagg Canyon Trail

N

287 191 89

To Grand Teton National Park

Grand Teton National Park Information & Ranger Station

Flagg Ranch Resort

P

Gas Station & Main Lodge

Flagg Ranch Campground

JOHN D. ROCKEFELLER JR. MEMORIAL PARKWAY

Grassy Lake (Ashton-Flagg Ranch) Road

Snake River

0   100   200   300 yards
0   100   200   300 meters

Ford

Bridge

Camp #1

P

start & finish

Huckleberry Hot Springs

Polecat Creek

Huckleberry Hot Springs

Grand Teton National Park's worst-kept secret is actually located just north of the park in the John D. Rockefeller Jr. Memorial Parkway area. Formerly the site of a private campground, all traces of development have been removed and the 100°-105°F springs have reverted back to their natural state.

Best Time

Locals soak here year-round, using cross-country skis to gain access in the winter. The shadeless pools can be too hot for pleasant soaking in full midday sun. Trail access can be a bit dodgy mid-April through mid-May due to heavy bear activity. Access beyond Flagg Ranch to Grassy Lake Road is often restricted during this period. If hiking in the fall during the hunting season, it's best to wear bright orange!

Finding the Trail

From Flagg Ranch, 2.5 miles south of Yellowstone National Park's South Entrance, follow signs for Grassy Lake Road (called Ashton-Flagg Ranch Road, Reclamation Road, or USFS Road 261 on older maps) through the resort's developed areas. Continue 1.1 miles west on the paved road to an unsigned turnout on the right, at a split-rail fence with a sign reading NO CAMPING, NO FIRES, immediately after the bridge over Polecat Creek. If you hit gravel, you have gone too far. From Grand Teton National Park in the south, head north on

TRAIL USE
Hike
LENGTH
1 mile, 1-2 hours
VERTICAL FEET
Negligible
DIFFICULTY
– **1** 2 3 4 5 +
TRAIL TYPE
Out & Back
SURFACE TYPE
Dirt

FEATURES
Child Friendly
Stream
Birds
Wildlife
Swimming
Geothermal

FACILITIES
Ranger Station
Restrooms

Some folks soak in their birthday suits, some don't. Families often use the springs. If you're offended by bare skin, it's probably best to steer clear of the area.

Hwys. 89/191/287 through the John D. Rockefeller Jr. Memorial Parkway and turn left at Flagg Ranch, just beyond the Snake River bridge.

Trail Description

From the unsigned trailhead pullout,▶1 follow the old roadbed (left over from the 1980s, when the Forest Service dismantled the developed pools and turned over control of the springs to the NPS) to the right at the first fork▶2 after 0.1 mile.

Stream

The wide ford of **Polecat Creek**▶3 can be trickier than it looks. The rocks are round and slippery, and the current is often stronger than it appears—grab a stick and bring sandals or wading shoes. Beyond the creek, watch for the steam rising from the first of three hot pots.▶4

Swimming

If you've got some extra time, pack a picnic and check out the waterfall, steamy grotto, and surrounding thermal meadows. After you've had your fill of soaking bliss, please pack out whatever you've packed in, plus something extra to leave the place a bit nicer than you found it, and retrace your steps to the parking area.▶5

MILESTONES

▶1 0.0 Start at unsigned parking turnout
▶2 0.1 Keep right at first fork
▶3 0.2 Ford Polecat Creek
▶4 0.5 Huckleberry Hot Springs
▶5 1.0 Return to parking area

Foraging Regulations

NPS regulations allow hikers to forage small amounts of berries for personal consumption. By all means, savor a few samples, but you'll cultivate better bear karma by leaving most of the crop for the park's ursine inhabitants.

Soak at Your Own Risk

The NPS posts signs warning of the possible presence of the pathogenic bacteria *Naegleria fowleri* in Huckleberry Springs, but no cases of the rare meningitis caused by the microscopic amoeba have been reported after bathing here. Just to be safe, do not submerge your head or nose below the water—the amoeba enters the brain via the nasal passages. Symptoms include a runny nose, sore throat, severe headache, and in the worst cases, death within a few days.

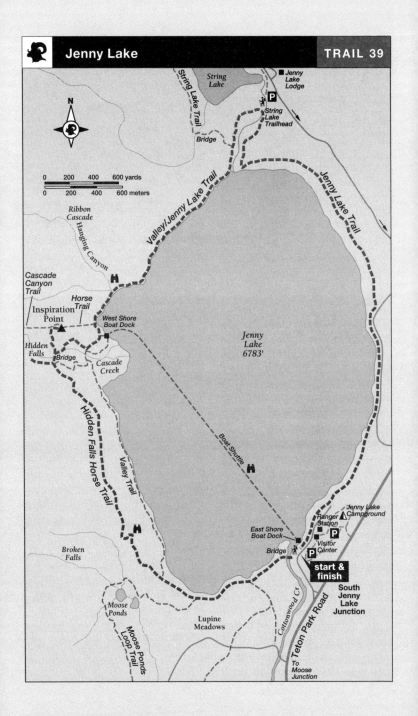

String Lake

Jenny Lake Lodge

String Lake Trail

P

String Lake Trailhead

Bridge

N

Jenny Lake Trail

0   200   400   600 yards
0   200   400   600 meters

Ribbon Cascade

Valley/Jenny Lake Trail

Hanging Canyon

Cascade Canyon Trail

Horse Trail

Inspiration Point

West Shore Boat Dock

Hidden Falls

Bridge

Cascade Creek

Jenny Lake 6783'

Hidden Falls Horse Trail

Valley Trail

Boat Shuttle

Jenny Lake Campground

Ranger Station

P

East Shore Boat Dock

Broken Falls

Visitor Center

P

Bridge

start & finish

South Jenny Lake Junction

Moose Ponds

Lupine Meadows

Moose Ponds Loop Trail

Cottonwood Ct

Teton Park Road

To Moose Junction

Jenny Lake

Grand Teton's most popular dayhike deserves all the accolades heaped upon it, but the route also suffers from the overcrowding the attention brings. The wide, well-maintained trail skirts the shoreline of the park's second-largest lake and is almost completely flat. A optional shuttle boat (one-way or round-trip) goes most of the way to the photogenic focal point, Hidden Falls.

TRAIL USE
Hike, Horse
LENGTH
7.0 miles, 3-4 hours
VERTICAL FEET
±525'
DIFFICULTY
– 1 2 **3** 4 5 +
TRAIL TYPE
Loop
SURFACE TYPE
Paved and Dirt

FEATURES
Child Friendly
Handicap Accessible
Lake
Waterfall
Autumn Colors
Birds
Cool & Shady
Great Views
Photo Opportunity
Geologic Interest

FACILITIES
Visitor Center
Restrooms
Picnic Tables
Phone
Water
Horse Staging

Best Time

It can be impossible to find parking around noon in summer, so aim to arrive early, or consider a late-afternoon start. When the shuttle boats are running, the trail is much less crowded and your chances of seeing wildlife increase exponentially. The loop around the lake is hikable from May through October and is a good, snow-free early- or late-season option.

Finding the Trail

From the south, take Hwys. 26/89/191 north out of Jackson for 8 miles past the park's southern boundary and turn left at Moose Junction. Continue 1 mile past the Visitor Center to the Moose Entrance Station. Go 7 miles north, and turn left at the South Jenny Lake Junction. Follow the signs for the East Shore Boat Dock for another 0.5 mile (making a couple of right-hand turns) through the developed area around the Visitor Center and Ranger Station to arrive at the trailhead parking area. From the north, starting at Jackson Lake Junction, take Teton Park

Road 12.5 miles south (past North Jenny Lake Junction) and turn right at the South Jenny Lake junction.

Jenny Lake was named in 1872 by the Hayden geological survey, after the Shoshone wife of pioneering trapper and guide Beaver Dick Leigh.

Logistics

Seasonal shuttle boats depart Jenny Lake's East Shore Boat Dock for the Cascade Canyon trailhead dock every 15 minutes daily, weather permitting, between May 15 and September 30. From June 1 to September 15, hours of operation are from 8 AM to 6 PM, with service reduced to 10 AM to 4 PM in May and the second half of September.

Fares are $5 or $7.50 (one-way or round-trip) for passengers 13 and older, and $4 or $5 for children over six years old. Kids six and under ride free. Call (307) 734-9227 for more information.

Alternatively, you can set up a car shuttle by leaving a vehicle at the String Lake trailhead to avoid the final 2.9-mile stretch that parallels the road.

Trail Description

From the **East Shore Boat Dock**▶1 near the Visitor Center, head out toward the Tetons around the southwest side of **Jenny Lake** (6783'). You'll cross Cottonwood Creek on a footbridge soon after passing the boat launch area. The wide trail here may feel more like a highway, especially if the shuttle boat is not running.

Just beyond the **Moose Ponds Loop Trail junction**▶2, the trail forks at an unsigned junction. Take the high route,▶3 an unsigned horse trail, for better views and to avoid the crowds. As the trail winds up above the lakeshore, there are several scenic viewpoints looking back out to the east across the lake to Jackson Hole. The lower, more crowded Valley Trail follows the lakeshore.

After 1.3 mile the trail's forks reunite near the spur trails leading to the **West Shore Boat Dock.▶4** If you wish to cut your hike short for some reason here, you can catch the shuttle boat back across the lake to the Visitor Center. Otherwise, follow the signs a few hundred yards to the base of 200-foot **Hidden Falls,▶5** really a cascade (a series of small falls) instead of one free-falling torrent of water. Semantics aside, it still exerts that romantic, mesmerizing effect unique to pristine falling water.

The area below the falls is a well-signed maze of well-beaten paths. Follow the signs for Cascade Canyon to avoid ending up at the boat dock.

Heading back towards the lake from the base of the falls, the well-marked trail crosses over **Cascade Creek** on a bridge at the mouth of the U-shaped canyon and ascends along the north side of the creek. It's well worth a bit of exertion to climb the 0.4 mile beyond the falls to **Inspiration Point** (7200').▶6

Note: If crowds look like they might pose a problem along the narrow trail to Inspiration Point, you can head a couple hundred yards north (right) from the boat dock and look for a horse trail that heads directly for the Cascade Canyon Trail. When it rejoins the main footpath, backtrack down the canyon (to the left) a few hundred yards to reach Inspiration Point.

After retracing your steps down from Inspiration Point back toward the boat dock, the **Jenny Lake Trail** (also known as the Valley Trail) hugs the lakeshore through a severe burn area, the aftermath of the lightning-sparked Alder Fire that consumed more than 300 acres in 1999. A few hundred yards beyond a scenic viewpoint, pause where a stream called **Ribbon Cascade** tumbles off the hillside to look up **Hanging Canyon**.

Look back up Cascade Canyon, to your left, for a glimpse of the Cathedral Group—from left to

Picknicking is prohibited near Hidden Falls and Inspiration Point due to past problems with people feeding black bears and squirrels.

 Waterfall

 Great Views

The terminal moraine around Jenny Lake was deposited by a glacier flowing out of Cascade Canyon during the Pinedale Glaciation period, which ended around 10,000 years ago.

right: Teewinot Mtn. (12,325'), the Grand Teton (13,770'), and Mt. Owen (12,928'). In Hanging Canyon, a steep, unofficial (unmarked and unmaintained) climbers' trail gains 2700 feet in less than 3 miles as it picks its way through boulder fields and climbs up the glacier-carved canyon past three lakes to Lake of the Crags, an imposing cirque.

You shouldn't encounter many hikers again until the **String Lake trailhead junction**▶7. Soon after the junction, the trail cuts away from the lakeshore and crosses a footbridge over the rapids between String Lake and Jenny Lake▶8 near the **String Lake parking lot**.

Along the final 2.9-mile stretch, the Teton views are impressive, but the traffic noise on the adjacent one-way scenic drive drowns out any illusion that you are in a pristine natural area. The trail hugs the eastern shore of Jenny Lake as it weaves in and out of lodgepole pine forest, before ending up back at the **South Jenny Lake parking area.**▶9

🚶 MILESTONES

▶1 0.0 Start at Visitor Center and East Shore Boat Dock

▶2 0.4 Right at Moose Ponds Trail junction

▶3 0.7 Fork left onto unsigned Hidden Falls Horse Trail

▶4 2.0 Left at West Shore Boat Dock cutoff

▶5 2.2 Hidden Falls

▶6 2.4 Inspiration Point

▶7 3.8 Right at the trail junction

▶8 4.1 Right after bridge over Jenny Lake inlet

▶9 7.0 Return to South Jenny Lake parking area

OPTIONS

Shuttle Boat

You can shortcut the first two miles of the hike by catching a shuttle boat across the lake to the West Shore Boat Dock. If you ride the boat in both directions, the round-trip hike to Hidden Falls and Inspiration Point is only 2 miles total. If you only want to take the shuttle boat one way, try starting at the String Lake trailhead near Jenny Lake Lodge and looping southwest around the less-trodden west shore, which cuts out the 2 most crowded miles.

Moose Ponds Loop

Done by itself from the East Shore Boat Bock, the 3-mile Moose Ponds Loop is a very pleasant, lightly traveled 90-minute outing. Four-tenths of a mile beyond the trailhead, drop down a moraine to your left from the overview point to the Moose Ponds. These three ponds and adjacent marshes at the base of Teewinot Mtn. offer a good chance to spot some waterfowl and wildlife, especially in the early morning or late evening. Willows, aspens, and wildflowers abound as you first approach the ponds. On the far (south) side of the ponds, the trail passes through a mature mixed subalpine fir and Engelmann spruce forest. Either retrace your steps, or follow the trail as it loops around the last pond, through the sagebrush flats in Lupine Meadows, to end up back near the South Jenny Lake parking area.

Cascade Canyon

Intrepid adventurers will want to continue upstream from Hidden Falls and Inspiration Point to the Forks of Cascade Canyon (an extra 9 miles round-trip, 3 to 4 hours, and 1000 feet elevation gain), a strenuous climb to views of the Cathedral Group. See Trail 36, page 279, for a full description.

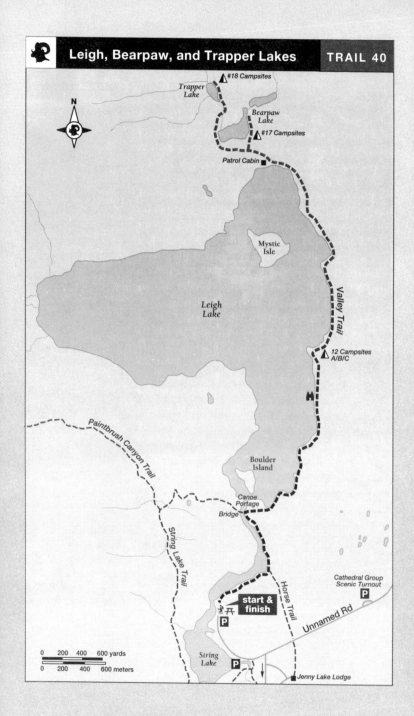

N

Trapper Lake

#18 Campsites

Bearpaw Lake

#17 Campsites

Patrol Cabin

Mystic Isle

Leigh Lake

Valley Trail

12 Campsites A/B/C

Paintbrush Canyon Trail

Boulder Island

String Lake Trail

Canoe Portage

Bridge

Cathedral Group Scenic Turnout

P

start & finish

P

Horse Trail

Unnamed Rd

String Lake

P

Jenny Lake Lodge

0   200   400   600 yards
0   200   400   600 meters

Leigh, Bearpaw, and Trapper Lakes

The easy outing to Leigh Lake is a favorite of families and those looking for a stress-free overnight option. The lake is big enough and just far enough away from the road to feel like it's in the backcountry, but close enough to attract parents with small children. It's also a favorite summer swimming hole and popular horseback riding destination. Campsites around the equally appealing Bearpaw and Trapper lakes provide an extra measure of seclusion.

Best Time

The hike is very pleasant at any time. The snow is usually gone by mid-May, and the trail is passable through October. Swimming is best in July and August. Beware of hypothermia-inducing temperatures in Leigh Lake before the end of June.

Finding the Trail

From the south, take Hwys. 26/89/191 north out of Jackson; proceed 8 miles past the park's southern boundary, and turn left at Moose Junction. Continue 1 mile past the Visitor Center to the Moose Entrance Station. Go 11 miles north, and turn left at the North Jenny Lake Junction. Continue 1.5 miles, and turn right near the Jenny Lake Lodge, just before the road becomes one-way. Follow the signs for a few hundred yards to the String Lake Picnic Area parking lot. From the north, starting at Jackson Lake Junction, go 9 miles south on Teton Park Road and turn right at North Jenny Lake Junction. Continue 1.5 miles and turn right into the picnic area parking lot.

TRAIL USE
Hike, Backpack, Horse
LENGTH
2.2 miles to Leigh Lake,
8.4 miles to Trapper
Lake; 2-3 hours
VERTICAL FEET
Negligible
DIFFICULTY
– 1 **2 3** 4 5 +
TRAIL TYPE
Out & Back
SURFACE TYPE
Dirt

FEATURES
Child Friendly
Lake
Autumn Colors
Birds
Wildflowers
Wildlife
Cool & Shady
Great Views
Photo Opportunity
Camping
Swimming

FACILITIES
Restrooms
Picnic Tables
Horse Staging

Trail Description

The glaciers hugging the sides of Mt. Moran are up to 100 feet thick.

Start from the trailhead (6875') near the northwest corner of the String Lake Picnic Area parking lot. ►1 The wide, packed-sand trail sees lots of horse traffic as it starts out through lodgepole pine forest. After a horse trail from **Jenny Lake Lodge** joins in on the right side, the trail meets the signed canoe portage ►2 for Leigh Lake, at 0.9 mile beyond the trailhead.

At the north end of **String Lake**, detour to your left to venture out onto the long, sturdy footbridge over the babbling brook that connects Leigh and String lakes.

From the canoe portage junction, follow the right fork and continue 0.1 mile north along the south shore of **Leigh Lake** (6877'). ►3 This is also a good area to forage for berries.

 Swimming

After 1.1 miles, you'll reach a wonderful sandy white swimming beach, ►4 where the views of Mt. Moran reflected in the lake are fit for the cover of a box of chocolates.

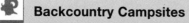

Backcountry Campsites

OPTIONS

Lake-lovers and unrepentant anglers will want to continue on to **Bearpaw** and **Trapper lakes**, and possibly even bushwhack a bit to reach remote **Bearpaw Bay** or **Little Grassy Island** campsites on the south shore of Jackson Lake.

Less than a mile farther along the lakeshore, you'll pass the first of three East Shore (12A, 12B, and 12C) **campsites,**▶5 all very pleasant spots to spend the night, and only 3 miles from the trailhead. They are also very popular with boating families. If you do spend the night here, take proper bear precautions; pitch your tent on a pad if provided; only build fires in grates; and beware of the waves (yes, waves) caused by wind on the lake.

Beyond the head of the lake and the **Leigh Lake Patrol Cabin**, the trail forks to the right for tree-lined **Bearpaw Lake**▶6 and several designated backcountry campsites in the 17-series, and to the left for **Trapper Lake**▶7 and another scenic campsite in the 18-series.

If you can pull yourself away, retrace your steps to the String Lake parking area.▶8

Just below Mt. Moran, Falling Ice Glacier often calves frozen blocks into the lake and contributes to Leigh Lake's unique blue-green tint.

 Camping

🚶 MILESTONES

▶1   0.0 Start at String Lake Picnic Area parking lot

▶2   0.9 Right at Leigh Lake Trail junction (Canoe Portage)

▶3   1.1 Leigh Lake

▶4   2.2 Sandy Beach

▶5   3.0 East Shore (12-series) campsites

▶6   3.7 Right at Bearpaw Lake junction (3.9 to Bearpaw Lake)

▶7   4.2 Trapper Lake

▶8   8.4 Return to String Lake parking lot

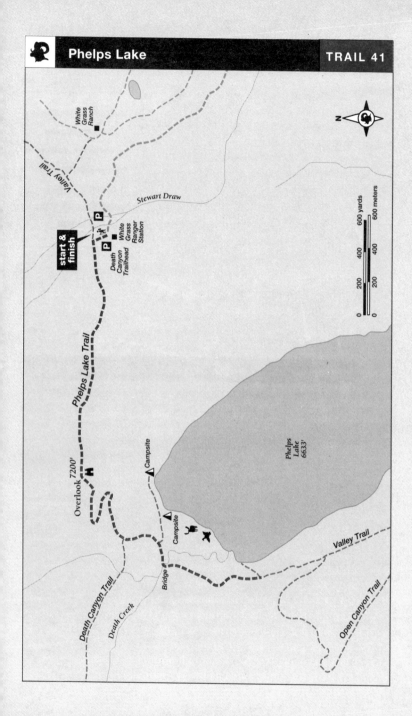

Phelps Lake

TRAIL 41

N

White
Grass Ranch

Valley Trail

Stewart Draw

P

White
Grass
Ranger
Station

start &
finish

P

Death
Canyon
Trailhead

600 yards

600 meters

Phelps Lake Trail

Overlook 7200'

Campsite

Campsite

Phelps
Lake
6633'

Valley Trail

Bridge

Death Canyon Trail

Death Creek

Open Canyon Trail

Phelps Lake

Beyond the scenic overlook of the park's fourth-largest lake, this rewarding route provides access to a group of three charming lakefront campsites that feel miles from the trailhead. Wildflowers, trout, moose, and black bears are abundant. Reserve campsites as far ahead as possible for this popular, family-friendly overnighter.

Best Time

Snow usually disappears from the trail by mid-June. Wildflowers appear soon after the snowmelt, and bird-watching is most diverse in early summer. Autumn colors peak in late August and early September. There's enough shade to make the trail pleasant at any time of day.

Finding the Trail

From south of the park in the town of Jackson, head 1 mile southwest through town on Hwys. 26/89/191 to the Hwy. 22 junction. Turn right and go west for 4.5 miles to Wyoming Hwy. 390 (Moose-Wilson Road). Turn right and go 7 miles north, past Teton Village and Jackson Hole Mountain Resort. Continue north through the park's Granite Canyon Entrance Station, where the road turns to dirt; proceed 5 miles north, past the Granite Canyon trailhead, and turn left on a paved road signed for Death Canyon. Bear left after 0.3 mile: The pavement ends after 0.5 mile, and the rough one-lane dirt road (no trailers or mobile homes allowed) gets worse for the next mile until it passes a larger

TRAIL USE
Hike, Backpack, Horse

LENGTH
4.0 miles, 2-3 hours

VERTICAL FEET
±420' to overlook,
±850' to lake

DIFFICULTY
− 1 **2** 3 4 5 +

TRAIL TYPE
Out & Back

SURFACE TYPE
Dirt

FEATURES
Child Friendly
Lake
Stream
Autumn Colors
Wildflowers
Birds
Wildlife
Cool & Shady
Great Views
Photo Opportunity
Camping
Swimming
Geologic Interest

FACILITIES
Restrooms
Horse Staging

Phelps Lake (6633') is full of cutthroat, brook, and lake trout. Moose and black bear are also frequently spotted foraging along the shore.

parking area (best for low-clearance vehicles). It dead-ends soon after at the crowded trailhead parking area near the White Grass Ranger Station.

From the north, look for the junction with Teton Park Road across from the Moose Visitor Center. Drive south for 3 miles on a narrow, windy, paved but scenic stretch of Moose-Wilson Road and turn right at the signed Death Canyon Trailhead Road junction.

Trail Description

From the Death Canyon trailhead (6780') near the seasonal **White Grass Ranger Station,** ▶1 keep to your left at the signed **Valley Trail** T-junction, ▶2 0.1 mile beyond the parking area.

For the next 0.8 mile, the well-beaten path—once a popular horseback riding route for dudes staying at the White Grass Ranch—rises gradually through meadows, mixed conifer forest, and colorful groves of aspens, crossing a couple of streams

 Great Views

flush with thimbleberries. Ignore all the unmarked horse trails that intersect the trail as it climbs to the overlook.

Once atop the lateral moraine-deposited over 15,000 years ago by a mass of ice pouring out of Death Canyon—there are nice picnic spots tucked among the boulders to the left, and good views over the lake to the Jackson Hole valley from the **Phelps**

🚶	MILESTONES
▶1	0.0 Start at Death Canyon (White Grass) trailhead
▶2	0.1 Left at Valley Trail T-junction
▶3	0.9 Phelps Lake Overlook
▶4	1.6 Left at Death Canyon Trail junction
▶5	2.0 Phelps Lake
▶6	4.0 Return to trailhead parking area

Lake Overlook (7200'). ▶3

For an easy, hourlong outing, some folks prefer to turn back here and return to the trailhead. To experience the variety of habitats around the lakeshore and for a better look up the glacial, U-shaped canyon, follow the switchbacks down the steeper southern face of the moraine for 0.7 mile, to the **Death Canyon Trail** junction. ▶4

The spur trail for the three lovely campsites, perched above the lake's northern shore, branches off to the left from the Phelps Lake Trail just beyond the Death Canyon junction.

For fishing access and some good bird-watching, continue south along the western lakeshore after crossing Death Creek on a footbridge, and follow a side trail down to the shore and inlet of Phelps Lake. ▶5 Retrace your steps back to the trailhead parking area. ▶6

The Death Canyon Patrol Cabin, 2 miles up-canyon on the Death Canyon Trail is a good, moderately strenuous detour through prime wildflower and moose habitat.

🦅 **Birds**

OPTIONS

Granite Canyon Car Shuttle

If you have two cars, you can extend the hike into a 6.1-mile point-to-point outing by leaving a vehicle at the signed Granite Canyon trailhead (6356'), on the west side of Moose-Teton Road, just north of the Granite Canyon Entrance Station.

Long-Distance Backpacking Routes

Popular overnight backpacking options that use the Death Canyon trailhead en route to the **Teton Crest Trail** include the 19.3-mile loop from Granite Canyon via Open Canyon; a 24.8-mile (one or two nights) route to Jenny Lake via Static Peak Divide; a more challenging 29.5-mile (two or three nights) route to the String Lake Picnic Area; a 25.7-mile (two nights) loop to Granite Canyon trailhead; and the demanding 36-mile (four nights) trip to String Lake via Paintbrush Canyon. Download or pick up a Backcountry Planning brochure for details. ▶

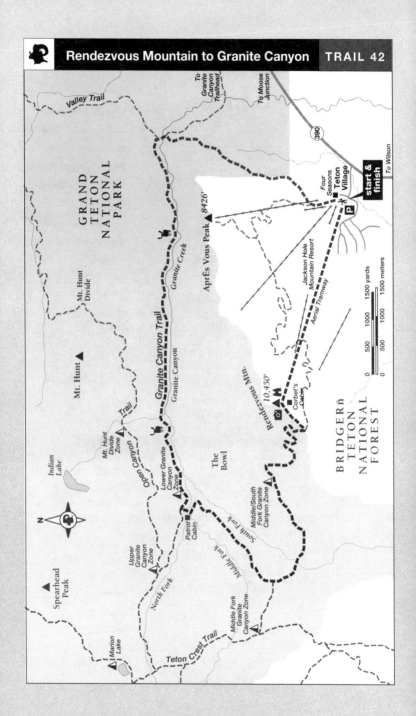

Rendezvous Mountain to Granite Canyon **TRAIL 42**

Valley Trail

To Granite Canyon Trailhead

To Moose Junction

390

To Wilson

Four Seasons

Teton Village

start & finish

P

GRAND TETON NATIONAL PARK

Aprês Vous Peak ▲ 8426'

Granite Creek

Mt. Hunt Divide

Jackson Hole Mountain Resort

Aerial Tramway

Mt. Hunt ▲

Granite Canyon Trail

Granite Canyon

Rendezvous Mtn. 10,450'

Corbet's Cabin

1500 yards
1000
500
0

1500 meters
1000
500
0

Indian Lake

Trail

Mt. Hunt Divide Zone

Open Canyon

Lower Granite Canyon Zone

The Bowl

Middle/South Fork Granite Canyon Zone

BRIDGERñ TETON NATIONAL FOREST

Spearhead Peak ▲

N

Upper Granite Canyon Zone

Patrol Cabin

South Fork

Middle Fork

North Fork

Marion Lake

Teton Crest Trail

Middle Fork Granite Canyon Zone

Rendezvous Mountain to Granite Canyon

Where else in the United States can you fill your lungs with such rarefied alpine air so early in the morning? This route is spectacular—and 95 percent downhill—so it gets traffic whenever the weather is decent and the tram is in service. Lower Granite Canyon is a riot of vegetation and wildlife. At times, there are so many birds and critters flitting about that it feels busy even when no other hikers are around.

Best Time

The tram operates from Memorial Day (late May) through late September, but inclement weather can halt operations, and snow can linger around Rendezvous Peak through July. Get an early start so you can enjoy a picnic lunch along the way and have plenty of time to hang out along the creek in the canyon. Better yet, reserve a backcountry campsite and make it an overnight trip. Fall colors peak around the autumnal equinox (September 21).

Finding the Trail

From Jackson, head 1 mile south on Hwys. 26/89/191 to the Hwy. 22 junction. Turn right and go west for 4.5 miles to Hwy. 390 (Moose-Wilson Road). Turn right and head north for 7 miles to Teton Village and Jackson Hole Mountain Resort. Turn left into the parking area and follow the signs to the aerial tram ticket booth. From the Moose Visitor Center, drive south for 8 miles on Moose-Wilson Road past the Granite Canyon trailhead and Granite Canyon Entrance Station to Teton Village.

TRAIL USE
Hike, Backpack, Horse

LENGTH
12.4 miles, 6-8 hours

VERTICAL FEET
+400'/-4100'

DIFFICULTY
– 1 2 3 **4 5** +

TRAIL TYPE
Loop

SURFACE TYPE
Dirt

FEATURES
Canyon
Mountain
Summit
Steep
Autumn Colors
Wildflowers
Birds
Wildlife
Great Views
Photo Opportunity
Camping
Geologic Interest

FACILITIES
Visitor Center
Restrooms
Phone
Water

Logistics

Horses are not allowed between the tram and the Middle Fork Cut-Off trail junction, an hour-to-90-minute hike down. Enjoy the singing mountain songbirds and woodpeckers drumming away.

This hike starts outside the park, high above Teton Village (locally known simply as "The Village") from **Jackson Hole Mountain Resort**. For information, see the Appendix (page 333).

The resort's **aerial tram** (round-trip tickets were $14-$18 in summer 2004; free for descent only) runs in summer from Memorial Day (late May) through late September. Hours of operation vary seasonally: from 9 AM to 5 PM in the low season, and from 9 AM to 6 PM in high season. The tram runs every half-hour and takes 12 minutes to climb more than 4000 feet to the top of Rendezvous Mtn.

High winds and inclement weather can disrupt tram service; contact the resort's Guest Service Center for updates on current conditions. Call (307) 739-2753. If you miss the last tram down from the summit, it's a long, 7.2-mile walk back down along the service road. Note that weather conditions at the summit are always much cooler and windier than at the base.

Trail Description

 Summit

Enjoy the expansive views from the **aerial tram**▶1 during the ride up **Rendezvous Mtn**. Upon exiting the tram platform, above treeline at the **summit** (10,450'),▶2 you can take care of any last-minute needs at **Corbet's Cabin**, where there are restrooms, plus pricey snacks and refreshments. Soak up the endless views, check out the Grand Teton in the telescope, then head left (south) along the ridge down the service road.

 Great Views

Tread lightly in this fragile alpine zone: Several varieties of delicate alpine wildflowers, lichens, and stunted krummholz Engelmann spruce and whitebark pine flourish in revegetation zones near the trail. Continue straight ahead at the first signed

 Wildflowers

junction after 0.4 mile, ▶3 your only chance to bail out and return to Teton Village. Soon after, at the second signed junction, enter **Grand Teton National Park** by turning right and following the signs for **Granite Canyon**. ▶4

The trail quickly drops into a big cirque aptly called **The Bowl**. The stunted spruce forest here marks timberline. After entering the **Middle/South Fork Granite Canyon camping zone**, the trail crosses several small stream culverts and bisects a wildflower meadow before crossing the **South Fork of Granite Creek**.

After 3.5 miles, beyond the **Middle Fork Cut-Off junction**, ▶5 follow the ridgeline between the Middle and South Forks of Granite Creek through open meadows down to a spruce-fir forest. A sign announces the end of the Middle Fork camping zone, then the trail crosses two babbling creek forks on sturdy wooden footbridges. Just beyond the second bridge, look for the **Granite Canyon Patrol Cabin** off-trail to your left at 5.2 miles. It's located just before the trail junction for Open Canyon, Marion Lake, and the Teton Crest Trail. ▶6 Turn right (east) here to start the gradual 4.7-mile descent on the **Granite Canyon Trail** to the mouth of the canyon.

Almost immediately after this junction, the trail enters fragrant forest and the **Lower Granite Canyon camping zone**. Several viewpoints high

Don't be startled by the well-camouflaged grouse that like to jump out of the woods just after the trail drops below treeline.

 Wildflowers

 Canyon

 Camping

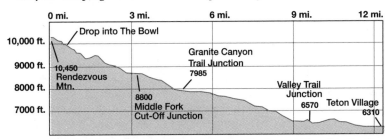

TRAIL 42 Rendezvous Mountain to Granite Canyon Elevation Profile

Wildlife

above **Granite Creek** afford views down to the canyon mouth. Before the trail eventually drops down alongside the creek, watch for moose and mule deer browsing in meadows—you may even see them foraging side by side.

Another sign indicates a group campsite, shortly before the trail passes below a small waterfall on the left and a stock bridge over the resulting stream. The trail drops through sagebrush meadows, past areas signed as closed for regrowth, before leveling off alongside a charming stretch of Granite Creek.

The cool, breezy lower half of the canyon is often choked with luxuriant vegetation. Ripe, rosy mountain-ash fruits are the most conspicuous eye-catchers. There are a couple of nice riverfront campsites, just before the canyon's right wall closes in to its narrowest point, opposite a large talus field riddled with raspberry bushes. From here, the trail levels off before a final abrupt descent, which begins where the trail trends away from the creek to exit the canyon.

Camping

The impact of heavy horse use becomes more apparent near the canyon mouth as the trail approaches the **Valley Trail**▶7 junction after 9.9 miles. The trail forks again 0.1 mile after crossing

NOTES

Loop and Overnight Options

If you're looking for a scenic workout, you can hike 7.2 miles (4100 vertical feet) up the service road and ride the aerial tram back down to the base area for free. If the weather looks dodgy up top, you might opt for one of several shorter, well-signed loops around the summit. Or, you can extend the trip by adding an overnight at Marion Lake (9240', 15.9 miles total), or in one of the three designated camping zones along the Granite Canyon Trail.

You can avoid the final dull Valley Trail stretch of the full loop by setting up a car shuttle at the Granite Canyon trailhead, just inside the park along the Moose-Wilson Road, 2 miles north of Teton Village.

On clear days the Grand Teton (13,770') is visible to the north from the aerial tram platform atop Rendezvous Mtn. (Trail 42).

Granite Creek for the final time on a stock bridge. Beyond this junction, follow signs for the Valley Trail and/or Teton Village, ignoring all unsigned horse trails that join in from the left.

The final 2.4 miles of the Valley Trail is the least appealing section of the entire route. It can be very dusty due to heavy equestrian use, with several mild ups and downs. It's an anticlimactic ending to an invigorating hike, but it does have some nice panoramas across Jackson Hole, fine displays of fall color, and deer and quail lying in wait alongside the trail.

A sign at the park boundary points the way (right) uphill to **Teton Village**. The trail passes briefly through a maintenance yard, then winds through an aspen grove before reaching a resort service road. Ignore all bike-route signs and turn left on the gravel service road, following the signs past the **Après Vous ski lift**. Continue down past a number of ski-in trophy houses and the Four Seasons lodge, to arrive at the base of the tram in the Village. ▶8

Yield to Moose: *In Lower Granite Canyon, I had a surprise encounter with a skittish cow moose and her very peeved bull (and his huge rack) who stared me down where the trail passes through their favorite willow thicket. I was unnerved enough to start singing to myself.*

MILESTONES

▶1 0.0 Start at Teton Village/Jackson Hole Mountain Resort parking area; buy tickets and board aerial tram

▶2 0.0 Exit tram platform and walk left on Rendezvous Mtn. Trail

▶3 0.4 Right at junction for Teton Village parking area

▶4 0.5 Right at Grand Teton National Park boundary

▶5 3.5 Right at Middle Fork Cut-Off junction

▶6 5.2 Right at Granite Canyon Patrol Cabin

▶7 9.9 Right at Valley Trail junction

▶8 12.4 Return to Teton Village

NOTES

Peak Après-Hike Experiences

When you return to civilization, why not stop for a drink? If you're feeling very civilized, drop into the stylish yet informal **Peak Lounge** at the Four Seasons, conveniently located next to the trail as it descends to the resort's base area.

For a less refined atmosphere, pop into the **Mangy Moose Restaurant and Saloon**, near the bottom of the tram in Teton Village for some live music, a free-range buffalo burger, or, best of all, a frosty pint of Moose Drool. Call (307) 733-4913 or see www.mangymoose.net to check the live music schedule.

Moosely Seconds Mountaineering

Moosely Seconds a discount retailer of top-quality mountaineering equipment, is the place to shop for last-minute gear. You can also rent gear: hiking boots, trekking poles, camping and climbing equipment, and mountain boots (for snow routes and ice climbs). Call (307) 739-1801; shop is closed in winter. If you're in town around Memorial Day weekend, don't miss their annual blowout sale. It's in the Dornan's commercial complex, near the park headquarters at Moose Junction.

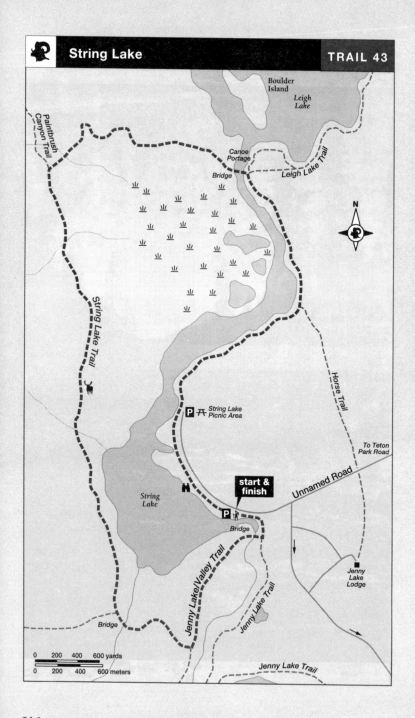

Boulder
Island

Leigh
Lake

Paintbrush
Canyon Trail

Canoe
Portage

Leigh Lake Trail

Bridge

N

String Lake Trail

Horse Trail

P ⚑ String Lake
Picnic Area

To Teton
Park Road

String
Lake

start &
finish

Unnamed Road

P

Bridge

Jenny Lake/Valley Trail

Jenny Lake Trail

Jenny
Lake
Lodge

Bridge

| 0 | 200 | 400 | 600 yards |
| 0 | 200 | 400 | 600 meters |

Jenny Lake Trail

String Lake

This is one of the most relaxing and easygoing—and thus very popular—hikes in the park. The nearly flat trail winds through a variety of habitats and traces the shoreline of the smallest in a string of tranquil piedmont lakes, all at the foot of the awe-inspiring Teton Range. Swimming and boating round out the recreational options.

Best Time

Whenever you can get in and out of the park, this hike is a good choice. There are a couple of short, sunny sections, but most of the route remains cool and shady all day long. Swimming is most enjoyable in July and August, after the lake has warmed up a bit.

Finding the Trail

From the south, take Hwys. 26/89/191 north out of Jackson; proceed 8 miles past the park's southern boundary, and turn left at Moose Junction. Continue 1 mile past the Visitor Center to the Moose Entrance Station. Drive 11 miles north, and turn left at North Jenny Lake Junction. Continue 1.5 miles, and turn right into the signed String Lake trailhead (not Picnic Area) parking lot, just before the road becomes one-way. From the north, starting at Jackson Lake Junction, go 9 miles south on Teton Park Road, and turn right at North Jenny Lake Junction. Continue 1.5 miles, and turn right into the trailhead parking lot.

TRAIL USE
Hike, Horse
LENGTH
3.4 miles, 1-2 hours
VERTICAL FEET
±270'
DIFFICULTY
– 1 **2** 3 4 5 +
TRAIL TYPE
Loop
SURFACE TYPE
Dirt and Paved

FEATURES
Child Friendly
Handicap Accessible
Lake
Autumn Colors
Wildflowers
Wildlife
Cool & Shady
Great Views
Photo Opportunity
Swimming
Geologic Interest

FACILITIES
Restrooms
Picnic Tables
Boat Launch
Horse Staging

317

Trail Description

From the **String Lake** trailhead parking area (6875'),▶1 the paved, wheelchair-accessible path winds around the peaceful lakeshore. The chief reason to start here instead of at the picnic area 0.3 mile north is to enjoy the unobstructed views and photo opportunities of the towering **Cathedral Group** (Teewinot Mtn., Mt. Owen, and the Grand Teton), which are often reflected in the lake's calm surface.

 Lake

Beyond the **picnic area,**▶2 the trail turns to packed sand and starts to see more horse traffic as it passes through lodgepole pine forest. After a horse trail from Jenny Lake Lodge joins in from the right, the trail meets the canoe portage to Leigh Lake, at 1.1 mile from the trailhead.▶3

 Great Views

Cross the babbling brook that links **Leigh Lake** and **String Lake** via a long, sturdy footbridge.▶4 Once across the bridge, you can't help but notice the large glacial erratic boulders. The well-worn footpaths around the rocks aren't beaten by climbers looking to practice boulder-scaling, but by savvy huckleberry seekers who flock here in early summer, trying to beat the bears to their treasure.

Beyond the berry patches, the trail ducks once again into mature mixed conifer forest and starts a steady but gentle climb up to the **String Lake Trail junction,**▶5 where the right fork leads steeply up into Paintbrush Canyon.

The trail opens up and traverses a few aspen-dotted meadows below Rockchuck Peak (11,144') and nearby Mt. Saint John as it heads south above the west shore of String Lake. Moose can sometimes be found in the willows here in the early morning hours. Shortly after the trail drops down to the shoreline, it passes through a small burn area. At this point you can make a short sidetrip to a scenic picnic spot at **Laurel Lake** (7625'). Before the trail crosses a footbridge over a feeder stream, follow an unmarked but well-worn path to the right, which climbs uphill for about a half-mile to the tiny lake.

 Great Views

After returning to the main trail, at the **Jenny Lake/Valley Trail junction,**►6 bear left to cross the bridge over String Lake's outlet stream and continue to back to the String Lake trailhead parking lot.►7

 MILESTONES

►1 0.0 Start at String Lake trailhead parking lot

►2 0.3 String Lake picnic area

►3 1.1 Left at Leigh Lake Trail junction

►4 1.2 Bridge across Leigh Lake outlet

►5 1.8 Left at String Lake Trail junction

►6 3.1 Left across bridge at Jenny Lake/Valley Trail junction

►7 3.4 Return to String Lake trailhead parking lot

Leigh and Jenny Lake Detours

OPTIONS

You can do the loop in either direction without increasing the difficulty. To extend the hike, add an out-and-back detour to the south shore of Leigh Lake (0.4-mile round-trip), or an extension to the north shore of Jenny Lake (0.4-mile round-trip). The backcountry campsites around Leigh, Bearpaw, and Trapper lakes are wonderful spots for overnight canoe trips and first-time family wilderness outings. For details, see Trail 40, page 301.

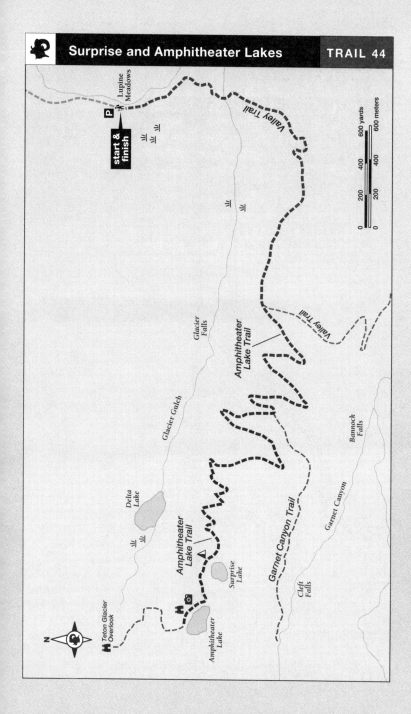

Lupine Meadows

Valley Trail

P

start & finish

600 yards

600 meters

Valley Trail

Glacier Falls

Amphitheater Lake Trail

Valley Trail

Glacier Gulch

Bannock Falls

Delta Lake

Garnet Canyon

Amphitheater Lake Trail

Garnet Canyon Trail

Surprise Lake

Teton Glacier Overlook

Cleft Falls

N

Amphitheater Lake

Surprise and Amphitheater Lakes

Welcome to the Tetons. Don't try this aerobic hike on your first day at altitude. It climbs nearly a thousand feet per mile—but the views are worth every last gasp of breath. The route is one of the park's most popular for good reason: It provides quick access to some of the most scenic alpine lakes in North America. Overachievers often add an extension to the stunning Teton Glacier Overlook.

Best Time

Snow often persists on higher portions of the route until as late as late June or early July, and it can start reappearing by mid-September. The lakes are ice-free for only a few months a year. The exposed switchbacks can be quite hot in the midday summer sun. Set out early to beat the crowds and to allow maximum time for enjoyment, recovery, and lakeside relaxation up top.

Finding the Trail

From the south, take Hwys. 26/89/191 north out of Jackson; proceed 8 miles past the park's southern boundary, and turn left at Moose Junction. Go past the Moose Visitor Center through the Moose Entrance Station. Continue north on Teton Park Road for 6.6 miles. Turn left at the signed Lupine Meadows junction. Follow the gravel road across the new Cottonwood Creek bridge for 1.5 miles, to the ample Lupine Meadows parking area and trailhead. From the north, starting at Jackson Lake Junction, go 13.3 miles south on Teton Park Road, and turn right at the Lupine Meadows junction.

TRAIL USE
Hike, Backpack
LENGTH
9.6 miles, 5-6 hours
VERTICAL FEET
±3000'
DIFFICULTY
– 1 2 3 4 **5** +
TRAIL TYPE
Out & Back
SURFACE TYPE
Dirt

FEATURES
Canyon
Mountain
Steep
Lake
Autumn Colors
Wildflowers
Birds
Wildlife
Great Views
Photo Opportunity
Camping
Geologic Interest

FACILITIES
Restrooms

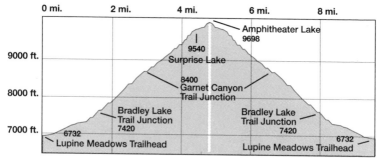

9000 ft.

8000 ft.

7000 ft.

0 mi. 2 mi. 4 mi. 6 mi. 8 mi.

Amphitheater Lake
9698

9540
Surprise Lake

8400
Garnet Canyon
Trail Junction

Bradley Lake
Trail Junction
7420

Bradley Lake
Trail Junction
7420

6732
Lupine Meadows Trailhead

6732
Lupine Meadows Trailhead

TRAIL 44 Surprise and Amphitheater Lakes Elevation Profile

Logistics

Amenities and last-minute supplies can be found near the Jenny Lake Visitor Center, a mile north of the Lupine Meadows junction. Bring plenty of water, since there's precious little between the trailhead and the tarns.

Trail Description

The Lupine Meadows trailhead parking area►1 (6732') is named after the colorful members of the pea family that dominate the surrounding sagebrush flats with luxuriant, blooming pastel displays every summer.

Geologic Interest

In sharp contrast to the open outwash plain deposited by glaciers around the parking area, the trail, a popular climbers' access route, quickly enters the cover of a mature, mixed conifer forest as it heads south on disintegrating asphalt.

After 1.7 miles, at the first junction with the Valley Trail, which leads down to Bradley Lake,►2 the Amphitheater Lake Trail forks off the Valley Trail and starts to switchback up an exposed ridge (known as a lateral moraine) between Burned Wagon and Glacier gulches, with views over the lake to Jackson Hole. Above here, ruffed grouse calmly

Wildflowers

sit along the trail, and wildflowers are often abundant on the sunny slopes.

Amphitheater Lake *occupies a stunning cirque at the foot of Disappointment Peak.*

Morgan Konn

> Obey the signs asking you to stay on the marked trail: Using the switchbacks both prevents erosion and preserves your knees.

Beyond the **Garnet Canyon Trail junction►3** (8400') at 3 miles, the straight-ahead switchback climb will knock the velvet off all but the most fit antlers. Pack an extra cache of chocolate (or other quick-energy food), and don't be surprised if you bonk halfway up the trail.

Stay on designated trails and use only official campsites to preserve the beautiful, fragile subalpine habitat surrounding the perfectly circular **Surprise Lake►4** (9540'). Just a few hundred yards above and beyond, **Amphitheater Lake►5** (9698') occupies a stunning cirque at the foot of Disappointment Peak (11,618').

After you have finished picnicking and exploring around the lakes, retrace your steps downhill to return to the trailhead parking area.**►6**

MILESTONES

►1 0.0 Start at Lupine Meadows parking area
►2 1.7 Right at Valley Trail junction (signed for Bradley Lake)
►3 3.0 Right at Garnet Canyon Trail junction
►4 4.6 Right at Surprise Lake
►5 4.8 Amphitheater Lake
►6 9.6 Return to Lupine Meadows parking area

OPTIONS

Garnet Canyon and Teton Glacier Overlook

You can extend the hike by adding a 2.2-mile, 2-hour detour up **Garnet Canyon**, to get to a large boulder field, spectacular views of the **Middle Teton** (12,804'), and a popular off-trail camping and climbing area. From Amphitheater Lake, you can continue for 0.3 mile one-way around the northeast shore, to the highly recommended **Teton Glacier Overlook**. It offers impressive views into the next valley and back over aquamarine Delta Lake to Jackson Hole.

Teton Glacier Overlook *overlooks Delta Lake and Jackson Hole.*

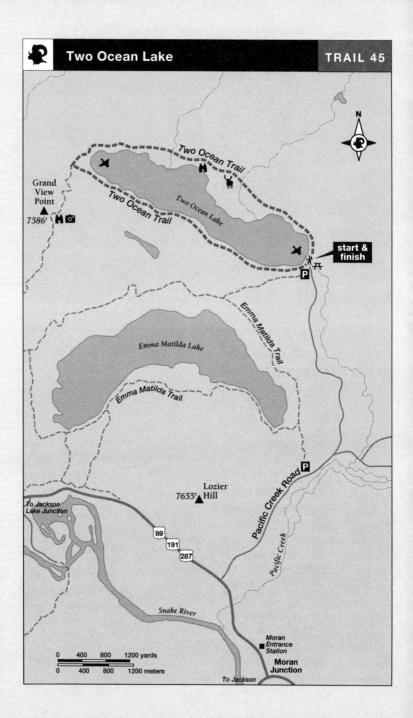

Two Ocean Lake

TRAIL 45

Two Ocean Trail

Grand
View
Point
▲
7586'

Two Ocean Trail

Two Ocean Lake

**start &
finish**

P

Emma Matilda Trail

Emma Matilda Lake

Emma Matilda Trail

N

Pacific Creek Road

P

Lozier
Hill
7655' ▲

To Jackson
Lake Junction

89
191
287

Pacific Creek

Snake River

Moran
Entrance
Station

**Moran
Junction**

To Jackson

0   400   800   1200 yards
0   400   800   1200 meters

Two Ocean Lake

This nearly level loop hike around a mountain lake is a perfect early- or late-season altitude acclimatization route. It also offers a nice escape from the crowds that flock to trails on the park's popular western side. Arrive early or stay late for the best chance at spotting deer, elk, or moose. Whenever you turn up, definitely allow time to ascend Grand View Point for some amazing views.

TRAIL USE
Hike, Horse
LENGTH
6.4 miles, 3-4 hours
ELEVATION GAIN/LOSS
±150'
DIFFICULTY
− 1 2 **3** 4 5 +
TRAIL TYPE
Loop
SURFACE TYPE
Dirt

Best Time

Since it is at a lower elevation than most of the park, Two Ocean Lake is typically accessible (depending on snow level and road conditions) from late May through early October. For spotting birds and wildlife, the early morning or late afternoon is best. On warm days, it's best to visit the sunnier, more exposed north shore in the morning to avoid the heat. The shady south shore is fine anytime. Thanks to its length and relative inaccessibility, the trail is often crowd-free, even on perfectly sunny summer days.

FEATURES
Summit
Lake
Autumn Colors
Birds
Wildflowers
Wildlife
Great Views
Photo Opportunity
Secluded
Geologic

Finding the Trail

From Moran Junction in the park's northeast sector, head 1 mile north on Hwys. 89/191/287 past the Moran Entrance Station. Turn right on paved Pacific Creek Road and go 2 miles; at the fork bear left onto the graded dirt road signed for Two Ocean Lake, and continue 2.3 miles to the signed parking area. Springtime downpours can cause the temporary closure of this road—if there's been recent heavy rain, double-check the road's status at a ranger station or

FACILITIES
Restrooms
Picnic Tables
Boat Launch
Horse Staging

Two Ocean Lake's name refers to an early assumption that since it's close to the Continental Divide, its waters must drain into both the Atlantic and Pacific Oceans. They don't, but the nearby Two Ocean Plateau, in Yellowstone's bottom-right corner, *is* bisected by the Continental Divide, and its waters *do* drain to both oceans.

Birds

Wildlife

visitor center; you may have to choose another trail. At other times, all vehicles should be able to navigate the unpaved section. To start on the north shore, look for the trailhead near the picnic area. For the south shore, look for the trailhead past the restrooms.

Logistics

The loop around Two Ocean Lake can be done in either direction with no change in elevation gain. You can start on the north or south shore, depending on whether you want to tackle the more difficult part first or leave it for last.

Trail Description

From the north shore trailhead,▶1 pass through the picnic area where a sign points the way 4.3 miles to Grand View Point. Cross a small bridge over the outlet stream of **Two Ocean Lake**▶2 (6896'), which meanders along Two Ocean Road for a couple of miles before its confluence with Pacific Creek. Waterfowl are abundant around the lake, and grizzlies have increasingly been sighted gorging themselves on berries, so remain bear aware.

After contouring along the open lakeshore for half a mile, the roller-coaster single-track trail trends northwest, away from the shore and enters a shady, mixed aspen and conifer forest. Ignore the horse trails that head down into the boggy meadows, and monitor the lakefront willow thickets for browsing moose. Even the main routes can get muddy in low-lying areas near feeder streams.

The trail continues along above the north shore, crossing several seasonal creeks that water meadows of sagebrush and prolific wildflowers. At around 1.5 miles beyond the trailhead, pick a spot midway along the shore to stop for a snack and enjoy the views of Mt. Moran and the Teton Range.▶3

Grand View Point *offers 360-degree views.*

Three miles from the trailhead, a sign announces the head of Two Ocean Lake▶4 at its open western end. A small, unmarked trail leads down to the lakeshore, where ducks, swans, and other waterfowl are often found basking in the bay.

 Birds

Back on the main trail and across a small bridge, a signed junction marks the route's most important decision-making moment.▶5

Continuing straight ahead for 1.3 miles takes you up the steep north side of **Grand View Point** (see Options, page 330) via a series of switchbacks. After the superb detour, what could be a fitting encore? Views from the lake's shady south shore are obscured by morainal ridges, so the final 3.1 miles are less spectacular than the first half of the hike.

 Great Views

From the junction for Grand View Point, the trail descends through pine forest to cross a couple of streams before gently climbing more than 100 feet above Two Ocean Lake's southern shoreline. The landscape on the home stretch of the trail varies: you'll encounter lodgepole pine and old-growth spruce-fir forests, clearings, bridged stream crossings, bogs and wildflower meadows—offering a look at a selection of flora not seen of the sunnier north shore.

After a final bridged crossing of a small bog, the trail crests a gentle rise at the Two Ocean parking and picnic area,▸6 on your left shortly after the signed junction for the trail to Emma Matilda Lake.

⚑ MILESTONES

▸1 0.0 Start at Two Ocean Lake parking area

▸2 0.1 Cross stock bridge

▸3 1.5 Find a shady picnic spot with grand Teton views

▸4 3.0 Western end of Two Ocean Lake

▸5 3.3 Straight to Grand View Point, or left to return to trailhead

▸6 6.4 Return to parking area

Grand View Point Side Trip

OPTIONS

The steep out-and-back detour from Two Ocean Lake up the north flank of **Grand View Point** (7586') adds at least an hour and 700 feet of elevation gain. On clear days, two volcanic outcroppings atop the well-named vista point make scenic picnic spots and offer amazing 360-degree panoramas, including eye-level views of the Teton Range. The second, balder clearing has the best views.

Top Rated Trails

Swimming hole *near Union Falls (Trail 34)*

Soaking at sunset *is one of the varied pleasures of backpacking the Bechler (Trail 25).*

Local Resources

Major Public Agencies

National Park Service
www.nps.gov
Phone numbers for specific divisions are listed below.

National Park Foundation/National Parks Pass
(888) 467-2757   www.nationalparks.org

Yellowstone National Park
www.nps.gov/yell
P.O. Box 168, Yellowstone National Park, WY 82190-0168

General Visitor Information: (307) 344-7381, TDD (307) 344-2386
Bechler Ranger Station: (406) 581-7074
Canyon Visitor Center: (307) 242-2550
Fishing Bridge Visitor Center: (307) 242-2450
Grant Village Visitor Center: (307) 242-2650
Madison Information Station: (307) 344-2821
Mammoth Visitor Center: (307) 344-2263
Norris Information Station: (307) 344-2812
Old Faithful Visitor Center (307) 545-2750
West Yellowstone Multiagency Visitor Center: (406) 646-4403
Central Backcountry Office: (307) 344-2163
Mammoth Backcountry Office: (307) 344-2160
Recorded camping and lodging report: (307) 344-2114
Road conditions: (307) 344-2117
Beartooth Highway road conditions: (888) 285-4636
Lake Hospital: (307) 242-7241
Mammoth Medical Clinic: (307) 344-7965
Old Faithful Medical Clinic: (307) 545-7325
Lost and found: (307) 344-2109

Grand Teton National Park
www.nps.gov/grte
P.O. Drawer 170, Moose, WY 83012-0170

General Visitor Information: (307) 739-3300 or (307) 739-3600,
TDD: (307) 739-3400 or (307) 739-3544
Colter Bay Visitor Center: (307) 739-3594
Jenny Lake Ranger Station: (307) 739-3343
Jenny Lake Visitor Center: (307) 739-3392
Moose Visitor Center: (307) 739-3399
Backcountry Permits Office: (307) 739-3602 or (307) 739-3309,
fax (307) 739-3438
Camping and lodging information: (307) 739-3603
River-flow information: (800) 658-5771
Road conditions: (307) 739-3614, in winter (307) 739-3682
Weather report: (307) 739-3611
Avalanche hazard and mountain weather forecast:
(307) 733-2664, www.jhavalanche.org
Lost and found: (307) 739-3450

Lodging

In Yellowstone National Park

Xanterra Parks and Resorts: Yellowstone's only in-park accommodation concessionaire (pronounced zan-TAIR-uh) runs four campgrounds, nine lodgings, and an RV park. The following contact information may change sometime after October 2005, when Xanterra's service contract is set to expire. The only other company bidding on the contract in Delaware North Companies Parks & Resorts (www.delawarenorth.com), which runs Yellowstone's general stores. www.travelyellowstone.com
P.O. Box 165, Yellowstone National Park, WY 82190
General information and same-day reservations: (307) 344-7901
Camping, lodging, and dining reservations: (307) 344-7311, TDD (307) 344-5395

In Grand Teton National Park

American Alpine Club's Grand Teton Climbers' Ranch: Open mid-June to mid-September, the unreservable dorm bunks ($10 per person) are the best budget lodging deal inside the park, hands down. (307) 733-7271, www. americanalpineclub.org

Dornan's: Runs the recommended **Spur Ranch Cabins** (one or two bedrooms $125-$185 or $175-$230) at Moose Junction. Open year-round. Three-night minimum from mid-June to mid-September. Has a good gourmet deli, wine shop, and grocery store; hearty meals are served al fresco at picnic tables or around a fire inside tepees. (307) 733-2522, www. dornans.com

Grand Teton Lodge Company: Manages a wide variety of accommodations: basic canvas tent cabins with wood-burning stoves ($37) and better-value cabins (shared bathroom, $38; private bathroom, $75-$140) at **Colter Bay Village**; as well as standard if overpriced hotel-style rooms at the well-situated **Jackson Lake Lodge** (doubles $173-$249, suites $425-$575); and finely appointed log cabins ($459) and exclusive suites ($614-$654) at the chic **Jenny Lake Lodge**. Package rates at the lodge include breakfast, horseback riding, and a five-course dinner. (307) 543-2811, (800) 628-9988, www.gtlc.com

Flagg Ranch Resort: Situated 6 miles north of Grand Teton National Park's northern boundary and 2 miles south of Yellowstone National Park's South Entrance. Open mid-May to mid-September; call for winter availability, which varies from year to year, depending on snowmobiling regulations. Doubles $145-$155; tent site for 1 or 2 people $25; RV site $45. Has a gas station and a decent restaurant. (307) 543-2861, (800) 443-2311, www.flaggranch.com

Jackson Hole Mountain Resort: In addition to the aerial tram at Teton Village, this year-round resort, 12 miles northwest of the town of Jackson, is home to world-class skiing and a slew of adventurous summer activities. The are 2500 acres of in-bounds terrain and a vertical drop of 4139 feet— the greatest continuous plunge in the USA. Half the runs traverse expert terrain, and the open backcountry gate system accesses more than 3000 out-of-bounds acres. Accommodation options range from private, budget-sparing rooms at the family-friendly Hostel X to studio condos and fully furnished, ski-in luxury chalets.

Jackson Hole Central Reservations: (307) 733-4005, (800) 443-6931, www.jacksonholewy.com

Jackson Hole Resort Lodging: (800) 443-8613, www.jhresortlodging.com

Signal Mountain Lodge: Two miles southwest of Jackson Lake Junction on Teton Park Road. Open early May through mid-October. Options include rustic log cabins (one or two rooms, $99-$129 or $142-$148); basic and deluxe motel rooms ($132 and $179); kitchenette bungalows ($140-$215); lakefront suites ($199-210); and one three-room cabin ($255). (307) 543-283, www.signalmtnlodge.com

Other Grand Teton Area Resources

Bridger-Teton National Forest
Grand Teton visitors often also end up camping, hiking, boating, or fishing in this National Forest, which borders the park on three sides.
(307) 739-5500, www.fs.fed.us/btnf

Buckboard Transportation Backpacker & Bicyclist Shuttles
(307) 733-1112, (877) 791-0211, www.buckboardtrans.com

Caribou-Targhee National Forest
This National Forest, which borders the park on its west side, is home to the Jedediah Smith and Winegar Hole Wilderness areas.
(208) 524-7500, www.fs.fed.us/r4/caribou-targhee

Jackson Hole and Greater Yellowstone Visitor Center
Jackson's helpful interagency center, staffed by friendly folks from the Chamber of Commerce, NPS, USFS, and USFWS, is loaded with detailed information and has extensive wildlife-related videos and exhibits. The bookstore is well-stocked, and there are public phones for making free calls for local lodging reservations. Sells all passes and permits. (307) 733-3616; 532 N. Cache Dr., Jackson, Wyoming. Open from 8 AM to 7 PM in summer, 8 AM to 5 PM in winter; closed Thanksgiving and Christmas.

More than 7500 elk overwinter from October through May at the US Fish and Wildlife Service's 25,000-acre **National Elk Refuge**, between Grand Teton National Park and the town of Jackson. Other inhabitants include 47 types of mammal and 175 bird species. (307) 733-9212, http://national elkrefuge.fws.gov

Wyoming Game and Fish Department issues hunting, fishing, and trapping licenses. Report poaching incidents to the hotline. 420 N. Cache Dr., Jackson, Wyoming (307) 733-2321; hotline in Wyoming (800) 442-4331, http://gf.state.wy.us

Major Nonprofit Organizations

Continental Divide Trail Alliance: (303) 838-3760, (888) 909-2382, www.cdtrail.org
Grand Teton National Park Foundation: (307) 732-0629, www.gtnpf.org
Grand Teton Natural History Association: (307) 739-3606, www.grandtetonpark.org
Greater Yellowstone Coalition: (406) 586-1593, www.greateryellowstone.org
The Murie Center: (307) 739-2246, www.muriecenter.org
National Parks Conservation Association: (800) 628-7275, www.npca.org
Teton Science Schools: (307) 733-4765, www.tetonscience.org
Yellowstone Association: (307) 344-2293, store orders (877) 967-0090, www.yellowstoneassociation.org
Yellowstone Institute
    (307) 344-2294, www.yellowstoneassociation.org/institute
Yellowstone to Yukon (Y2K) Conservation Initiative
    (406) 327-8512, in Canada (403) 609-2666, www.y2y.net
Yellowstone Park Foundation: (406) 586-6303, www.ypf.org

Outfitters, Guides, and Tour Operators

Yellowstone: Contact the NPS (or see www.nps.gov/yell/planvisit/services) for a current list of outfitters permitted to lead guided dayhiking, backpacking, fishing, bicycling, llama- and horse-packing, cross-country skiing, wildlife watching, and photo safari trips inside Yellowstone National Park.

Grand Teton: Contact the NPS (or see www.nps.gov/grte/trip/activities/concessioners.htm) for a current list of outfitters authorized to lead guided dayhiking, backpacking, climbing, fishing, rafting, kayaking, cross-country skiing, snowshoeing, and horseback riding trips within Grand Teton National Park.

Internet Resources

Visitor Information

Cody Country Chamber of Commerce: www.codychamber.org
Cooke City/Silver Gate/Colter Pass Chamber of Commerce:
    www.cookecitychamber.com
Gardiner Chamber of Commerce: www.gardinerchamber.com
Idaho Travel and Tourism Guide: www.visitid.org
Jackson Hole Chamber of Commerce: www.jacksonholechamber.com
West Yellowstone Chamber of Commerce:
    www.westyellowstonechamber.com
Wyoming Travel and Tourism: www.wyomingtourism.org
Yellowstone Country Montana: www.yellowstone.visitmt.com

Miscellaneous

Blogging Yellowstone: Share and download news, views, photos, and trail
    updates from around Greater Yellowstone at the author's personal
    weblog: http://ynp.blogspot.com
Geyser Observation and Study Association: www.geyserstudy.org
Mammoth Hot Spring Webcam: www.nps.gov/yell/mammothcam.htm
Mt. Washburn FireCam: www.nps.gov/yell/firecam.htm
Old Faithful Webcam: www.nps.gov/yell/oldfaithfulcam.htm
USGS Yellowstone Volcano Observatory: http://volcanoes.usgs.gov/yvo
Windows into Wonderland electronic field trip:
www.windowsintowonderland.org

Useful Books

Guidebooks

Adkison, Ron. *Exploring Beyond Yellowstone: Hiking, Camping, and Vacationing in the National Forests Surrounding Yellowstone and Grand Teton.* Berkeley, CA: Wilderness Press, 1996.

Florence, Mason, Andrew Dean Nystrom, and Marisa Gierlich. *Lonely Planet Rocky Mountains.* Oakland, CA: Lonely Planet Publications, 2001.

Henry, Jeff. *Yellowstone Winter Guide.* Boulder, CO: Roberts Rinehart, 1998.

Mayhew, Bradley, Tim Cahill, and Andrew Dean Nystrom. *Lonely Planet Yellowstone & Grand Teton National Parks.* Oakland, CA: Lonely Planet Publications, 2003.

Geology

Bryan, Scott T. *The Geysers of Yellowstone.* Niwot, CO: University Press of Colorado, 1995.

Fritz, William J. Roadside *Geology of the Yellowstone Country.* Missoula, MT: Mountain Press Publishing, 1985.

Good, John M. and Kenneth L. Pierce. *Interpreting the Landscape: Recent and Ongoing Geology of Grand Teton and Yellowstone National Parks.* Jackson, WY: Grand Teton Natural History Association, 1997.

Smith, Robert B., and Lee J. Siegel. *Windows into the Earth: The Geologic Story of Yellowstone and Grand Teton National Parks.* New York: Oxford University Press, 2000.

Natural History

Brock, Thomas D. *Life at High Temperatures.* Yellowstone NP, WY: Yellowstone Association, 1994.

Craighead Jr., Frank C. *For Everything There Is A Season: The Sequence of Natural Events in the Grand Teton-Yellowstone Area.* Helena, MT: Falcon Press, 1994.

Halfpenny, James C. *Scats and Tracks of the Rocky Mountains.* Helena, MT: Falcon Press, 2001.

Halfpenny, James C. *Yellowstone Wolves in the Wild.* Helena, MT: Riverbend Publishing, 2003.

Herrero, Stephen. *Bear Attacks: Their Causes and Avoidance.* New York: Lyons Press, 2002.

Koch, Edward D., and Charles R. Peterson. *Amphibians & Reptiles of Yellowstone and Grand Teton National Parks*. Salt Lake City: Univ. of Utah Press, 1995.

McEneaney, Terry. *Birds of Yellowstone: A Practical Habitat Guide to the Birds of Yellowstone National Park, and Where to Find Them*. Boulder, CO: Roberts Rinehart, 1988.

McNamee, Thomas. *The Return of the Wolf to Yellowstone*. New York: Owl Books, 1998.

Phillips, Michael K., et al. *The Wolves of Yellowstone*. Stillwater, MN: Voyageur Press, 1998.

Raynes, Bert, and Darwin Wile. *Finding the Birds of Jackson Hole*. Jackson, WY: D. Wile Publisher, 1994.

Schreier, Carl. *A Field Guide to Wildflowers of the Rocky Mountains*. Moose, WY: Homestead Publishing, 1996.

Robson, Gary D., and Elijah Brady Clark. *Who Pooped in the Park? Yellowstone National Park*. Helena, MT: Farcountry Press, 2004.

Schullery, Paul. *The Bears of Yellowstone*. Worland, WY: High Plains Publishing, 1992.

Shaw, Richard J.. *Plants of Yellowstone & Grand Teton National Parks*. Salt Lake City: Wheelwright Press, 2001.

Varley, John D., and Paul Schullery. *Yellowstone Fishes: Ecology, History and Angling in the Park*. Mechanicsburg, PA: Stackpole Books, 1998.

Wilkinson, Todd, and Michael H. Francis. *Watching Yellowstone & Grand Teton Wildlife*. Helena, MT: Riverbend Publishing, 2004.

Yellowstone Resources and Issues Handbook. National Park Service, Division of Interpretation, Yellowstone National Park, 2004.

History

Haines, Aubrey L. *Yellowstone Place Names: Mirrors of History*. Niwot, CO: University Press of Colorado, 1996.

Haines, Aubrey L. *The Yellowstone Story: A History of Our First National Park: Vols. 1 & 2*. Niwot, CO: University Press of Colorado, 1996.

Janetski, Joel C. *Indians in Yellowstone National Park*. Salt Lake City: University of Utah Press, 2001.

Russell, Osborne. *Journal of a Trapper*. New York: MJF Books, 1997.

Schullery, Paul. *Searching for Yellowstone: Ecology and Wonder in the Last Wilderness*. Helena, MT: Montana Historical Society Press, 2004.

Whittlesey, Lee H. *Death in Yellowstone: Accidents and Foolhardiness in the First National Park*. Boulder, CO: Roberts Rinehart, 1995.

Whittlesey, Lee H. *Yellowstone Place Names*. Helena, MT: Montana Historical Society, 1988.

Literature

Cahill, Tim. *Lost in My Own Backyard: A Walk in Yellowstone National Park*. New York: Crown Journeys, 2004.

Ferguson, Gary. *Hawks Rest: A Season in the Remote Heart of Yellowstone*. Washington, D.C.: National Geographic Adventure Press, 2003.

Ferguson, Gary. *Walking Down the Wild: A Journey Through the Yellowstone Rockies*. Helena, MT: Falcon Press, 1997.

Hoagland, Bill, ed. Ring of Fire: Writers of the Yellowstone Region. Cody, WY: Rocky Mountain Press, 2000.

Krakel, Dean. *Downriver: A Yellowstone Journey*. San Francisco: Sierra Club Books, 1987.

Schullery, Paul. *Mountain Time: A Yellowstone Portrait*. Boulder, CO: Roberts Rinehart, 1995.

Photography

Adams, Ansel. *The Tetons and the Yellowstone*. Boston, MA: Little Brown, 1970.

Holdsworth, Henry H. *Yellowstone & Grand Teton Wildlife Portfolio*. Helena, MT: Farcountry Press, 2003.

Lange, Joseph K. *Photographer's Guide to Yellowstone & the Tetons*. Mechanicsburg, PA: Stackpole Books, 2000.

Murphy, Tom. *The Light of Spring: The Seasons of Yellowstone*. Livingston, MT: Crystal Creek Press, 2003.

Murphy, Tom. *Silence & Solitude: Yellowstone's Winter Wilderness*. Helena, MT: Riverbend Publishing, 2001.

Maps

The maps included in this book will be sufficient for on-trail navigation and following the hikes as they are described in this book. If you're planning off-trail exploration or longer overnight trips, you should pick up some of the following maps.

National Geographic's recently revised **Trails Illustrated** topographic series are the most detailed and user-friendly maps of Yellowstone. The series covers the entire park with four waterproof, tear-resistant maps ($8.95 each) at a scale of 1:63,360, with a contour interval of 50 feet and selected GPS waypoints. The *Grand Teton National Park* map (no. 202) covers the entire park at 1:78,000 on one side, with a more detailed 1:24,000 inset covering many of the most popular backcountry camping zones on the reverse. Call (303) 670-3457 or (800) 962-1643; www.nationalgeo-graphic.com/trails.

Earthwalk Press publishes the seven-color, 1:106,250 *Yellowstone National Park Hiking Map & Guide* ($4.95 or $8.95 for a waterproof version), which has 80-foot contour intervals and depicts the burn areas from the 1988 fires. The similar 1:72,500 *Grand Teton National Park Hiking Map & Guide* has a shaded topo relief map of entire park and a 1:48,000 close-up of Granite and Moran canyons. Call (800) 828-6277; 5432 La Jolla Hermosa Ave., La Jolla, CA 92037.

The 1:24,000 topographic quadrangle series published by the **United States Geological Survey** covers all of Greater Yellowstone with 80 maps, but the level of detail (and number of maps required for a multiday hike) is a bit of overkill unless you plan to do some serious off-trail exploring. If you can find them, the discontinued 15-minute topo series maps are a handy size, but much of the trail information is now outdated. Call (888) 275-8747; http://geography.usgs.gov.

Digitized, GPS-compatible versions of the 1:24,000 USGS topo quads are available on CD-ROM from National Geographic for the **TOPO!** software suite in both Mac and PC versions. The **TrailSmart** *60 US National Parks* ($50) collection, available only for PCs, covers the most popular parks, including Yellowstone and Grand Teton.

Index

Author

Andrew Dean Nystrom

Andrew Dean Nystrom is a writer, photographer, and travel planning consultant who specializes in adventure travel in Latin America and the western United States. His home base is a garden cottage straddling an earthquake fault in Northern California. Since earning a BA in Conservation Geography and Environmental Education from the University of California at Berkeley, he has contributed to a dozen Fodor's and Lonely Planet guidebooks, covering locales as varied as California, the Rocky Mountains, the US Southwest, Mexico, Bolivia, and Argentine and Chilean Patagonia and Tierra del Fuego. His writing has been translated into a dozen languages.

In 2004, he was invited by the National Geographic Society's Sustainable Tourism Initiative to participate as an expert advisor in their destination stewardship survey of North American national parks. The survey results will be published in the summer of 2005 in *National Geographic Traveler* magazine.

Andrew contributes regularly to two nationally syndicated newspaper columns: *Travel 101* and *Travels with Lonely Planet*. He is also the coauthor of Lonely Planet's *Yellowstone & Grand Teton National Parks* guide.

Contact him at laughtears@yahoo.com or visit his weblog at http://ynp.blogspot.com.

Photographer

Morgan Konn

Morgan Konn is a photographer, writer, and fine artist. She has published photographs in several travel and outdoor publications, and is the co-author of Lonely Planet guides to Bolivia, Mexico, and Thailand. She has written travel articles for various newspapers, including the *San Francisco Chronicle*, *Miami Herald*, and Portland's *Oregonian*. She licenses her travel photographs via the stock agency Lonely Planet Images (www.lonelyplanetimages.com).

Morgan holds a BA in Fine Arts from the University of Pennsylvania. She is a member of the Society of Photographic Educators, and is currently an MFA candidate at San Jose State University.

Series Creator

Joe Walowski

Joe Walowski conceived of the Top Trails series in 2003, and was series editor of the first three titles: *Top Trails Los Angeles*, *Top Trails San Francisco Bay Area*, and *Top Trails Lake Tahoe*. He currently lives in Seattle.